MW00904674

Women's Reflections on the Complexities of Forgiveness

Wanda Malcolm, Nancy DeCourville, Kathryn Belicki

Editors

Routledge
Taylor & Francis Group
New York London

Routledge
Taylor & Francis Group
270 Madison Avenue
New York, NY 10016

Routledge
Taylor & Francis Group
2 Park Square
Milton Park, Abingdon
Oxon OX14 4RN

Routledge is an imprint of Taylor & Francis Group, an Informa business

Printed in the United States of America on acid-free paper
10 9 8 7 6 5 4 3 2 1

International Standard Book Number-13: 978-0-415-95505-8 (Hardcover)

Library of Congress Cataloging-in-Publication Data

Women's reflections on the complexities of forgiveness / edited by Wanda Malcolm, Nancy DeCourville, and Kathryn Belicki.
p. cm.
ISBN 0-415-95505-X
1. Forgiveness. 2. Women--Psychology. I. Malcolm, Wanda. II. DeCourville, Nancy. III. Belicki, Kathryn.

BF637.F67W66 2007
155.9'2--dc22 2007019105

Visit the Taylor & Francis Web site at
http://www.taylorandfrancis.com

and the Routledge Web site at
http://www.routledge.com

For Stan: friend, husband, gift from God

Wanda Malcolm

For my son, Neill McKay, who is truly the light of my life

Nancy DeCourville

For Denis: You are the answer to one of my first prayers

Kathryn Belicki

Contents

About the Editors

Wanda Malcolm, PhD, is a registered psychologist trained in emotion-focused therapy whose primary work is in private practice with adult individuals and couples. She is also an adjunct member of faculty at Brock University and Wycliffe College (Toronto School of Theology, the University of Toronto). Her clinical research interests focus on gaining a deeper understanding of when and how to facilitate adaptive forms of forgiveness within therapy.

Nancy DeCourville, PhD, is an associate professor in the Department of Psychology at Brock University, cofounder of the Brock Forgiveness Research Group, and a statistical consultant. Her research is oriented toward understanding the disjunctions between theoretical construals and the lived experiences of phenomena including drunkenness, affirmative action, and forgiveness. She has a particular interest in understanding the implications of differences between academic notions of forgiveness and the way that people actually experience forgiveness.

Kathryn Belicki, PhD, MTS, is a registered psychologist, professor of psychology at Brock University, and cofounder of the Brock-Forgiveness Research Group. Her current interest in forgiveness and forgiveness-seeking arose from her prior research on the impact of childhood trauma and abuse on adult physical and psychological well-being. Her recent research has focused on documenting various forms of forgiveness and forgiveness-seeking as well as varying motives for forgiving and for seeking forgiveness.

Contributors

Marjorie E. Baker, PhD, is an associate professor of social work at Wright State University in Dayton, Ohio. She was named social worker of the year (2001) by the regional and state chapters of the National Association of Social Workers. Marjorie has authored several articles and has presented her work at conferences nationwide for over 15 years. Her expertise and area of research include personal empowerment applied to forgiveness, self-forgiveness, end-of-life issues, and single parenting.

Helen Chagigiorgis, MA, is a doctoral candidate in clinical psychology in the Department of Psychology at the University of Windsor, Ontario, Canada, where she works under the supervision of Dr. Sandra Paivio. Her research interests include psychotherapy process and outcome, emotion focused/experiential therapy, emotion and emotional processes in psychotherapy, forgiveness in psychotherapy, and psychotherapy integration.

Lise DeShea, PhD, is a statistician in the Quality Assurance Division of the Oklahoma Health Care Authority in Oklahoma City, Oklahoma. She earned her master's and doctoral degrees in quantitative psychology at the University of Oklahoma. Her research focuses on the measurement of forgiveness, as well as its relationship with spirituality, religiosity, and personality traits.

Julie Juola Exline, PhD, is an associate professor of psychology at Case Western Reserve University in Cleveland, Ohio. As a researcher, she uses techniques from clinical and social psychology to study topics such as forgiveness, humility, altruistic love, and spiritual struggles. To bring a clinical perspective to her work, she is pursuing licensure in psychology as well as training in spiritual direction.

Suzanne Freedman, PhD, is an associate professor of human development at the University of Northern Iowa in Cedar Falls, a position she has held since 1994. She was the recipient of the APA Dissertation Award in 1993 for her groundbreaking research on forgiveness and incest survivors. She has been studying the topic of forgiveness for 19 years and her publications focus on the psychology of forgiveness with both adults and adolescents. Suzanne has presented her research on forgiveness at numerous national and international conferences, as well as at invited workshops.

Michelle M. Green, MA, is a doctoral candidate in the Department of Psychology at Brock University, St. Catharines, Ontario, Canada. Her research focuses on the pathways connecting forgiveness with mental and physical health. In addition, she is examining sex differences in the relationship between physiological measures of stress and affective disorders.

Virginia Todd Holeman, PhD, is a professor of counseling at Asbury Theological Seminary in Wilmore, Kentucky. She is a psychologist in Ohio and a licensed marriage and family therapist in Kentucky. She is a member of the Christian Association for Psychological Studies and is a clinical member of the American Association of Marriage and Family Therapy. She is the author of *Reconcilable Differences: Hope and Healing for Troubled Marriages* (2004, InterVarsity Press).

Kathleen A. Lawler-Row, PhD, joined the faculty at the University of Tennessee in Knoxville after a postdoctoral fellowship year at

Harvard University. In 2006, she became professor and chair of the Department of Psychology at East Carolina University, where she also directs the Health Psychology doctoral program and continues her research on forgiveness and health.

Ann Macaskill, PhD, is a professor of health psychology at Sheffield Hallam University in the United Kingdom. Ann is a chartered health psychologist and is trained in counseling and cognitive behavior therapy. She has published a self-help book and several papers on forgiveness and is currently studying the impact of families on forgiveness.

Kimberly Matheson, PhD, is a professor of psychology at Carleton University in Ottawa, Ontario, Canada. Her research focuses on how women contend with their disadvantaged social status. She employs a stress and coping perspective, including an emphasis on the social support dynamics that operate in situations that entail discrimination (including partner abuse).

Megan McCarthy, BA, received the Cara Chefurka Memorial Book Prize for her undergraduate research on alcohol abuse and was a laureate of the CPA Certificate of Academic Excellence for her thesis on forgiveness and apology. She has presented her research findings at conferences in Ontario and Quebec. Her research interests include child and adolescent development, addiction, and forgiveness.

Sandra Paivio, PhD, is a professor of psychology at the University of Windsor, Ontario, Canada, where she is involved in research, teaching, and clinical training. She also maintains a part-time private practice. Sandra has authored numerous articles on affective processes and psychotherapy processes and outcome, as well as coauthored (with Les Greenberg) the book *Working With Emotions in Psychotherapy*. She has dedicated her work to the development and evaluation of emotion-focused therapy for trauma (EFTT), which specifically focuses on resolving issues stemming from child abuse trauma.

Nancy A. Peddle, PhD, is the chief executive officer of LemonAid Fund, which aids individuals who have experienced violence to change their lives and their communities. Peddle's expertise has taken her to over 20 countries, focusing on trauma recovery. She was the first director of the International Society for the Prevention of Child Abuse and Neglect, and a research fellow at Prevent Child Abuse America.

Sandra Rafman, PhD, is a developmental and pediatric psychologist at McGill University Health Centre–Montreal Children's Hospital and the Université du Québec à Montréal. Her publications, research, and clinical interventions focus on children and families who experience trauma. Sandra has a particular interest in the interaction of the political and psychological, and she argues for the inclusion of a moral dimension in the study of children's responses to traumatic events.

Kimberly A. Reed, PhD, is an assistant professor at Emory and Henry College in Emory, Virginia, where she continues her research on forgiveness, spirituality and religion, and the teaching of psychology.

Jessica Rourke, MA, is a doctoral candidate in the Department of Psychology at the University of Victoria, British Columbia, Canada. Her research focuses on forgiveness-seeking motivations and behaviors, and how they are affected by such things as degree of guilt and personality of the offender. She has presented her work on forgiveness at both national and international conferences.

Renate Ysseldyk, MA, is a doctoral candidate in the Department of Psychology at Carleton University in Ottawa, Ontario, Canada. Her research focuses on how both religious and nonreligious coping efforts, including forgiveness, might influence the psychological and physiological effects of interpersonal stressors. In addition, she is investigating how specific coping styles might buffer the stressful effects of religious identity threat.

Anne L. Zell, MA, is a doctoral candidate in social psychology in the Department of Psychology at Florida State University, Tallahassee, Florida. She will be taking up an assistant professor position at Augustana College, Sioux Falls, South Dakota, in the fall of 2007. Her research focuses on topics such as humility, appeasement, self-regulation, and responses to praise and criticism.

Acknowledgments

This book grew out of a vision, shared by the three of us, of providing a venue in which women felt free to present their perspectives on the complexities of forgiveness. We anticipated that this would add a distinctive voice to the field and enrich our understanding of this fascinating, sometimes frustrating, ambiguous phenomenon—one that impinges on everyone's life, one way or another, sooner or later. There is a big difference, however, between having an idea and delivering a finished project! The book you hold in your hands would not have been possible without the interest and involvement of the group of women who met at the Glenerin Inn in May 2005. We want to express our heartfelt appreciation to each one of them because that meeting inspired us to pursue the idea of a book written by women about forgiveness. The women, who gathered in a beautiful estate home that has been transformed into an inn on the outskirts of Toronto, came from North America, Great Britain, Japan, and Sierra Leone and included:

Marjorie Baker
Deborah Bowen
Helen Chagigiorgis
Becky Cornock
Lise DeShea

Julie Exline
Suzanne Freedman
Marion Goertz
Larissa Goertzen
Michelle Green
Virginia Todd Holeman
Ann Laviolette
Kathleen Lawler-Row
Ann Macaskill
Masami Matsuyuki
Megan McCarthy
Catalina Woldarsky Meneses
Erica Nairne
Nancy Peddle
Sandra Rafman
Sharon Ramsay
Jessica Rourke
Ann Sprague
Tammy Stewart-Atkinson
Elizabeth Walker
Renate Ysseldyk

We especially want to thank Elizabeth Walker, who, with her characteristic skill and grace as a hostess, volunteered significant time both before and during the 2-day event to help us ensure that the meeting was an enjoyable and successful event. She was the "go-to" person who took care of all sorts of details so that we could interact with the other participants, confident in the knowledge that everything would run smoothly under Elizabeth's oversight. Even after the event drew to a close, she played a crucial role, inviting Nancy Peddle to be a guest in her home rather than her staying in an impersonal hotel room before she flew back to Sierra Leone, as well as being the on-call person for Lise DeShea's international student from Japan, who was mysteriously detained by immigration when she attempted to return to graduate school in the United States! Thank you, Elizabeth; you are a cherished friend.

We would also like to acknowledge the financial assistance provided by our respective institutions, which allowed us to reduce some of the cost to the participants. Our thanks go out to Dr. David Siegel, dean of the faculty of social sciences at Brock University, and to Dr. Earl Davey, provost of Tyndale University College (where Wanda, at the time, was an assistant professor of psychology).

On the editorial front, we would like to thank Michelle Green for undertaking the onerous tasks of checking the references and correcting the formatting for each chapter in the book. Fred Coppersmith, the senior editorial assistant from Routledge, has our gratitude for his patient and helpful response to our many questions.

Last but by no means least, the people we live with have been there in the background, encouraging and supporting us while we worked on this project. Thank you, Denis, Leah, Stan, Sylvia, Tyler, and Van.

Wanda Malcolm, Brampton, Ontario

Nancy DeCourville, St. Catharines, Ontario

Kathryn Belicki, St. Catharines, Ontario

Women's Reflections on the Complexities of Forgiveness

WANDA MALCOLM, KATHRYN BELICKI, AND NANCY DeCOURVILLE

This is not a book about forgiveness in women; it is a book by women about forgiveness. The chapters have been contributed by women who have given considerable thought and energy to the task of understanding the controversies and conundrums of forgiveness and who, on the basis of their clinical and empirical work in the field, have significant things to say about the complexities of forgiveness that are worth considering.

When we first began to think about this project, we had in mind a book *about* forgiveness in women. We were stirred by a statement made by Connie Kristiansen (2004), when she spoke as chair of a symposium on forgiveness, that forgiveness is women's work. This was consistent with our own experience. It fit well with Wanda Malcolm's observation that women are more likely to volunteer to participate in psychotherapy research and also are more likely to come to therapy than men. The result is that we are more often studying women's forgiveness efforts than men's (a fact readily apparent from a cursory look at the demographics of most forgiveness studies other than those that focus on work with couples).

Kathy Belicki came to researching forgiveness from a background of studying the impact on adult functioning of childhood abuse, primarily sexual abuse, in which girls are more frequently victims than boys. It is noteworthy that—in contrast to the forgiveness research community, where there tends to be a largely positive view of forgiveness—within those studying and working with survivors of sexual abuse, the attitude toward forgiveness is decidedly more ambivalent. For example, the book that became the grassroots manual of choice, *The Courage to Heal* (Bass & Davis, 1988), espoused quite a negative view of forgiveness.

Many women's lived experience teaches them that compared with men, they can expect to have less financial, political, and professional or expertise-related power, with the consequence that they may also have greater difficulty owning power and living out of a grounded sense of personal power. This is likely to put women in subordinate positions in their personal and professional relationships with men; hence, forgiveness for the sake of repairing relationships may have great appeal to women, but it may also put them at risk of injury again if the hurtful other is inclined to misuse or abuse the power differential.

As one who has taught courses in the psychology of women, Nancy DeCourville is particularly sensitive to the notion of differential power. There has been little research on power and its impact on forgiveness: The little that has been done suggests that this is an important variable that merits more attention. For example, Aquino, Tripp, and Bies (2001) found that power interacted with vengefulness in complex ways. They found that employees of lower status were less forgiving than those of higher status and that people were more vengeful toward offenders of lower status. Mary Trainer observed that, when women are "assigned to passive and reactive roles in which they are not expected to act out feelings of anger, hostility and revenge and are expected to forgive, to be weak and accepting [of] injuries that occur" (1981, pp. 18–19), they are more likely to engage in forms of forgiveness that fall short of a self-empowered and empowering freedom to respond adaptively to interpersonal hurtfulness. This form of forgiveness, which Trainer refers to as role-expected forgiveness, can become "a weapon in the hands of the powerful to maintain the status quo, increasing perceptions of impotence."

Members of groups that hold positions of lower social, financial, or political power may also be told by authority figures (e.g., clergy and respected members of their own group who are afraid of what will happen if one of them resists someone of the more powerful group) that they "ought" to forgive; hence, they carry the burden of responsibility for addressing the hurtfulness, regardless of whether the offender acknowledges the harm done or seeks to make amends. Of course, having less power or status, while more common among women, is an issue not only for women, but also for men. An example of this comes from an interview study conducted by Nancy DeCourville and Kathy Belicki. One man who participated in that study recounted a particularly moving story of forgiveness. He indicated clearly that he had forgiven those who hurt him, but the quality of his forgiveness seemed very different from that of others. The difference did not come out so much in his words but in his tone of voice and general demeanor, which conveyed a sense of defeat and powerlessness.

The Field of Forgiveness Research Is a "Typical" Research Field for Women

There is research suggesting that, although not true of all female academics, many are inclined to conduct interdisciplinary research in new fields where there is less accumulated methodological wisdom and that in the process of doing so, they are inclined to question established definitions and conceptualizations (Aisenberg & Harrington, 1988). In fact, this is one of the strengths of women's research: They will use research methods that run counter to traditional or mainstream practices when conventional methods are not the best means of addressing the questions they pose about the phenomena they choose to study (Babbi & Benaquisto, 2002). This is evident in the present volume from the number of authors who have drawn on case studies (Malcolm, chapter 14) or qualitative research (Baker, chapter 4; DeCourville, Belicki, & Green, chapter 1; Freedman, chapter 6; Holeman, chapter 13; Macaskill, chapter 3; Peddle, chapter 10) to further their understanding of the complexities of forgiveness.

Aisenberg and Harrington (1988) have observed that women often prefer to work in fields that are important to human experience and hence focus their research on topics with immediate relevance to daily life. In addition to knowledge derived from positivist methods that work best for investigating objective, quantifiable phenomena, women are disposed to incorporate both experientially based and contextualized knowledge (i.e., knowledge or "truth" that varies according to the context in which it is encountered) into their research methodology (Babbi & Benaquisto, 2002), and they are more likely to situate that knowledge within its cultural context. Many women resist a reductionist approach to knowing. The result is that they are more willing to tolerate ambiguity in the answers they get to questions they have asked and have less need for the greater certainty that comes from abstraction (Aisenberg & Harrington, 1988). As a result of these research choices, their research tends to be slower to "mature" and is more likely to be published in less mainstream venues (Simeone, 1987).

The study of forgiveness is exactly such a field. It is an exciting one that has brought together thinkers from many disciplines, but it is also a field replete with methodological limitations including definitional, conceptual, and measurement issues. Many of the studies described in this volume rely on convenience samples of inadequate sizes. As a consequence, some of the reported research lacks the rigor that typifies older, more established fields. Nonetheless, most of the women who have taken the lead in contributing chapters to this book are experienced researchers and/or clinicians who are aware of the limitations of their research and, given the benefits that attend intrinsically motivated and satisfying work, accept that such limitations come with choosing to work in this field.

It was for these kinds of reasons that we became increasingly excited about a book *about* forgiveness in women, written by women. However, reality then intervened. As we called a meeting of potential authors who could contribute to the project, it quickly became clear that among those women whose principal focus is the study of forgiveness, there simply was not enough theoretical focus on forgiveness in women or the kind of related research that would be required to pull together a meaningful book on the topic.

The interest certainly was there. We planned a very small meeting for potential contributors and intentionally did not advertise, simply contacting people directly. Nonetheless, word swiftly spread. We were very pleased by the number of women who heard that there was a meeting to discuss "women's perspectives on forgiveness" and wanted to be there. The idea obviously struck a chord with other women, but with some regret, we stayed with our original intention to gather only a small group so that we could comfortably engage in extensive conversation.

If Not a Book Written by Women ***About*** *Forgiveness in Women, What Then?*

In the end, 28 of us gathered, and it was a meeting like nothing the three editors had ever experienced: Almost immediately, a new idea dawned. What about a book *by* women *about* forgiveness? From our experience of the meeting, we believed that such a book would be different from other books on forgiveness.

What did we experience in that meeting? There seemed to be more "thinking outside the box." There was a remarkable diversity of opinion about every aspect of forgiveness and a great tolerance for differing perspectives. Along with that, there was more opposition to statements that are beginning to emerge as "truisms" within the field than we had heard when two of us had attended a large international conference on forgiveness. There seemed to be little need or demand for unanimity and agreement, and there was greater tolerance for the ambiguities within the field. Those who gathered seemed to be delighted by the differences, intrigued by the ambiguities, and truly interested in hearing more about alternative positions to their own. A delightful spirit of collegiality and cooperation prevailed. For example, Lise DeShea provided everyone with a computer disk containing copies of the forgiveness scales and subscales that she had included in her investigation on the reliability and validity of forgiveness measures. Not one of us could remember attending a coed conference marked by such an absence of territoriality.

Many of the qualities we experienced at that meeting are mirrored in this book. There are several contradictory views. For example, Suzanne Freedman (chapter 6) argues for the careful delineation of true forgiveness and Marjorie Baker (chapter 4) makes a case for the need to differentiate adaptive self-forgiveness from other forms that are narcissistic and would undermine women's efforts to recover from drug and alcohol addictions. Renate Ysseldyk and Kim Matheson (chapter 8) also call for greater definitional precision, arguing that this is necessary if researchers hope to succeed in identifying psychological mechanisms linked to forgiveness. In contrast, Kathy Belicki and her colleagues (chapter 9) resist defining forgiveness in such a narrow way, seeing benefit in riskier, "messier" forms of forgiveness. DeCourville and her coauthors (chapter 1) suggest that we would be better off acknowledging and attempting to document the different forms that forgiveness takes, in order to align our research and clinical efforts with the real-world variability in people's understandings of forgiveness.

On the one hand, Suzanne Freedman (chapter 6) and Marjorie Baker (chapter 4) are enthusiastic about the potential benefits of therapeutic facilitation of other- and self-forgiveness, and Kathleen Lawler-Row and Kimberly Reed (chapter 5) provide evidence of associations between forgiveness and enhanced physical, mental, and spiritual health. On the other hand, Helen Chagigiorgis and Sandra Paivio (chapter 7) and Wanda Malcolm (chapter 14) tend to be more tempered in their enthusiasm about promoting forgiveness within therapy; they argue that self-repair work, which includes clients' processing their feelings about the hurtful other and what she or he did, takes precedence over the goal of arriving at a stance of forgiveness. As Helen Chagigiorgis and Sandra Paivio put it, "[C]lients need to feel better about and stronger within themselves before they can fully confront offenders and unequivocally hold them responsible for harm." Furthermore, Helen Chagigiorgis and Sandra Paivio consider it of utmost importance that clients (particularly those who have suffered traumatic abuse as children) determine for themselves what constitutes a positive outcome of therapy.

Similarly, Wanda Malcolm holds to the view that it is always the client's right to determine if, or when, she or he might forgive a hurtful other. She argues that too much pressure to forgive could invalidate the client's experience and undermine the client's perception of the self as strong enough to come to terms with the pain and suffering involved in experiencing an interpersonal injury at the hands of a loved one. Kathleen Lawler-Row (chapter 5) also notes the role of time and self-repair work in the kind of forgiveness that leads to good physical, mental, and spiritual health.

Renate Ysseldyk and Kim Matheson (chapter 8) report research that demonstrates an association between both dispositional and state forgiveness and coping strategies. They point out the potential for forgiveness to be a maladaptive method of coping if it is associated with self-blame and passive resignation, as was the case with participants in their study who remained in or returned to psychologically abusive relationships. This dovetails nicely with the concern expressed by Helen Chagigiorgis and Sandra Paivio (chapter 7) that forgiveness might not be the best alternative for recovering from the trauma of childhood abuse if it prevents clients from asserting themselves as undeserving of the abuse or discourages them from holding the abuser responsible for his or her actions.

In keeping with the idea that forgiveness might not be the best route to recovery, it is fascinating to note that two sets of authors (Chagigiorgis & Paivio, chapter 7, and Peddle, chapter 10) studying different populations (childhood abuse survivors and war refugees, respectively) found that while those who forgave also met other criteria of resolution or recovery, the reverse was not true: Not all who met the criteria for recovery or resolution forgave. Furthermore, Chagigiorgis and Paivio did not find significant differences in outcome between those whose resolution included forgiveness and those who did not forgive. This echoes the research findings of Warwar, Greenberg, and Malcolm (under review), who found that clients who forgave were always among those who had let go of distressing feelings against the person who injured them and among those who made marked improvements from pre- to post-therapy. However, the reverse was not true: Not everyone who let go of distressing feelings and made marked improvements on outcome indices forgave. This kind of finding is a corrective for uncritical endorsements of forgiveness that may be perceived by the public to mean that forgiveness is the only valid or always the best way to recover from interpersonal hurtfulness.

In the spirit of not accepting conventional wisdom unquestioned, Kathy Belicki, Jessica Rourke, and Megan McCarthy (chapter 9) ponder the potential downside of empathy and note that being able to take the perspective of the injurer increases the likelihood not only of adaptive forgiveness, but also of accepting excuses that may put a person at risk of being injured again. Just to keep readers on their toes, they also explain how excuses may sometimes be the kindest response to being confronted with wrongdoing because an explanation of the mitigating circumstances allows the harm-doer to affirm that even if she or he did not intend the harm, what she or he did was wrong, and the hurt person has a right to be upset.

The Complexities of Forgiveness

Along with significant contradictions and overlap among the authors who contributed to this volume, almost all of the chapters share a common characteristic: The authors tend to view forgiveness as a complex issue. Furthermore, without any direction from us, most saw the writing of their chapters as an opportunity to reflect on some puzzling feature of forgiveness. For example, Julie Exline and her colleagues (Exline, Baumeister, Bushman, Campbell, & Finken, 2004) had earlier recognized that an inflated sense of self-entitlement is likely to serve as an obstacle to forgiveness. In this book, she and Anne Zell (chapter 12) describe their efforts to instill humility, a possible antidote for an inflated sense of self-entitlement. In discovering how difficult it is to identify and then instill an adaptive form of humility, they provide us with a greater appreciation for the challenges faced by those of us who hope our research will prove useful to clinical work.

Ann Macaskill (chapter 3) took up the challenging task of looking at how just- and unjust-world views may affect how forgiving people are. She also undertook a qualitative investigation of the ways in which people respond to traumatic, uncontrollable situations that cannot be attributed to human agency (e.g., natural disasters) and how this differs from forgiveness in the wake of human hurtfulness. One of her noteworthy findings is that like interpersonal hurtfulness, acceptance of traumatic, uncontrollable situations evokes a need to hold someone responsible for what happened, even when doing so is recognized to be (at least in the case of natural disasters) irrational behavior.

The understandings of forgiveness that emerge from this volume are less definitive than readers might like. However, it is precisely this lack of definitiveness that gives rise to a richer, less simplistic conceptualization of forgiveness and the process of forgiving than would be possible if unanimity had been the goal. Sandra Rafman (chapter 11) has contributed a chapter that is unique to the current forgiveness field. She draws our attention to the poignant dilemmas that children face as they try to make sense of their experience of the trauma of war or political violence—particularly when that trauma has included the loss of parents or having been the witness of horrific acts that have destroyed their moral universe and left them without a moral "compass" to guide their response to those who perpetrated the violence or their response to themselves if they have been forced to engage in immoral acts in order to survive. Working with a similar population, Nancy Peddle (chapter 10) unpacks the experience of war refugees from the former Yugoslavia, Africa, and Europe, and looks at the links among forgiveness, resilience, and recovery from war trauma. In the process of doing so, she finds a pattern that is similar to one identified by Kathleen Lawler-Row and Kimberly Reed (chapter 5): People's inclinations to forgive increase with age.

Virginia Holeman (chapter 13) draws our attention away from an exclusive focus on the person doing the forgiving to the role of apology and, more extensively, to the process of repentance as these are involved in seeking to repair the harm one has done as a consequence of acting hurtfully.

We sought to provide a venue in which women felt free to present their perspectives on the complexities of forgiveness. Our expectation was that this would add a distinctive voice to the field and enrich our understanding of a phenomenon that impinges on everyone's life, one way or another, sooner or later. We invite those who read the book to come to their own conclusions about whether we have succeeded in what we set out to do.

References

Aisenberg, N., & Harrington, M. (1988). *Women of academe: Outsiders in the sacred grove.* Amherst: The University of Massachusetts Press.

Aquino, K., Tripp, T. M., & Bies, R. J. (2001). How employees respond to personal offense: The effects of blame attribution, victim status, and offender status on revenge and reconciliation in the workplace. *Journal of Applied Psychology, 86*, 52–59.

Babbi, E., & Benaquisto, L. (2002). *Fundamentals of social research* (1st Canadian ed.). Toronto: Thomson Canada Limited.

Bass, E., & Davis, L. (1988). *The courage to heal: A guide for women survivors of child sexual abuse.* New York: Harper & Row.

Exline, J. J., Baumeister, R. F., Bushman, B. J., Campbell, W. K., & Finken, E. J. (2004). Too proud to let go: Narcissistic entitlement as a barrier to forgiveness. *Journal of Personality and Social Psychology, 87*(6), 894–912.

Kristiansen, C. (2004). *Moderator's comments for a symposium on forgiveness.* Paper presented at the annual meeting of the Canadian Psychological Association, St. John's, Newfoundland, Canada.

Simeone, A. (1987). *Academic women: Working towards equality.* South Hadley, MA: Bergin & Garvey Publishers, Inc.

Trainer, M. F. (1981) *Forgiveness: Intrinsic, role-expected, expedient, in the context of divorce.* Unpublished doctoral dissertation, Boston University, Boston, MA.

Warwar, S., Greenberg, L., & Malcolm, W. M. (under review). *Differential effects of emotion focused therapy and psycho-education in facilitating forgiveness and letting go of emotional injuries.*

1

Subjective Experiences of Forgiveness in a Community Sample

Implications for Understanding Forgiveness and Its Consequences*

NANCY DeCOURVILLE, KATHRYN BELICKI, AND MICHELLE M. GREEN

Introduction

In the course of human relationships, it is virtually impossible to avoid hurting others and being hurt by them. One response to interpersonal offenses is to forgive the offender, thereby opening the door to reconciliation and increasing the likelihood of living "happily ever after." This assumption that forgiveness is beneficial to individuals and relationships, even when it is not stated explicitly, is implicit in much of the research investigating its correlates, antecedents, determinants, and consequences.

It has been suggested that forgiveness is important to repairing the damage that occurs as a result of hurtful, interpersonal events in the work place (Aquino, Grover, Goldman, & Folger, 2003) and in the context of close relationships (Fincham & Beach, 2001). In fact, Fenell (1993) claimed that forgiveness is one of the most important factors contributing to marital longevity and satisfaction. Others have argued that forgiveness may be beneficial to the mental and physical

* The authors are grateful to the Social Sciences and Humanities Research Council of Canada and the Brock University Advancement Fund for their financial support of this research.

health of individuals (e.g., Mauger et al., 1992; McCullough, 2000; Thoresen, Harris, & Luskin, 2000). In contrast, only a few scholars have countered that forgiveness may be maladaptive because the offended individual may be placed at risk of repeated harm (Bass & Davis, 1994; Katz, Street, & Arias, 1997).

One serious challenge facing forgiveness researchers is determining exactly what it means to forgive. It is unlikely that scholars will arrive at a consensual definition of forgiveness, due, at least in part, to the many issues involved in defining this construct, including whether it is interpersonal, intrapersonal, or both; whether it is situational, dispositional, motivational, or some combination of these; whether it is affective, cognitive, or behavioral, or involves all three; and whether it is a process or a discrete event or act.

These issues are evident from differences in how forgiveness is defined by scholars and from the proliferation of measures described in the literature (DeShea, this volume). For example, Enright and the Human Development Study Group (1991) maintain that forgiveness involves replacing negative affect, cognitions, and behaviors directed at the transgressor with positive affect, cognitions, and behaviors, whereas Thompson et al. (2005) argue that moving to a neutral position with respect to the transgressor is sufficient. In other work, McCullough (2000) has taken a motivational approach, defining forgiveness as a composite of changes in three sets of motives (i.e., avoidance, revenge, and benevolence) underlying reactions to the transgressor.

In contrast, there is considerable agreement among scholars on what forgiveness is *not* (e.g., Enright, Freedman, & Rique, 1998; Rye et al., 2001). The majority agrees that forgiveness is not: forgetting the offense; denying that an offense occurred; accepting that an offense occurred, but ignoring its consequences; excusing an offense on the basis of mitigating circumstances; condoning or justifying an offense; pardoning or granting amnesty to an offender; or the same as reconciliation.

Definitional issues have been acknowledged by researchers, including Fincham and Beach (2001), who pointed out that there is a tendency for both researchers and laypersons to assume a common understanding of the term "forgiveness." This tendency is a barrier to communicating about and researching forgiveness because people undoubtedly differ in how they define and practice forgiveness. Nonetheless, research has generally employed definitions derived by scholars, with seemingly little concern with how forgiveness is actually experienced and defined by laypersons.

This omission has not escaped notice. Indeed, Rye et al. (2001) have argued that "social scientists need to study whether most people practice forgiveness in accordance with the conceptualizations provided by social scientists, philosophers, and religious leaders" (p. 261). They have noted that it is important to understand how people experience forgiveness because the consequences may differ as a function of how they forgive. Witvliet (2001) also recognized the importance of considering the perspectives of laypersons in trying to understand the relation between forgiveness and health and well-being, noting that individuals' responses to forgiveness-related questions are influenced by what forgiveness means to them. Thus, if there are important differences between how forgiveness is defined by researchers and how it is experienced/defined by laypersons, the potential impact of such discrepancies on our understanding of forgiveness is, as yet, unknown.

As an illustration of the possible impact of differing definitions of forgiveness, consider the finding that the relations between forgiveness and health and well-being (i.e., mental, physical, relationship), whether examined experimentally or in correlational research, tend to be modest at best (McCullough & Witvliet, 2002). Based on these modest relations, it could be argued that forgiveness is not particularly beneficial to health and well-being. A plausible alternative explanation is that forgiveness *is* beneficial, but that the relationship between forgiveness and health is more complex than that revealed through simple correlations. For example, forgiveness may have differential effects on health as a function of such factors as personality, characteristics of the offense (e.g., severity), characteristics of the offender (e.g., type of relationship), and social–psychological influences (e.g., social support); researchers have begun to examine these complexities (e.g., Green, 2005; Lawler et al., 2005). A third possibility, suggested by Thompson and Snyder (2004), is that forgiveness may be beneficial to physical, mental, and relationship health and well-being, but that the nature and degree of the beneficial effects depend, at least in part, on how forgiveness is defined and experienced.

There is some support for this notion in results reported by Trainer (1981), who hypothesized and tested the validity of three types of forgiveness: expedient forgiveness (to fulfill a social goal such as a need to "get along with" an offending coworker or family member), role-expected forgiveness (expected or required by a particular social role, such as employee or parent), and intrinsic forgiveness (involving a positive change in emotions, cognitions, and behaviors relative to the offender). Trainer reported that expedient forgiveness was accompanied by hostility, which has been shown to be associated with poor cardiovascular health (Miller, Smith, Turner, Guijarro, & Hallet, 1996, cited in McCullough & Witvliet, 2002). In addition, her results suggested that role-expected forgiveness may be accompanied by fear, anxiety, and resentment, which also tend to be associated with lower levels of well-being. Finally, intrinsic forgiveness involves a change in attitudes and feelings toward the offender and may be beneficial to health and well-being, although, to our knowledge, this has not been demonstrated empirically.

If actual experiences of forgiveness are accurately represented by the manner in which forgiveness is defined by scholars, research efforts should be directed at investigating the possible mechanisms underlying the forgiveness–health relationship. However, if actual experiences of forgiveness differ from academic definitions of the construct, a more pressing candidate for research may be to develop measures of forgiveness that reflect individuals' experiences. This, in turn, would enhance the potential to advance our understanding of its effects, if any, on health and well-being.

There is research suggesting that laypersons' definitions and experiences of forgiveness are different from how forgiveness is defined in the literature. Brenneis (2002) asked 88 male clergy members undergoing residential psychological treatment to respond in writing to the question, "What does forgiveness mean to you?" The goal was to compare the extent to which these clergy members agreed with representations of forgiveness in the literature. Results clearly showed differences: Respondents focused on emotional or affective elements of their experience almost to the exclusion of the cognitive, behavioral, and moral concerns prominent in published definitions of forgiveness.

In other research, Zechmeister and Romero (2002) examined individuals' experiences of forgiveness indirectly through the use of 215 written personal accounts of situations in which participants were offended and forgave (or not) and in which they offended another and were forgiven (or not). Results indicated that there were differences between how forgiveness was experienced and how it is defined by researchers (e.g., some victims continued to experience anger directed at the offender, despite having indicated that they had forgiven).

Kanz (2000) also examined how people defined and experienced forgiveness in a sample of 155 undergraduates. In that study, participants were asked to respond to questions based on how forgiveness is represented in the literature (e.g., whether reconciliation is a necessary part of forgiveness). Although the patterns of responses tended to be in agreement with the manner in which forgiveness is conceptualized by researchers, there were areas of disagreement. For example, the majority of respondents indicated that reconciliation was a necessary part of forgiveness, that they felt guilty if they did not forgive, and that forgiveness could cause emotional problems.

More recently, Mullet, Girard, and Bakhshi (2004) addressed the question of how people conceptualize forgiveness by presenting a large sample ($N = 1{,}029$) of individuals with 93 statements designed to represent aspects of forgiveness presented in the literature—for example, "To forgive necessarily means to start feeling affection toward the offender again" (p. 80). Results of exploratory and confirmatory factor analyses revealed substantial disagreement with how forgiveness is conceptualized by researchers, including the notion that forgiveness involves "a change of heart toward the offender" (p. 85).

Thus, there is a growing body of research documenting discrepancies between researchers' and laypersons' definitions of forgiveness. However, as with virtually any research (including the research described in this chapter), there are limitations to the studies described previously. Brenneis's (2002) sample comprised clergy members who could be characterized as troubled. Moreover, they were asked to define forgiveness in response to a particular injury—that of having been hurt by the authority who required that they undergo treatment.

Zechmeister and Romero (2002) reviewed abbreviated accounts (on average, nine sentences each) in which participants were asked to describe situations in which they had either been hurt by or had hurt another. Thus, although Zechmeister and Romero examined the accounts for descriptions of forgiveness and unforgiveness, understanding the experience was not the primary goal of their work. The research conducted by Kanz (2000) required that participants respond "yes" or "no" to the items they included in their survey, thus excluding the possibility of more nuanced beliefs on the part of respondents. Finally, Mullet et al. (2004) were concerned primarily with examining specific aspects of definitions of forgiveness. The research reported here was designed specifically to try to understand how people experience and define forgiveness for themselves.

Our Study

Participants were 19 women and 10 men who responded to a call for volunteers placed in the university newsletter and subsequently picked up by several regional newspapers. Participants ranged in age from 17 to 80 ($M = 46.79$, $SD = 17.33$). Their educational backgrounds ranged from grade 9 through completion of a graduate degree. More than half of the participants were married ($n = 17$, 58.6%); five were single (17.2%), three were separated (10.3%), two were divorced (6.9%), and two were widowed (6.9%). Participants included homemakers, entrepreneurs, factory workers, teachers, a dietician, writers, laborers, students, retired persons, a counselor, church ministers, and clerical/office employees. All but two participants indicated that they believed in God, and all who indicated their religious affiliation reported that they were Christian (e.g., Anglican, Roman Catholic, Mennonite). Thirteen (44.8%) of the participants indicated at least weekly attendance at church. The remainder did not attend church ($n = 8$, 27.6%), attended only occasionally ($n = 5$, 17.2%), did not respond ($n = 1$, 3.4%), or were not asked this question ($n = 2$, 6.9%).

Approximately 100 community members left voice messages expressing an interest in hearing more about the study. They were contacted by telephone and given details on the nature of the research. Given the large number of callers, it was decided that the first 30 who agreed to participate would be interviewed. One individual agreed to participate initially, but did not appear as scheduled. The individual was invited to reschedule, but declined. No explanation was asked for or given. Appointments were scheduled either at the university or at the respondent's home, depending on the participant's preference. At the scheduled appointment, the study was again explained and the participants invited to ask questions about any aspect of the research. Participants then signed the informed consent, retaining a copy for themselves, and were given $30 and the cost of parking as a token of appreciation for their participation. They were thanked for their participation and invited to contact us if they had any questions or wished to add anything to what they had said in the interview. Subsequent to the interviews, several individuals wrote or telephoned to express their thanks for having had the opportunity to talk about their experiences. One participant called to describe another incident of forgiveness in her life.

Information was obtained by means of 1.5- to 2-hour, semistructured interviews conducted by the first two authors and a mature honors student with extensive interviewing experience. All interviews were tape recorded and transcribed verbatim. A typical interview* began by asking participants to describe a situation in which they had been hurt and had forgiven the person who hurt them. Participants were also queried about situations in which they had been hurt, but had not forgiven; had hurt someone else and had been forgiven; and had hurt someone else and had not been forgiven. They were asked to explain what forgiveness meant to them as well as to answer general questions about issues debated in the literature, such as whether some acts are unforgivable and whether forgiveness is relevant in the case of unavoidable accidents or when someone other than the participant is injured (someone close or a stranger). Finally, participants were asked to provide information on their age, education, and occupation, and about their religious or spiritual practices.

Verbatim transcripts were read repeatedly with an eye for elements that have been discussed in the literature as essential to defining

* A copy of the interview protocol that served as a guideline for the interviews is available from Nancy DeCourville.

forgiveness. Specifically, we looked for evidence to suggest that forgiveness involved a conscious choice, transformation of negative affect (hatred) to positive (love) or neutral (indifference), transformation of negative cognitions (bad person) to positive (good person) or neutral (indifferent), and transformation of negative behaviors (vengeful acts) to positive (approach) or neutral (ignore). We also examined the transcripts to determine whether, or to what extent, our participants' views and experiences incorporated elements that have been described as not characteristic of forgiveness (i.e., forgetting, accepting, excusing, condoning, pardoning, denying, or reconciling) and for elements that represented novel views of forgiveness.

As indicated earlier, participants were asked to describe a situation in which they had forgiven someone (virtually all participants described more than one situation over the course of the interview). Ten participants reported childhood abuse (physical, sexual, psychological, or some combination of these); 19 spoke of a variety of incidents in adulthood, including motor vehicle accidents involving an intoxicated driver, infidelity, accusations of personal misconduct, and interpersonal conflicts in the context of intimate or work relationships.

Many of the participants had difficulty articulating a definition of forgiveness, although most attempted to do so. In many instances, the attempts to understand just what individuals meant by forgiveness required substantial probing of their experiences.

Forgiveness Is a Choice

One important element in academic definitions is that forgiveness is a "willed change of heart" (North, 1998, p. 21). Consistent with this notion, many stated very clearly that they had made a conscious decision to forgive. For one woman, making the decision to forgive is what she termed her philosophy of life. In her words, "[S]o, I thought the only way to end this and to stop walking around pretending ... and so it was a very easy decision." Another participant said,

> [N]o amount of external stuff can make you forgive. You have to ... it has to be an internal choice that you make and sometimes those external things can help you get there, but it can't be the thing that makes you do it.

Moreover, the motivations for forgiving differed among those who indicated that they had made a decision to forgive. Most said that they chose to forgive because they knew that forgiveness would relieve them of the burden of negative emotions. Others chose to forgive because they believed that they were obligated to do so by religious or personal convictions. These individuals also indicated that they felt better after forgiving. One woman seemed to be motivated by emotional and physical health concerns: "Just to reiterate how essential it [forgiveness] is to a healthy, functioning life. I've witnessed too many people who've been hurt and because of unforgiveness … they have robbed themselves of a good life."

Others came to forgiveness differently. One woman, who had been physically and emotionally abused by her father in childhood, recalled her thoughts following an occasion during which she saw her father interacting lovingly with her own children and realized, suddenly, that she had forgiven him. She said:

> Yeah, it [forgiveness] came in a moment. Like an epiphany moment, you know. It was just one of those moments in time—but the feeling, I can always remember that, of just release and that lightness of being that I'm talking about. Like, I can't explain even the words that would apply to that.

Another woman also reported having forgiven spontaneously: "I was driving to work one morning and I went, 'Ohh, I think I've forgiven him.' I really do, and it was like a weight was lifted off me. I knew I'd forgiven him." A slightly different perspective was voiced by a man who said, "It's almost like—I can't even choose—forgiveness will happen. It's almost as if you realize deep down that you're going to have to interact with this person and if you don't forgive them, life will become more difficult."

Replacing Negative Thoughts, Feelings, and Behaviors With Positive Thoughts, Feelings, and Behaviors

Some of our participants indicated that they now had good feelings about the person who had hurt them, but others were simply indifferent. A few made it clear that, although they had forgiven, they certainly did not have good thoughts on the occasions in which the offender came to mind. This is illustrated by a statement made by one man: "There's probably a little malice yet. Will I ever get rid of it? I don't know."

Forgiveness as "Letting Go" of Negative Feelings

Many of our participants experienced forgiveness as a release from negative feelings, including bitterness, hatred, and anger—in fact, this was probably the most cited benefit of forgiveness. This is illustrated by the account of a woman who had been raped by a stepbrother and abused by her stepfather in childhood and forgave these offenders many years later. "I really feel released from all that acid, the burning acid. It's as though, going through those processes of forgiving your perpetrators, you take, you neutralize the pain, you know?" In a similar vein, another participant who had also been physically and psychologically abused by her father, defined forgiveness as "releasing negative energy and constrictive energy that is damaging you, that you have to forgive in order to get rid of that, and once you do that, there's this lightness of being that you have." These women indicated that they forgave so as to feel better.

Forgiveness to Feel Better

Scholars have been very clear on the notion that forgiveness is not done just to feel better, but this is exactly what so many of our participants said. In fact, some were adamant about wanting to feel better as their main (and, for some, the only) reason for forgiving.

Forgiveness as an Obligation

Several of our participants said that they felt obliged to forgive, as a result of either church teachings or personal standards of morality. This sense of obligation was clear from one woman, who said, "I *have* to learn to forgive others," but seemed to experience this obligation as a welcome task, rather than as a burden.

Contrast that with the experience of one man who felt obligated to forgive, but for whom the obligation seemed to be onerous. When asked to explain what he meant by forgiveness, he said:

> I had a lot of anger … malice … hatred—all those things. Now, if we think of forgiveness, we think of the opposite of that. Of extending to them loving, kindness, doing well to them. We don't hold any malice in our heart; we don't hold any hatred; we try to turn it all into a loving—a loving situation.

This man had been deeply offended by church authorities and shunned by its members, a very traumatic situation because his church was one of the most important elements in his life. Several times over the course of the interview, he said, "I *had* to forgive—that's part of God's word." His tone of voice and manner made it seem as though forgiveness was something that he *was compelled* to do; there was a sense of almost grim determination. That this man still felt some anger and hurt was evident from comments he made later in the interview. Nevertheless, he stated more than once that he had forgiven. Incidentally, this man's idea of forgiveness clearly indicated that it did not involve *forgetting*—a sentiment expressed by others:

> We would lay that all down and it would be forgotten.… Now, forgiveness is a little bit like when I was a boy, there was a fairly large boulder laying in the field and Dad always had implements, and one day he went back and dug a big hole beside it … and we rolled the stone in the hole and covered it over and it seemed like I—when we walked that field, it was always "that's where Dad buried the stone" … so, that's sort of forgiveness, we try to bury it. I don't think we forget it, but we try not to dig it up again.

Forgiveness as Aggression

One woman, who had been sexually assaulted by a babysitter, spoke of forgiving him as a release from anger and bitterness and said that there were different kinds of forgiveness: "There's two different ways to forgive, though; there's just forgiving in your own mind, and then there's the other type of forgiveness where you go out and you force them to acknowledge that ... they've hurt you." This woman had also been neglected and emotionally abandoned by her mother, whom she blamed for not recognizing that she had been assaulted. At the interview, she reported having forgiven her mother for the neglect, but her forgiveness was somewhat aggressive and hurtful in itself. She had said, "I forgive you for being a total ass and total idiot and being totally unaware, and uncaring about your child's well-being and I only thank God that you didn't have any more children." As an explanation, she said:

> When I went up to my mother and said, "I forgive you for being a totally inattentive parent," part of that was for me to acknowledge verbally that this occurred and this is how it affected me. So part of that was totally, strictly for me and my benefit. You know that was me venting what I needed to vent. The other part was to force her to acknowledge that she had a role in it.

Later in the interview, this participant reiterated what she had said earlier about two kinds of forgiveness and added, "You're waving a white flag but really you've got a sword in your other hand."

Forgiveness as Intrapersonal Versus Interpersonal Phenomenon

In contrast with those who forgave for themselves, some included consideration of the offender in their definition of forgiveness. One woman, who had been sexually molested as a child, defined forgiveness as

> allowing other people to have the grace to live their lives and make their mistakes without holding them in a box you created for the rest of your life. It's realizing that, I mean, how other people live their lives *does* impact you, but you can't constrain them in that action for the rest of both of your lives or neither life is going to be happy, meaningful, productive.

This woman's approach to forgiving involved talking things out with people who had hurt her, as well as with those whom she had hurt. For her, getting to forgiveness necessarily involved the offender.

Another woman also spoke of forgiveness as a release, but saw it as a release for *both* the offended party and the offender. This woman, who had been seriously injured in a collision with a drunk driver and continued to suffer the effects of that incident, said, "Forgiving is loving … and it's healing … I think it's healing for the other person too … once you forgive a person who has hurt you, you release them." Yet, another participant saw forgiveness as something she did entirely for herself:

> It's nothing to do with the other person … I used to think forgiveness was about forgiving the other person but as I've gotten older, I realize that it has nothing to do with that. It just has nothing to do with the other person.

Several of our participants indicated that an important component of forgiveness was to tell their offenders that they (the victim) had forgiven. In fact, one woman said that, without this step, "your forgiveness is not complete." Others said that this step was unnecessary, or irrelevant to their experiences of forgiveness. One man said that he would not tell his offender because "if I say I forgive him, then I have accused him of a major error." Another man, who had been abandoned by his father at a young age, said:

> Forgiveness, I think, is to let *him* know that I forgave him for it. So that even in his mind, he won't be sitting back and wondering … so that I think forgiveness *requires* that you let the other person know as well.

Acceptance

As mentioned earlier, forgiveness researchers typically agree with the notion that forgiveness is not acceptance. However, several participants specifically used that term when they talked of their experiences. One woman, who had experienced conflict at work that affected her and her coworkers, said, "I think that it means just acceptance, accepting the person, accepting the situation for what it is, that that happened." After some difficult months, she confronted the individual with whom she had had the conflict and eventually came to a resolution: It was not exactly what she had hoped for, but she was satisfied that she had done her best and had forgiven the offender.

Conditions for Forgiveness

Two recurring themes in people's definitions and experiences of forgiveness were the conviction that the offense would not recur, and the idea that the offender must be remorseful. These are evident in the following definition, provided by a young woman whose father had been physically and emotionally abusive toward her throughout her childhood. Forgiveness means:

> I've put aside the wrong that was done to me because I know that he loves me and that it would never happen again, that he regrets what he did and that, in order to have a healthy relationship, I can't hold onto it because it's going to destroy me, it's going to destroy him and any chance we have at happiness as a father and daughter.

For this woman, forgiveness was contingent on the offender's actions. She had been unable to forgive until her father apologized to her. She also made this contingency clear when she spoke of her mother, whom she believed to be responsible for instigating many of the father–daughter conflicts out of jealousy. She said that she was unable to forgive her mother because the latter would not acknowledge that she had done anything wrong; although she longed to be able to forgive her mother and to reconcile with her, she could not do so until her mother admitted to having hurt her.

Separating the Person From the Act

Another recurring theme in people's descriptions is illustrated by this next definition, provided by a young woman who had been bullied and harassed by schoolmates—that is, the idea of separating the person from the act. She said that forgiveness meant "not having anger inside me any more, and being able to look at them as a person rather than what they did to me." Another said, "That's why I could forgive him ... separate what he did from that person."

Reconciliation

It was very clear that, for some, reconciliation and forgiveness were synonymous. Indeed, at least one individual said that she knew she had forgiven one person *because* they were now close friends. When asked whether reconciliation was part of forgiveness, one woman responded, "In the ideal situation, yes. I don't think it's always possible. It may not even also always be healthy." Another said, "When forgiving someone, we have two ways to go: either put the past behind us and seek reconciliation or live with the pain for the rest of your life."

Understanding/Justifying

Several of our participants emphasized the importance of understanding why their respective offenders had hurt them, but there were differences in the nature of this understanding. Some made up a story about why the offender did what she or he did to hurt them, and then they acted as if this were fact. In some cases, this sounded very much like justifying or excusing the behaviors rather than empathic perspective taking, which has been shown to be related to forgiveness. According to one man,

> You would have to look at that person and feel that they … somehow lost it or whatever and you have to forgive him. And, I would have to use the basis that he didn't understand, he didn't know, he was mentally ill or some kind of a thing that would have to help me through that forgiveness.

The woman for whom forgiveness of her father's abuse "came in a moment" described how, some years after she had forgiven him, she began to consider how his wartime experiences had probably affected his behavior: He had suffered from war nerves and had never had any help: "So then, of course, the family he had were going to be the victims." This same woman was able to forgive the man who killed her brother only after she was able to convince herself that the latter had not intended to do so even though she had never actually communicated with him. Another example of this notion of understanding, which more closely resembles empathy, came from a man who had been assaulted physically. He said that he had been able to forgive a coworker who had assaulted him because he understood the man's very difficult life situation: "[I] could visualize the trauma he was going through. I was trying to put myself in his position."

Impermanence

Another point that some of our participants made was that they were surprised to find themselves revisiting an incident that they believed they had forgiven and having to go through the process of forgiving more than once. All of those who spoke of this indicated that the process became easier and that "re-forgiving" happened more quickly each time.

Intra-individual Differences

Several of our participants spoke of more than one incident in which they had forgiven an offender. We noticed that experiences of forgiveness varied not only between individuals but also within individuals, indicating that situational forces and the nature of the offense influenced the extent to which they forgave their offenders. One participant had been able to forgive a family friend who had sexually assaulted her repeatedly. This same respondent, to her own expressed consternation, had been unable to forgive a colleague who had demeaned her in the presence of other coworkers by commenting negatively on her appearance. She speculated that her ability to forgive the former was validated by the fact that the damage inflicted on her body had healed and that the offender, whom she still saw occasionally, was clearly not "living the good life." In contrast, many years after the incident, she continued to feel hurt, angry, and humiliated at the thought of the insult to which she had been subjected and that however hard she tried, she was unable to forgive her former colleague. This point of view was echoed by another participant, who said:

> I would say things that don't affect my sort of immediate sense of self, who I believe myself to be, are very easy to forgive. If they affect who I do believe myself to be or who I think I am, if they really challenge that thinking, then that's harder.

It seems that forgiving has less to do with the objective nature of the offense and more to do with the meaning of the offense to the individual. For example, one woman was raped by a stranger about 30 years before the interview and had never been able to get over it. At the time of the interview, she indicated that she was still afraid and definitely had not forgiven, acknowledging that her feelings about that particular incident differed from other serious offenses committed against her: "Now there I can't separate *that* [person from the act] ... You know, I'm thinking that person. How hateful. See, that doesn't go with the other stuff I'm saying because that was a personal invasion, I think."

Conclusion/Implications

These results indicate that people differ in how they define and experience forgiveness. Indeed, if we were to rely on how forgiveness is depicted in the literature, we would have to conclude that relatively few of our participants described experiences that could be called forgiveness. Moreover, none of the participants' definitions matched those presented in the literature, although some shared elements of definitions provided by scholars, including forgiveness as a choice and forgiveness as a transformation of negative thoughts, behaviors, and feelings to positive or neutral. Our findings argue for broadening existing definitions (at least operational definitions as reflected in measures of forgiveness) to include, as much as possible, the experiences of those who have forgiven, despite the fact that there has been at least one call to narrow the manner in which forgiveness is defined (e.g., "definitional drift," Enright et al., 1998, pp. 50–51).

It is clear from our results that like many researchers, laypersons also assume that forgiveness is beneficial to mental and physical health, to maintenance of good relationships, and to repair of damaged relationships. This may well prove to be the case, but answering this question will not be an easy task. Consistent with Trainer's (1981) findings, it may be that only certain aspects of forgiveness, such as reduction in negative emotions (most likely anger and hostility) or certain ways of forgiving, will be associated with better health and enhanced well-being.

One option is to continue to develop measures that incorporate elements that have been identified by individuals as important to their notions of forgiveness in addition to those described by scholars. This option will require abandoning notions of what is "true" forgiveness and what forgiveness is not because some of the latter (e.g., justifying, reconciling) are important to the process of forgiving for individuals.

Understanding the forgiveness–well-being relationship may be facilitated by taking a more person-centered, rather than variable-centered, approach. This could be accomplished by examining how forgiveness-related variables cluster within individuals and looking at the extent to which these configurations, or types, are shared by others, reminiscent of Trainer's (1981) work. These types could then be used to examine the relationship between forgiveness and well-being (physical, psychological, or relationship). Such an approach would render moot the issue of whether someone has, objectively, forgiven or not—an issue that has been raised in the literature. For example, Fincham and Beach (2001) wrote that "to say I forgive you does not thereby constitute forgiveness" (p. 171). In contrast, Neblett (1974) argued that there are situations in which "saying 'I forgive you' *does* constitute forgiveness. And ... that it is a mistake to imagine that there is some specific and definable activity, which activity, and no other, constitutes forgiveness" (p. 269). Given the finding that the best predictor of morbidity and mortality is an individual's self-assessment of physical health (Idler & Benyamini, 1997), it is reasonable to conclude that the best predictor of forgiveness and its consequences would be the individual's self-assessment. It is time we listened.

References

Aquino, K., Grover, S. L., Goldman, B., & Folger, R. (2003). When push doesn't come to shove: Interpersonal forgiveness in workplace relationships. *Journal of Management Inquiry, 12,* 209–216.

Bass, E., & Davis, L. (1994). *The courage to heal: A guide for women survivors of child sexual abuse.* Toronto: Fitzhenry & Whiteside.

Brenneis, M. J. (2002). Understandings, definitions, and experiences of clergy in residential psychiatric treatment. *Counseling and Values, 46,* 84–95.

Enright, R. D., Freedman, S., & Rique, J. (1998). The psychology of interpersonal forgiveness. In R. D. Enright & J. North (Eds.), *Exploring forgiveness* (pp. 46–62). Madison: University of Wisconsin Press.

Enright, R. D., & the Human Development Study Group (1991). The moral development of forgiveness. In W. M. Kurtines & J. L. Gewirtz (Eds.), *Handbook of moral behavior and development* (Vol. 1, pp. 123–152). Hillsdale, NJ: Lawrence Erlbaum Associates.

Fenell, D. L. (1993). Characteristics of long-term first marriages. *Journal of Mental Health Counseling, 15,* 446–460.

Fincham, F. D., & Beach, S. R. H. (2001). Forgiving in close relationships. In F. H. Columbus & S. P. Shohov (Eds.), *Advances in psychology research* (pp. 163–197). Hauppauge, NY: Nova Science Publishers.

Green, M. M. (2005). *Stress, social support, and health risk behaviours as mediators of the forgiveness–health relation.* Unpublished master's thesis. Brock University, St. Catharines, Ontario, Canada.

Idler, E. L., & Benyamini, Y. (1997). Self-rated health and mortality: A review of 27 community studies. *Journal of Health and Social Behavior, 38,* 21–37.

Kanz, J. E. (2000). How do people conceptualize and use forgiveness? The Forgiveness Attitudes Questionnaire. *Counseling and Values, 44,* 174–188.

Katz, J., Street, A., & Arias, I. (1997). Individual differences in self-appraisals and responses to dating violence scenarios. *Violence and Victims, 12,* 265–276.

Lawler, K. L., Younger, J. W., Piferi, R. L., Jobe, R. L., Edmondson, K. A., & Jones, W. H. (2005). The unique effects of forgiveness on health: An exploration of pathways. *Journal of Behavioral Medicine, 28,* 157–167.

Mauger, P. A., Perry, J. E., Freeman, T., Grove, D. C., McBride, A. G., & McKinney, K. E. (1992). The measurement of forgiveness: Preliminary research. *Journal of Psychology and Christianity, 11,* 170–180.

McCullough, M. E. (2000). Forgiveness as human strength: Theory, measurement, and links to well-being. *Journal of Social and Clinical Psychology, 19,* 43–55.

McCullough, M. E., & Witvliet, C. V. O. (2002). The psychology of forgiveness. In C. R. Snyder & S. J. Lopez (Eds.), *Handbook of positive psychology* (pp. 446–458). New York: Oxford University Press.

Mullet, E., Girard, M., & Bakhshi, P. (2004). Conceptualizations of forgiveness. *European Psychologist, 9,* 78–86.

Neblett, W. R. (1974). Forgiveness and ideals. *Mind, 83,* 268–275.

North, J. (1998). The "ideal" of forgiveness: A philosopher's exploration. In R. D. Enright & J. North (Eds.), *Exploring forgiveness* (pp. 15–34). Madison: University of Wisconsin Press.

Rye, M. S., Loiacono, D. M., Folck, C. D., Olszewski, B. T., Heim, T. A., & Madia, B. P. (2001). Evaluation of the psychometric properties of two forgiveness scales. *Current Psychology, 20,* 260–277.

Thompson, L. Y., & Snyder, C. R. (2004). Measuring forgiveness. In S. J. Lopez & C. R. Snyder (Eds.), *Positive psychological assessment: A handbook of models and measures* (pp. 301–312). Washington, DC: American Psychological Association.

Thompson, L. Y., Snyder, C. R., Hoffman, L., Michael, S. T., Rasmussen, H. N., Billings, L. S., et al. (2005). Dispositional forgiveness of self, others, and situations. *Journal of Personality, 73,* 313–359.

Thoresen, C. E., Harris, A. H. S., & Luskin, F. (2000). Forgiveness and health: An unanswered question. In M. E. McCullough, K. I. Pargament, & C. E. Thoresen (Eds.), *Forgiveness: Theory, research, and practice* (pp. 254–280). New York: The Guilford Press.

Trainer, M. F. (1981). *Forgiveness: Intrinsic, role-expected, expedient, in the context of divorce.* Unpublished doctoral dissertation, Boston University, Boston, MA.

Witvliet, C. V. O. (2001). Forgiveness and health: Review and reflections on a matter of faith, feelings, and physiology. *Journal of Psychology and Theology, 29,* 212–224.

Zechmeister, J. S., & Romero, C. (2002). Victim and offender accounts of interpersonal conflict: Autobiographical narratives of forgiveness and unforgiveness. *Journal of Personality and Social Psychology, 82,* 675–686.

2

Measuring Forgiveness

LISE DESHEA

Introduction

> Forgiveness is not an occasional act. It is a permanent attitude.
>
> **Martin Luther King, Jr.**

> Everyone says that forgiveness is a lovely idea, until he has something to forgive.
>
> **C. S. Lewis**

Researchers have wrestled with definitions of forgiveness at least since the early 1990s when the topic began to draw increased interest among psychologists. Worthington (2005) suggested that the multitude of definitions indicates the possibility that there may be many kinds of forgiveness that can be grouped into two broad categories: an individual's experience of forgiveness and a complex interpersonal process of forgiveness. Even with differing definitions of forgiveness, researchers and clinicians can choose a forgiveness scale without subscribing to a particular viewpoint, as most forgiveness scales do not define the term. The connection between people's understanding of forgiveness and numeric values for forgiveness is quite a leap, however, and not one to be taken without looking at the research on the measurement of forgiveness. Most of this measurement has involved self-report questionnaires, or *scales*. This chapter will describe the available scales measuring forgiveness and compare the evidence regarding reliability and validity. Recommendations also will be made on the use of certain scales in specific situations, as well as some suggestions on what remains to be explored about the measurement of forgiveness and its interface with forgiveness definitions and theory.

Most forgiveness research has focused on the viewpoint of the harmed person, the one with the task of forgiving a transgression. As the quotations at the beginning of this chapter illustrate, forgiveness can be classified as a transient state or an enduring personality trait. Most of the scales in use today target another person for forgiveness; a few scales target a situation or oneself. For the purposes of this chapter, a *scale* refers to a quantitative measure intended to stand as one instrument, and a *subscale* is a section of a scale that produces a separate score. For example, the 18-item Transgression-Related Interpersonal Motivations Scale (TRIM-18; McCullough, Root, & Cohen, 2006) is referred to as a scale. It produces three scores, representing motivations regarding Revenge, Avoidance, and Benevolence; these components are referred to as subscales. Many scales were under development in the mid-1990s and were published soon thereafter, so at least a dozen measures of state forgiveness of others, and even more trait measures, have been published.

How does one evaluate the quality of a scale, and how does one decide which scale is best for one's purposes? Among many possible criteria, users look for a scale that will match their purpose for measuring forgiveness; the backgrounds of the respondents; the amount of time available for people to complete the scale; possibly, the cost of the scale (to the author's knowledge, the only scale available solely through purchase is the Enright Forgiveness Inventory); and evidence supporting such use of the scale. Many of these criteria can be met with easy answers. Most of the scales included in the study to be described in this chapter were developed for research purposes or, secondarily, for clinical purposes. The task of choosing a scale is simplified by deciding whether a measure of a person's current level of forgiveness of a specific person or situation is needed; if so, the list of scales is limited to the state scales. Most forgiveness scales have been created for administration to adults; forgiveness among children has attracted little research; only one known child-specific scale has been developed (Scobie & Scobie, 2003). Shorter scales with brief, simple statements may be chosen for administration under time constraints or to people with lower reading ability. (Appendix A gives the number of items in the scales; aside from the scenario scales, most of the instruments involve relatively simple statements.)

More questions remain: What evidence exists that supports the use of a scale for a given purpose and what information does the scale provide? Faced with reading every scale and its associated journal publication, one easily could be overwhelmed by the prospect of having to evaluate each measure according to these questions. This chapter will summarize the research findings about forgiveness scales and provide a framework for thinking about forgiveness measurement.

Trait Forgiveness Scores as Estimates of a Characteristic

When measuring a desk, one obtains a number to describe a *characteristic* that it possesses—its height in centimeters, its length in feet, possibly a rating from 1 to 10 on its appropriateness for use by people in wheelchairs. Similarly, one obtains a number on a forgiveness scale to serve as an estimate of a human characteristic we call *forgiveness* or, according to some authors, *forgivingness*. The scale limits the inferences that a researcher or clinician can make about the human characteristics being measured. By itself, the English word *forgive* can bring to the Western mind a number of preconceived notions and common sayings: "forgive and forget," "forgive us our trespasses as we forgive those who trespass against us," and so forth.

A loaded term like *forgiveness* can result in responses from people who want to "look good" to others. In fact, research consistently shows that forgiveness scores often correlate positively with measures of socially desirable responding. For example, DeShea, Tzou, Kang, and Matsuyuki (2006) found that most trait forgiveness measures correlated with Impression Management, but fewer of these scales correlated with Self-Deception. Therefore, users of trait forgiveness scales clearly must be aware that respondents may bias their responses in order to make a favorable impression on others. Researchers should make an effort to assure participants of the confidentiality of their responses, perhaps by use of codes to identify individuals, thus reducing the pressure to respond in socially desirable ways.

Trait measures also differ considerably in their scope and intent. For example, Brown's (2003) Tendency to Forgive Scale consists of four items. Another trait measure, Jones, Iver, and Lawler's (2002) Forgiving Personality Scale, includes 33 items. Do these two scales provide the same information? Yes and no. Their scores tend to be strongly correlated, but by virtue of being much longer, the Jones et al. scale has the potential to provide a greater amount of information—if the person administering the scale needs it. On one hand, a clinician may be interested in a client's answer to each question, which could serve as jumping-off points for therapeutic discussions. On the other hand, a researcher conducting a quantitative study may need only the summary score from a short scale to include in a packet of many questions that address a constellation of related personality characteristics or interpersonal situations. The question of whether a very short scale is the best choice in the larger scheme of best research practices goes beyond the scope of this chapter, and the reader is referred to McCullough and Root (2005) and Hoyt and McCullough (2005) for further information and discussion on this issue.

Reliability and Validity

People with graduate training in any number of disciplines are familiar with the concepts of reliability and validity. A scale is said to be reliable if it produces consistent data. (To be precise, the *data* are reliable; the scale does not change from one administration to another; Thompson & Vacha-Haase, 2000.) The most common way of looking at reliability is internal consistency: Do the responses on the various items of a scale correlate with each other? The clinician or researcher in the market for a forgiveness scale can rest easy on this question because all trait forgiveness scales studied by the present author produced reliable data in multiple studies. Cronbach's alphas from a study in which almost all the known forgiveness scales were administered to the same sample (DeShea et al., 2006) are given in appendix A. (Caution is urged in comparing these values because, all things being equal, a longer scale will result in a higher reliability coefficient.)

Determining the validity of a scale is a more complex undertaking. Messick defined *validity* as "an integrated evaluative judgment of the degree to which empirical evidence and theoretical rationales support the adequacy and appropriateness of inferences and actions based on test scores or other modes of assessment" (1989, p. 13)—a daunting definition for a daunting task. The definition deserves to be parsed so that the limits of any validation study become clear. Starting from the end of the definition, one uses scores to make decisions and inferences about the respondents. One weighs the adequacy and appropriateness of those decisions and inferences based on an *integrated judgment*; that is, there is no single number or bit of evidence that will determine whether the data produced by a scale are valid. One takes into account a constellation of information in the process of considering whether appropriate inferences are being made. Both theoretical rationales and empirical evidence (data) must be considered in that process.

At a minimum, judgments about the validity of data collected with a certain scale will depend upon whether the conditions for data collection are similar to the conditions under which the scale's developers tested their measures. Just as physical tools might have been tested only under certain conditions (e.g., ordinary indoor temperature ranges), scales also may have been checked with only one homogeneous sample, limiting the degree to which users may generalize the results. In fact, most forgiveness scales have been tested on predominantly young Euro-American samples of college students, although forgiveness research increasingly is being conducted in a variety of cultures (e.g., Azar & Mullet, 2002; Kadiangandu, Mullet, & Vinsonneau, 2001; McLernon, Cairns, Hewstone, & Smith, 2004; Sandage, Hill, & Vang, 2003; Scobie, Scobie, & Kakavoulis, 2002; Vinsonneau & Mullet, 2001).

When administering a scale for a new purpose or to people who differ from the validation samples, one must remember that the scale may behave differently in that setting. For example, a collectivistic society most likely would view forgiveness as a process involving the community, not simply something that occurs between two individuals. A man from a country such as Zimbabwe would be able to respond to questions about his tendency to forgive a person who harmed him, but in his culture the harm may be viewed as a transgression against the man's clan by the other person's clan, and the forgiveness would involve groups of people. So a score on a forgiveness scale developed in the United States would fail to capture forgiveness as it is understood in Zimbabwe.

Even within a western country such as the United States, forgiveness by Latinos, for example, has not been explored systematically to this author's knowledge. Those who would administer forgiveness scales to Latinos would be taking the scale into new territory. In fact, when studying forgiveness in a different culture, one must remember one's own cultural biases. What would not be a transgression in Western society could be highly offensive in another culture. In sum, *the scale itself does not become valid* simply because one or a few published studies claim to have observed evidence of one kind of validity or another.

Many kinds of validity may be examined in a scale-development study. The scale's authors may wish to demonstrate that scores on the scale correlate with scores on a scale measuring a related construct. Such a correlation would be evidence of construct validity. In terms of forgiveness measures, the constructs of empathy and perspective-taking often have been used to demonstrate this kind of validity. Scores on two forgiveness scales should correlate more strongly with each other than either scale correlates with measures of empathy and perspective-taking. A scale's authors also may wish to demonstrate that scores on the scale are unrelated to scores on a scale measuring an unrelated construct, which would demonstrate another kind of validity known as *discriminant validity*. Research has shown that scores on forgiveness scales have tended not to correlate with certain "Big Five" personality factors (openness, extraversion, and conscientiousness), which may be interpreted as evidence of discriminant validity. At the same time, forgiveness tends to correlate with agreeableness and neuroticism (or its opposite, emotional stability), which would demonstrate construct validity.

This pattern of correlations with the five personality factors is not uniform across forgiveness measures. As clinicians or researchers choose a forgiveness measure, they may wish to identify a scale that correlates with *some* but not *all* personality factors. Any number of rubrics could be chosen to evaluate trait forgiveness scales' construct and discriminant validity. For the purposes of this chapter, the previously described correlations (and lack of correlations) with empathy, perspective-taking, and the five personality factors will serve as one such rubric.

Summary of Trait Forgiveness Results

The following section will summarize whether a number of trait other-forgiveness scales produce scores that meet the following criteria: They correlate (a) with scores from other scales measuring the same kind of forgiveness, (b) with Empathic Concern and Perspective-Taking (Davis, 1983), and (c) with Agreeableness and Emotional Stability (but not other personality factors, thus showing some evidence of discriminant validity). The following results were taken from a study (DeShea et al., 2006) in which all the scales were presented to the same sample so that comparisons among the scales could be made; this offered an advantage over prior studies. As is true of all validation studies, the generalizability of this research is limited by the sampling method (convenience sampling) and characteristics of the sample (dominated by female Euro-American college students).

Most of the scales measuring trait forgiveness of others correlated with each other. The Trait Forgivingness Scale (Berry, Worthington, O'Connor, Parrott, & Wade, 2005), which consists of eight items, showed especially strong correlations with similar measures, with an average correlation of .56 (median $r = .60$). Several scales met the preceding criteria: Ashton, Paunonen, Helmes, and Jackson's Forgiveness/Nonretaliation (1998); Brown's Attitude Toward Forgiveness (2003); Pollard, Anderson, Anderson, and Jennings's Personal Relationships Forgiveness (1998; as scored by the present author, summing responses to 20 items after reverse-scoring certain items); Tangney, Boone, Fee, and Reinsmith's Forgiveness of Others (1991); the Trait Forgivingness Scale (Berry et al., 2005); and the Transgression Narrative Test of Forgivingness (TNTF; Berry, Worthington, Parrott, O'Connor, & Wade, 2001). The Forgiveness as a Positive Response to an Offender (F-PRO; Wade & Worthington, 2003) showed weaker but statistically significant correlations with similar scales, perhaps indicating that it taps a specific kind of forgiveness, as it was designed to do. Interestingly, it did not correlate with Impression Management or Perspective-Taking.

Five scales failed to discriminate among the personality factors (i.e., their scores correlated with all five factors of personality) and thus would be judged under this rubric as lacking discriminant validity. These scales are Forgiving Personality (Jones et al., 2002),

Heartland-Other (Thompson et al., 2005), Heartland Self-Forgiveness (Thompson et al., 2005), and Forgiveness of Others and Forgiveness of Self subscales (Mauger et al., 1992). In addition, the Heartland Situations (Thompson et al., 2005) correlated with all but one of the personality factors.

Three of the scenario-based scales draw suspicion: Kanz's Forgiveness Questionnaire (2000), Rye and colleagues' Forgiveness Likelihood (2001), and DeShea Willingness to Forgive (2003). These scales failed to correlate with Empathic Concern and, aside from their stronger correlations with each other, shared weaker correlations with other measures of other-forgiveness. One might infer that the respondents were reacting differently to scenarios than to statements about forgiveness (e.g., "I forgive more easily when the person apologizes"). Do scenario-based scales provide the same kind of information as scales that are based on ratings of agreement with statements about forgiving? The scenario-based scales' correlational results as well as the increased time required for respondents to read and respond to scenarios make these scales less attractive alternatives.

Further study would be needed to determine why the scenario-based scales elicited qualitatively different responses. Perhaps these scales gave participants the opportunity to ease their cognitive load and rely solely on the information in the scenario, instead of doing the more challenging task of truly imagining their immediate reactions in those situations. Another vignette-type of scale, Tangney and colleagues' Self-Forgiveness measure (1991), also fails on two points: The expected correlations with Agreeableness and Perspective-Taking were in the opposite direction from the hypothesis. Oddly, these researchers' Self-Forgiveness scores correlated negatively with Impression Management and failed to correlate with two other trait self-forgiveness scales: the Heartland Self (Thompson et al., 2005) and the Forgiveness of Self (Mauger et al., 1992). Given that Thompson and colleagues' Heartland Self and Mauger and coworkers' Forgiveness of Self measures correlated $r = .48$ with each other, it appears Tangney's Self-Forgiveness may be the odd one out.

Another measure with problematic results was the Mullet Personal/Social Circumstances subscale (Neto & Mullet, 2004), which consists of statements about the ability to forgive when personal or social circumstances are favorable or unfavorable. This subscale correlated negatively with Agreeableness and not at all with Perspective-Taking, Empathic Concern, Emotional Stability, or any of the other measures of other-forgiveness. Mullet and colleagues are among the researchers doing a great deal of cross-cultural research on forgiveness, and the value of their contribution cannot be understated. For an American sample, however, one may wish to save time and omit the Personal/Social Circumstances subscale.

State Forgiveness Measures

Measures of state forgiveness have their own peculiar challenges and cannot be judged based on the same pattern of correlations used to compare the trait measures. For instance, one may tend to score high on a measure of trait Empathic Concern for others while also reporting feeling extremely unforgiving thoughts and emotions toward a transgressor regarding a current interpersonal wrong. McCullough, Fincham, and Tsang (2003) described forgiveness as unfolding across time, requiring repeated measures to quantify the change in valence that is at the center of many definitions of forgiveness. (McCullough and Root, 2005, recommend multilevel modeling with at least three occasions of measurement.) Most state forgiveness scales provide a score that is akin to a snapshot capturing a single moment in time, not a fluid, evolving process. Repeated measures would amount to a series of still photos that approximate a movie of the forgiveness process.

An impressive development in the measurement of state forgiveness is the Gordon and Baucom Forgiveness Inventory (2003), the only process measure published as of this writing. Gordon and Baucom's scale produces three scores, representing three stages of the forgiveness process. According to this model of forgiveness, Stage 1 is the impact stage, when the injured party is reeling from the effect of the transgression. Previous conceptions of the relationship are called into question, and the injured party doubts the other person's trustworthiness. This phase can be marked by revenge and feelings of powerlessness. Gordon and Baucom called Stage 2 the "meaning" stage, when the injured person tries to make sense of why the transgression happened; understanding why the event happened can increase the person's feeling of being in control of his or her life. The previously held assumptions are reworked, and if the parties remain in relationship with each other, they may try to restore the balance of power between them. Stage 3 is the recovery or "moving on" stage, when the injured party is putting the transgression behind him or her. She or he may begin to see that she or he will remain stuck emotionally if punishment of the transgressor continues. The injured party may or may not continue the relationship, but as forgiveness unfolds, the injured person gains a more balanced view of the painful events.

In extending the validation of the Gordon and Baucom (2003) scale, Dixon, DeShea, and Gordon (2006) showed that people who scored high on Stage 1 also tended to score high on McCullough and colleagues' (2006) TRIM-Revenge and TRIM-Avoidance subscales, while scoring low on the TRIM-Benevolence subscale. Scores on the Stage 2 subscale tended to be uncorrelated with the three TRIM scores; those with high scores for Stage 3 had low scores on Revenge and Avoidance and high scores on Benevolence. This process measure deserves serious consideration by those interested in determining how far a person has progressed in the process of forgiving specific interpersonal offenses. (Noll and McCullough also have developed a process measure of forgiveness that is under review at this writing and not included in the study by DeShea et al., 2006.)

Summary of State Forgiveness Scales

Almost all of the scales produced acceptably reliable data. An exception was the Understanding subscale of the Interpersonal Relationship Resolution Scale (IRRS; Hargrave & Sells, 1997), which had an extremely low alpha in two studies (DeShea, Holeman, Muhomba, & Howell, 2005; DeShea et al., 2006). The IRRS items are dichotomous (e.g., "Yes, I believe this most of the time" vs. "No, I have difficulty believing this"), which can reduce variability and lead to lower reliability estimates. In both studies, some of the five Understanding items received lopsided endorsement for one of the two response options, which also would affect the reliability estimate. A strength of Hargrave and Sells's scales is that they were developed to match the researchers' model of forgiveness, which emerged from a theory of contextual family therapy. Further research could determine whether replacing the forced-choice format with a Likert-type response scale would solve this subscale's reliability problem.

Most of the state forgiveness measures correlated adequately with each other, indicating construct validity, and many would serve well for repeated measurements to track respondents' unfolding forgiveness. The Gordon and Baucom Forgiveness Inventory (2003) stands head and shoulders above other state measures, but others that performed well include Brown and Phillips's Offense-Specific Forgiveness Measure (2005); McCullough and colleagues' TRIM-18 (2006); Rye and colleagues' Forgiveness Scale (2001), consisting of subscales measuring Presence of Positive Emotions and Absence of Negative Emotions; and DeShea & Wahkinney's State Self-Forgiveness Scales (2003).

What We Need to Know

Scale validation should be an ongoing process. Scale users must keep in mind that new research could point to problems with their favorite scales, which may frustrate clinicians and researchers who think they have found a scale that will fit their purposes. Scores on a forgiveness scale are the result of an interaction between the written statements and the individual respondents. So a scale that provides a good measurement for one group of people may not be the best choice for a different group.

Reducing forgiveness to one or a few numbers falls short of capturing the dynamic process of forgiveness, which is viewed by each person through his or her cultural lenses. The preceding discussion may persuade the reader of the value of using more than one scale to assess trait or state forgiveness. Moreover, one may consider whether forgiveness is genuine or socially induced, decisional or emotional, and whether unforgiveness is more than the lack of forgiveness. Harris and Thoresen (2005) said many kinds of unforgiveness—angry, depressed, or passive—may exist. They wrote that "no current assessment instrument or method captures the full complexity of these constructs" (p. 329). In fact, one may consider quantitative scales to be overgeneralizations, like the average height of the Rocky Mountains, failing to represent the landscape as well as a topographic map would.

These limitations notwithstanding, the Gordon and Baucom (2003) process measure discussed previously is among the most promising additions to clinicians' and researchers' forgiveness toolbox. Finding people's current location in the process of forgiving a specific interpersonal transgression may provide discussion points for therapy, as well as a way of comparing people in research studies who have suffered the same wrong, such as marital infidelity. What about those who seek forgiveness or are granted forgiveness? Much less is known about their viewpoint. Forgiveness measures could be developed that capture more than one viewpoint in the process. Further, some of the most fascinating work involving forgiveness has included measurement of physical and neurological reactions (e.g., see Witvliet, Ludwig, & Vander Laan, 2001). Whether the brain changes permanently as a result of forgiving or harboring grudges remains to be explored.

None of the forgiveness scales discussed in this chapter provides *the* answer in the measurement of forgiveness. The basic decision about the kind of research to conduct (e.g., quantitative surveys using scales) limits the kinds of observations and inferences that can be made. The next generation of quantitative researchers will have to learn more advanced statistical methods, such as hierarchical linear modeling, so that they can analyze their results while taking situational variables into account. They also should explore different ways of assessing forgiveness, such as Kachadourian, Fincham, and Davila's (2005) method of having respondents list their intimate partners' characteristics. In their approach, those who showed more ambivalence about their partner are assumed to have experienced less forgiveness.

Even more subtle methods of measuring forgiveness and unforgiveness could be developed so that socially desirable responding might be sidestepped. Rather than responding to statements about how forgiving they are, respondents could read passages about forgiveness situations and then evaluate the quality of the argument for or against forgiveness. This methodology was the basis of the Racial Arguments Scale, a subtle measure of racism (Saucier & Miller, 2003); people who are less forgiving may be more critical of an argument in favor of forgiving a particular transgression.

The selection of a scale should be made mindfully. Just as a carpenter chooses tools based on what she or he wishes to build, researchers and clinicians should choose measurement methods based on the questions they wish to answer, instead of finding something to build using a tool they happened to find.

References

Ashton, M. C., Paunonen, S. V., Helmes, E., & Jackson, D. N. (1998). Kin altruism, reciprocal altruism, and the Big Five personality factors. *Evolution and Human Behavior, 19,* 243–255.

Azar, F., & Mullet, E. (2002). Interpersonal forgiveness among Lebanese: A six-community study. *International Journal of Group Tensions, 30,* 161–181.

Berry, J. W., Worthington, E. L., Jr., O'Connor, L., Parrott, L., III, & Wade, N. G. (2005). Forgiveness, vengeful rumination, and affective traits. *Journal of Personality, 73,* 183–226.

Berry, J. W., Worthington, E. L., Jr., Parrott, L., III, O'Connor, L., & Wade, N. G. (2001). Dispositional forgivingness: Development and construct validity of the Transgression Narrative Test of Forgivingness (TNTF). *Personality and Social Psychology Bulletin, 27,* 1277–1290.

Brown, R. P. (2003). Measuring individual differences in the tendency to forgive: Construct validity and links with depression. *Personality and Social Psychology Bulletin, 29,* 759–771.

Brown, R. P. (2004). Vengeance is mine: Narcissism, vengeance, and the tendency to forgive. *Journal of Research in Personality, 38*, 576–584.

Brown, R. P., & Phillips, A. (2005). Letting bygones be bygones: Further evidence for the validity of the tendency to forgive scale. *Personality and Individual Differences, 38,* 627–638.

Davis, M. H. (1983). The effects of dispositional empathy on emotional reactions and helping: A multidimensional approach. *Journal of Personality, 51,* 67–184.

DeShea, L. (2003). A scenario-based scale of willingness to forgive. *Individual Differences Research, 1,* 201–217.

DeShea, L., Holeman, V. T., Muhomba, M., & Howell, P. (2005, August). *A rose by any other name: Two models of forgiveness.* Poster presented at the annual conference of the American Psychological Association, Washington, DC.

DeShea, L., Tzou, J., Kang, S., & Matsuyuki, M. (2006, January). *Trait forgiveness II: Spiritual vs. religious college students and the five-factor model of personality.* Poster presentation at the annual conference of the Society for Personality and Social Psychology, Palm Springs, CA.

DeShea, L., & Wahkinney, R. L. (2003, October). *Looking within: Self-forgiveness as a new research direction.* Paper presented at the meeting of A Campaign for Forgiveness Research, Atlanta, GA.

Dixon, L. J., DeShea, L., & Gordon, K. C. (2006, November). *A study of the validity of the Forgiveness Inventory.* Poster presented at the annual meeting of the Association for Behavioral and Cognitive Therapies, Chicago, IL.

Gordon, K. C., & Baucom, D. H. (2003). Forgiveness and marriage: Preliminary support for a synthesized model of recovery from a marital betrayal. *American Journal of Family Therapy, 31,* 179–199.

Hargrave, T. D., & Sells, J. N. (1997). The development of a forgiveness scale. *Journal of Marital and Family Therapy, 23,* 41–64.

Harris, A. H. S., & Thoresen, C. E. (2005). Forgiveness, unforgiveness, health, and disease. In E. L. Worthington, Jr. (Ed.), *Handbook of forgiveness* (pp. 321–333). New York: Routledge.

Hoyt, W. T., & McCullough, M. E. (2005). Issues in the multimodal measurement of forgiveness. In E. L. Worthington, Jr. (Ed.), *Handbook of forgiveness* (pp. 109–123). New York: Routledge.

Jones, W. H., Iver, V., & Lawler, K. A. (2002). *Assessing forgiveness as a dimension of personality.* Unpublished manuscript, University of Tennessee.

Kachadourian, L. K., Fincham, F. D., & Davila, J. (2005). Attitudinal ambivalence, rumination and forgiveness of partner transgressions in marriage. *Personality and Social Psychology Bulletin, 31,* 334–342.

Kadiangandu, J. K., Mullet, E., & Vinsonneau, G. (2001). Forgivingness: A Congo–France comparison. *Journal of Cross-Cultural Psychology, 32,* 504–511.

Kanz, J. E. (2000). How do people conceptualize and use forgiveness? The Forgiveness Attitudes Questionnaire. *Counseling and Values, 44,* 174–188.

Luskin, F. M. (1999). The effect of forgiveness training on psychosocial factors in college-age adults. *Dissertation Abstracts International, 60,* 1026.

Mauger, P. A., Freedman, T., McBride, A. G., Perry, J. E., Grove, D. C., & McKinney, K. E. (1992). The measurement of forgiveness: Preliminary research. *Journal of Psychology and Christianity, 11,* 170–180.

McCullough, M. E., Fincham, F. D., & Tsang, J. (2003). Forgiveness, forbearance, and time: The temporal unfolding of transgression-related interpersonal motivations. *Journal of Personality and Social Psychology, 84,* 540–557.

McCullough, M. E., & Root, L. M. (2005). Forgiveness as change. In E. L. Worthington, Jr. (Ed.), *Handbook of forgiveness* (pp. 91–102). New York: Routledge.

McCullough, M. E., Root, L. M., & Cohen, A. D. (2006). Writing about the benefits of an interpersonal transgression facilitates forgiveness. *Journal of Consulting and Clinical Psychology, 74,* 887–897.

McLernon, F., Cairns, E., Hewstone, M., & Smith, R. (2004). The development of intergroup forgiveness in Northern Ireland. *Journal of Social Issues, 60,* 587–601.

Messick, S. (1989). Validity. In R. L. Linn (Ed.), *Educational measurement* (3rd ed., pp. 13–103). New York: American Council on Education.

Neto, F., & Mullet, E. (2004). Personality, self-esteem, and self-construal as correlates of forgivingness. *European Journal of Personality, 18,* 15–30.

Pollard, M. W., Anderson, R. A., Anderson, W. T., & Jennings, G. (1998). The development of a family forgiveness scale. *Journal of Family Therapy, 20,* 95–109.

Rye, M. S., Loiacono, D. M., Folck, C. D., Olszewski, B. T., Heim, T. A., & Madia, B. P. (2001). Evaluation of the psychometric properties of two forgiveness scales. *Current Psychology, 20,* 260–277.

Sandage, S. J., Hill, P. C., & Vang, H. C. (2003). Toward a multicultural positive psychology: Indigenous forgiveness and Hmong culture. *Counseling Psychologist, 31,* 564–592.

Saucier, D. A., & Miller, C. T. (2003). The persuasiveness of racial arguments as a subtle measure of racism. *Personality and Social Psychology Bulletin, 29,* 1303–1315.

Scobie, G. E. W., & Scobie, E. D. (2003). Measuring children's understanding of the construct of forgiveness. In P. H. M. P. Roelofsma, J. M. T. Coreleyn, and J. W. van Saane (Eds.), *One hundred years of psychology and religion* (pp. 105–121). Amsterdam: VU University Press.

Scobie, G. E. W., Scobie, E. D., & Kakavoulis, A. K. (2002). A cross-cultural study of the construct of forgiveness: Britain, Greece and Cyprus. *Psychology, the Journal of the Hellenic Psychological Society, 9,* 22–36.

Staub, E. (2003). *The psychology of good and evil: Why children, adults, and groups help and harm others.* New York: Cambridge University Press.

Subkoviak, M. J., Enright, R. D., Wu, C., Gassin, E. A., Freedman, S., Olson, L. M., et al. (1995). Measuring interpersonal forgiveness in late adolescence and middle adulthood. *Journal of Adolescence, 18,* 641–655.

Tangney, J. P., Boone, A. L., Fee, R., & Reinsmith, C. (1991). *Individual differences in the propensity to forgive: Measurement and implications for psychological and social adjustment.* Unpublished manuscript, George Mason University, Fairfax, VA.

Thompson, B., & Vacha-Haase, T. (2000). Psychometrics *is* datametrics: The test is not reliable. *Educational and Psychological Measurement, 60,* 174–195.

Thompson, L. Y., Snyder, C. R., Hoffman, L., Michael, S. T., Rasmussen, H. N., Billings, L. S., et al. (2005). Dispositional forgiveness of self, others, and situations. *Journal of Personality, 73,* 313–359.

Vinsonneau, G., & Mullet, E. (2001). Willingness to forgive among young adolescents: A European–Maghrebi comparison. *International Journal of Group Tensions, 30,* 267–278.

Wade, N. G., & Worthington, E. L., Jr. (2003). Overcoming interpersonal offenses: Is forgiveness the only way to deal with unforgiveness? *Journal of Counseling and Development, 81,* 343–353.

Witvliet, C. V. O., Ludwig, T. E., & Vander Laan, K. L. (2001). Granting forgiveness or harboring grudges: Implications for emotion, physiology, and health. *Psychological Science, 121,* 117–123.

Worthington, E. L., Jr. (2005). More questions about forgiveness: Research agenda for 2005–2015. In E. L. Worthington, Jr. (Ed.), *Handbook of forgiveness* (pp. 557–573). New York: Routledge.

Appendix A: Scales' and Subscales' Reliability

	CRONBACH'S ALPHA	REFERENCE
Trait scales and subscales (no. of items)		
Ashton Forgiveness/Nonretaliation (16)	.74	Ashton, Paunonen, Helmes, & Jackson, (1998)
Brown Attitudes Toward Forgiveness (6)	.73	Brown & Phillips (2005)
Brown Tendency to Forgive (4)	.73	Brown (2003, 2004)
Willingness to Forgive (12 scenarios)	.92	DeShea (2003)
Jones Forgiving Personality Scale (33)	.95	Jones, Iver, & Lawler (2002)
Mullet Forgivingness scales		Neto & Mullet (2004)
Personal/Social Circumstances (7)	.82	
Forgiveness vs. Revenge (6)	.82	
Blockage to Forgiveness (5)	.91	
Heartland Forgiveness Scale (six per subscale)		Thompson et al. (2005)
Self	.74	
Others	.81	
Situations	.77	
Kanz Forgiveness Attitudes Questionnaire (26 scenarios)	.93	Kanz (2000)
Mauger scales		Mauger et al. (1992)
Forgiveness of Self (15)	.84	
Forgiveness of Others (15)	.87	
Pollard scale, scored as instructed by its authors		Pollard, Anderson, Anderson, & Jennings (1998)
Realization (8)	.68	
Recognition (8)	.69	
Reparation (8)	.73	
Restitution (8)	.68	
Resolution (8)	.73	
Pollard Family of Origin Forgiveness (after reversing, all scores summed) (20)	.90	Pollard, Anderson, Anderson, & Jennings (1998)
Pollard Personal Relationships Forgiveness (after reversing, all scores summed) (20)	.77	Pollard, Anderson, Anderson, & Jennings (1998)

(*continued*)

Appendix A (*continued*)

	CRONBACH'S ALPHA	REFERENCE
Tangney Multidimensional Forgiveness		Tangney, Boone, Fee, & Reinsmith (1991)
Self (eight scenarios)	.82	
Others (eight scenarios)	.90	
Trait Forgivingness Scale (10)	.83	Berry, Worthington, O'Connor, Parrott, & Wade (2005)
Transgression Narrative Test of Forgivingness (five scenarios)	.78	Berry, Worthington, Parrott, O'Connor, & Wade (2001)
State scales and subscales included in the study		
Jones Acts of Forgiveness (45)	.97	Jones, Iver, & Lawler (2002)
Brown Offense-Specific Forgiveness (7)	.91	Brown & Phillips (2005)
Forgiveness as Positive Responses to an Offender (6)	.88	Wade & Worthington (2003)
Gordon & Baucom Forgiveness Inventory		Gordon & Baucom (2003)
Stage 1 (7)	.73	
Stage 2 (8)	.63	
Stage 3 (7)	.76	
Interpersonal Relationship Resolution Scale		Hargrave & Sells (1997)
Insight (5)	.61	
Giving Opportunity for Compensation (7)	.75	
Understanding (5)	.10	
Overt Act of Forgiveness (5)	.75	
Luskin Forgiveness Self-Efficacy (14)	.90	Luskin (1999)
Transgression-Related Interpersonal Motivations (18)		McCullough, Root, & Cohen (2006)
Avoidance (7)	.94	
Revenge (5)	.87	
Benevolence (6)	.90	
Rye Forgiveness Scale		Rye et al. (2001)
Absence of Negative (10)	.88	
Presence of Positive (5)	.81	

(*continued*)

Appendix A (*continued*)

	CRONBACH'S ALPHA	REFERENCE
State Self-Forgiveness Scales		DeShea (2003)
Self-Forgiving Feelings/Actions (8)	.91	
Self-Forgiving Beliefs (9)	.79	
Enright Forgiveness Inventory		Subkoviak et al. (1995)
Affective (20)	.98	
Behavioral (20)	.97	
Cognitive (20)	.97	
Pseudo (5)	.81	
Scales not included in the study		
Rwandan Reconciliation Scale		Staub (2003)
Process of Forgiveness Scale		Noll & McCullough (unpublished)
Children's Forgiveness Scale		Scobie & Scobie (2003)

Source: Results taken from DeShea, Tzou, Kang, & Matsuyuki (2006).
Note: All things being equal, adding items will increase reliability. Caution is urged when comparing alphas for data from scales of different lengths. Unless otherwise specified, the scales measure forgiveness of others.

3

Just-World Beliefs and Forgiveness in Men and Women

ANN MACASKILL

Introduction

While there is now more empirical research on forgiveness, the factors that lead one person to be more forgiving than another are still not well understood. Personality is one obvious source of individual differences that influences how forgiving an individual is, but it does not provide the full explanation. Mullet, Neto, and Riviére (2005) reviewed 27 published studies that examined the relationship between personality and forgiveness, and concluded that personality accounted for between 20 and 30% of the observed differences in forgiveness of others and forgiveness of self. This leaves a considerable amount of variance still to be accounted for in our search to understand the factors that influence how forgiving an individual is. The research reported here goes beyond personality variables to examine how our models of reality may affect how forgiving we are. The contentious issue of measuring forgiveness of situations is also examined.

Belief in a Just World as a Theory of Reality

It is well established that as individuals experience life, they develop theories about the nature of reality (Beck, Rush, Shaw, & Emery, 1981; Cantor, 1990; Ellis & Dryden, 1997). These theories act as cognitive filters, influencing the perception, evaluation, and memory of events and encouraging people to see the world as meaningful (Epstein, 1990).

Just-world belief is an example of one such theory about the nature of reality. Lerner (1965) first suggested that individuals are motivated to believe that the world is just and that individuals get what they deserve: Good things happen to good people, bad things to bad people. There is more than 30 years of research demonstrating that just-world belief is a fundamental attribution error but that it has significant adaptive value, allowing individuals to ignore the randomness and essential uncontrollability of their physical and social worlds, and to act as if the world is stable and orderly (Cantor, 1990; Furnham, 1985, 2003; Furnham & Proctor, 1989; Lerner, 1965, 1977; Lerner & Miller, 1978). Individuals with high levels of belief in a just world are motivated to behave in fair and just ways (Bierhoff, Klein, & Kramp, 1991) and they also expect to be treated justly (Dalbert, Lipkus, Sallay, & Goch, 2001). When they are treated unjustly, as in situations involving forgiveness, they are strongly motivated to rectify or rationalize the injustice done to them to minimize their distress (Lerner, 1997, 1980; Schmitt, 1998). They may resort to unjustified victim blaming to protect their belief (De Judicibus Lerner, 1997; & McCabe, 2001).

Belief in a Just World and Forgiveness of Others and Self-Forgiveness

The findings in the just-world research literature are somewhat disparate, making specific predictions difficult. Nonetheless, a brief discussion of the concept suggests several ways in which it may influence forgiveness. It may be that individuals who believe strongly in the concept of a just world will be less forgiving when they suffer misfortune that they feel is undeserved. Conversely, their concept of just-world belief may help them cope by believing that justice will ultimately prevail, so they feel no need to hold a grudge or seek revenge. In relation to self-forgiveness, strong belief in a just world may result in individuals being less forgiving of themselves when they have behaved unjustly toward others. They may seek to rationalize or rectify the injustices done to increase their levels of self-forgiveness.

Belief in a Just World and the Concept of Situational Forgiveness

While there is general agreement in the literature on the validity of measuring interpersonal forgiveness and self-forgiveness, situational forgiveness has proved to be more contentious (Snyder, 2003). Situational forgiveness has been argued to be relevant when the source of a transgression is viewed as being beyond anyone's control (Thompson & Snyder, 2003). Examples include illnesses, natural disasters, and acts of fate in which it is not possible to identify a specific individual as the target of blame.

Conceptualizing situations as the source of distress is familiar within the cognitive therapy literature, where Beck et al. (1995) and Ellis and Dryden (1997) outline three possible sources of distress: the individual, other people, and situations. For cognitive therapists, the focus of situational distress is a more global target that is perceived to be the source of the individual's hurt. Victims may blame fate as causing them to be unlucky, or blame God, nature, the political system, general human stupidity, and so on. Thompson and Snyder (2003) argue that the need for situational forgiveness arises in these situations.

Macaskill (2005) has argued that the term "forgiveness" does not appropriately describe the adjustments made in response to aversive events outside anyone's control. Rather, it would seem that individuals reduce their anger and come to accept the situations that have occurred. In fact, the items in Thompson and Snyder's (2003) Forgiveness of Situations subscale actually appear to measure this acceptance process, rather than forgiveness, because they do not include the word "forgiveness" but instead employ the language of "acceptance." Moreover, given that it is not a moral agent that can be held responsible for its actions, a situation is, rationally, an inappropriate target to forgive. Finally, within the forgiveness literature, the term "situational forgiveness" has a meaning different from that of Thompson and Snyder's. Specifically, it refers to how forgiving an individual is in response to a particular scenario. This may involve forgiving the transgressor or the self for behavior occurring in a particular situation and is contrasted with dispositional forgiveness. Using the same term to label a different concept is confusing. For these reasons, the Thompson and Snyder concept of situational forgiveness will be labeled "acceptance of uncontrollable, traumatic situations" as this more accurately describes the process they are measuring. In this chapter, I will occasionally abbreviate this to "acceptance of situations."

Exline and Martin (2005) have demonstrated a similar phenomenon in relation to individuals experiencing anger toward God. They treat this as a phenomenon outside the domain of interpersonal forgiveness, arguing that talking about forgiving God is inappropriate, as many individuals believe that God is not capable of moral wrongdoing. Here, resolving anger rather than forgiveness is the solution. This would seem to exemplify an instance of the situational forgiveness described by Thompson and Snyder (2003). Despite these difficulties with labeling the concept, Thompson and Snyder as well as Macaskill (2007) have demonstrated that acceptance of uncontrollable, traumatic situations accounts for unique variance in aspects of psychological well-being relevant to forgiveness.

This study utilizes the Heartland Forgiveness Scale developed by Thompson and Snyder (2003), which measures acceptance of uncontrollable, traumatic situations as well as dispositional forgiveness of self and others. Within this measure, forgiveness is defined as the renunciation of anger or resentment, and reframing of the target event so that it ceases to be perceived negatively and is then viewed either positively or neutrally. This reframing process involves changes in the cognitions, emotions, and behaviors that the victim holds toward the target transgressor or memories of the event. Within this definition, by forgiving, the victim becomes free of any negative attachment to the event, having either neutral or positive feelings. This position with respect to neutral feelings differs from most other definitions but is similar to the pragmatic definition of forgiveness as closure, reported by Macaskill (2005) in a study of general population definitions of forgiveness.

Just- or unjust-world belief should be particularly relevant to the acceptance of situations where there is no obvious target to blame. If you think the world should be fair but it is "treating" you unfairly, how do you respond when you cannot reasonably blame anyone? To explore this further, the concept of acceptance of uncontrollable, traumatic situations is examined in more detail, utilizing mainly qualitative approaches to explore how individuals perceive such situations and to see whether they try to make causal attributions. The nature of such attributions and how they relate to acceptance are examined.

Belief in a Just World Measurement Issues

The early measurement of belief in a just world assumed that it was a one-dimensional bipolar concept with just-world belief at one end and unjust-world belief at the other (Rubin & Peplau, 1973, 1975). However, the relationships between the just and unjust subscales of measures of just-world belief were very low, suggesting that the concepts may be independent (Dalbert et al., 2001; Furnham & Proctor, 1989; Heaven & Connors, 1998). Dalbert et al. suggest that the distinction is important, as different behavior is associated with each world view. As we have discussed, individuals believing in a just world aim to behave justly to others, believe that others will treat them fairly, and trust their environment. Belief in an unjust world may lead individuals to be distrustful of the environment, not always to expect fair treatment and, therefore, to be more accepting of their own and others' transgressions. To explore this distinction further, this study used separate scales to measure belief in a just and an unjust world, and examined their relationship with each other, with forgiveness, and with acceptance of uncontrollable, traumatic situations.

The research literature has relatively little to say about whether there are sex differences in just-world beliefs, so this was also examined. Worthington (2005) noted that sex differences in actual levels of forgivingness are not widely reported although significantly different relationships between personality variables and interpersonal and self-forgiveness have been reported for men and women (Maltby, Macaskill, & Day, 2001; Neto & Mullet, 2004). Following the recommendation of Neto and Mullet, the data were explored for any possible sex differences.

To summarize, this research examined the relationships between theories about the nature of reality—namely, belief in a just world or belief in an unjust world and forgiveness of others, self-forgiveness, and acceptance of uncontrollable situations. Acceptance of situations was examined in more detail using qualitative approaches.

Preliminary Study

To conceptualize "situational forgiveness"—that is, acceptance of uncontrollable, traumatic situations—in a form that would be readily understood by participants, a focus group was held with six students: three men, and three women. They were all second-year students studying for a psychology degree. The Thompson and Snyder (2003) definition of situational forgiveness was given to the group and they were asked to think of situations that might provide an easily understood focus for questions on acceptance of uncontrollable, traumatic situations. Many topics were discussed, such as accidents and ill health, but with both of these it was thought that targets to blame could often be identified. The decision was that natural disasters provided a suitable topic. This also had the advantage of being a current issue with the recent tsunami in Asia and the hurricane in the United States. The consensual view was that if individuals are thinking rationally, a target of blame cannot be identified in natural disasters like tsunamis and hurricanes.

Description of the Study

Ranging in age from 18 to 43 years ($M = 20.1$, $SD = 5.49$), 190 university students (67 male and 123 female) participated voluntarily. With the exception of four participants who were British Asian, all participants were Caucasian. Students completed three standardized questionnaires: the Heartland Forgiveness Scale (Thompson & Snyder, 2003), the General Belief in a Just World Scale (Dalbert, Montada, & Schmitt, 1987), and the Belief in an Unjust World Scale (Dalbert et al., 2001).* To explore acceptance of uncontrollable, traumatic situations in more detail, three questions were included in the questionnaire that required respondents to provide qualitative data. One question asked respondents to rate how common it was for individuals to look for someone or something to blame for such disasters, using a 5-point Likert scale (1 = *very common*, 5 = *very uncommon*), and to explain why. A second, open-ended question asked individuals why they thought that natural disasters like tsunamis or hurricanes occurred. Finally, respondents were asked to say whether they thought it was logical to look for someone to blame.

* With the exception of the Belief in a Just World Scale, all the alpha coefficients were above the recommended .70 (Kline, 2000). In line with the Dalbert et al. (1987) recommendation for questionnaires with few items, the index of homogeneity was calculated for Belief in a Just World Scale ($r_{est} = .38$) and Belief in an Unjust World Scale ($r_{est} = .37$), which are both satisfactory. To compare male and female responses, independent t-tests with a Bonferroni correction were computed. An alpha level of .05 was used for all the statistical tests.

Relationships Between Belief in a Just or Unjust World and Forgiveness

Men had slightly higher scores than women on the Forgiveness of Others subscale and the Unjust World Belief Scale. The Unjust World Belief Scale was significantly associated with all of the forgiveness measures for men and women. The association was strongest for forgiveness of others ($r = .74$, $p < .01$), followed by self-forgiveness ($r = .59$, $p < .01$), and then acceptance of uncontrollable, traumatic situations ($r = .46$, $p < .01$). The finding with forgiveness of others is consistent with the argument that believing that the world is unjust means there is no expectation of fair treatment and the individual is likely to perceive and evaluate an event involving unfair treatment as less distressing (Dalbert et al., 2001; Lerner, 1965). Therefore, such mistreatment is easier to forgive compared with the situation of an individual who believes in a just world and expects to be treated fairly.

The strength of the correlations led to the suspicion that the scales might be measuring the same concept. However, close examination of the scales suggests that the questions examine different constructs. The Forgiveness of Others Scale is focused on how individuals treat others who have hurt or mistreated them (e.g., "Although others have hurt me in the past, with time, I have come to see them as good people"), while the Unjust World Belief Scale is a measure of an individual's beliefs about how the world operates in terms of delivering justice (e.g., "I feel that even important decisions are often unfair"). The two measures seem distinct. If we consider that theories of reality, such as the belief in an unjust world, act as cognitive filters influencing how individuals perceive and evaluate events (Epstein, 1990), the high correlations are less surprising.

With regard to self-forgiveness, Lerner (1997) and De Judicibus and McCabe (2001) report that, at a preconscious level, individuals believing in an unjust world do not engage in self-blame to the same extent as individuals who believe in a just world, and this relationship is supported. This corresponds with the Dalbert et al. (2001) observation that individuals believing strongly in an unjust world do not expect fair treatment (Dalbert et al., 2001; Furnham & Proctor, 1989; Heaven & Connors, 1998).

While I found a strong relationship between self-forgiveness and belief in an unjust world, the findings with belief in a *just* world were much weaker. Women who believed that the world is just were less self-forgiving ($r = -.25$, $p < .01$). The just-world belief literature reports that individuals with high levels of just-world belief feel obligated to treat others fairly (Bierhoff et al., 1991; Dalbert et al., 2001). Failure to treat others fairly is likely to result in believers judging themselves more harshly and hence being less self-forgiving, and this seems to have occurred here, but only to a small extent and only for women. As an aside, women were found to be more self-forgiving with age ($r = .22$, $p < .05$). Similar age effects on forgiveness have been reported previously (Neto & Mullet, 2004).

In both men ($r = -.38$, $p < .01$) and women ($r = -.49$, $p < .01$) belief in a just world was associated with lower acceptance of uncontrollable traumatic situations. If, as Cantor (1990) and Lerner (1980) suggest, belief in a just world allows individuals to feel that the world is stable and orderly, it may be that when presented with evidence such as natural disasters, such individuals are more likely to attribute blame to protect their world view; consequently, they are less accepting. Individuals who believe in an unjust world may simply see such situations as examples that justify their belief system. This is examined in more detail in a later section of this chapter.

As mentioned previously, some researchers have suggested that the concepts of just world and unjust world may be independent (Dalbert et al., 2001; Furnham & Proctor, 1989; Heaven & Connors, 1998) with different behavior associated with each world view (Dalbert et al., 2001). For men, the correlations between just-world belief and unjust-world belief were low and not statistically significant, suggesting that the concepts are unrelated. However, for women, there was a low but statistically significant negative correlation between just- and unjust-world beliefs ($r = -.23$, $p < .01$), suggesting some degree of relationship between the concepts. Heaven and Connors also reported similar sex differences, which require further research.

To examine the predictive value of just- and unjust-world beliefs and age on the forgiveness measures, standard multiple regression analyses were conducted separately for men and women. For forgiveness of others and for self-forgiveness, only unjust-world beliefs emerged as a significant predictor for both women and men. In fact, unjust-world beliefs accounted for a much larger proportion of the variance in forgiveness of others and self-forgiveness scores relative to the variance that is typically explained by personality measures (Mullet et al., 2005). Specifically, it accounted for 56.7% and 49.2% of the variance in forgiveness of others in men and women, respectively, and 40.2% and 30.3%, respectively, of the variance in self-forgiveness.

This finding—that if there is no expectation of just treatment, it is easier to be forgiving—is an important one that merits further research. Future research could usefully examine the relationships among personality traits, just- and unjust-world beliefs, and forgiveness to assess their combined predictive value. In addition, research focusing on forgiveness of specific incidents should be undertaken in contrast to the general measure used in this study to examine dispositional forgiveness. This could be done using scenarios, as in McCullough and Hoyt (2002), or by asking individuals to reflect on incidents that they have personally experienced, as in Enright and North (1998). Here, in addition to unjust-world beliefs, it would be relevant to use a measure of belief in a *personal* just world, as Dalbert (1999) has argued that this measure is more relevant when judgments are being made about forgiveness in specific, personal situations. Other alternative world schemas could also be explored.

In terms of acceptance of uncontrollable, traumatic situations, both unjust- and just-world beliefs were significant predictors, accounting for 28.4% and 26.5% of the variance for men and women, respectively. For both women and men, unjust-world beliefs were the stronger predictor. If an individual's schema is that the world is unjust, evidence of injustice merely serves to confirm that model (Dalbert et al., 2001; Furnham & Proctor, 1989). Consequently, the individual will be more accepting, as observed here. Furthermore, it was predicted that individuals who believe that the world is just would be less accepting of uncontrollable, traumatic situations, and this was confirmed.

Reflection on Belief in a Just World and Observed Sex Differences

As we have seen, the lack of significant relationships between belief in a just world and forgiveness of others could be due to the variability in responses that appear to be related to belief in a just world. It may be that some individuals who believe in a just world find a target to blame to protect their belief in a just world, as reported by Lerner (1997) and De Judicibus and McCabe (2001), and this would make them less likely to forgive. Other individuals, while believing in a just world, may have a longer perspective about when justice will occur and so will be less resentful or vengeful, and more forgiving, believing that the transgressor will get his or her just desserts eventually (Lerner, 1965).

While there were no sex differences in the predictors for any of the forgiveness measures, they did account for different proportions of variance, and men also had higher levels of unjust-world beliefs. These differences confirm the value of exploring sex differences, as advocated by Neto and Mullet (2004). There may well be differences in the processes of forgiveness or in the way that the world is construed, as there were in this study.

While this part of the study demonstrated the usefulness of the concept called "situational forgiveness" by Thompson and Snyder (2003), in that it proved to be a meaningful concept for participants and demonstrated a different pattern of relationships with the belief in a just or unjust world schema, the processes that individuals use to make sense of such occurrences are still unclear. The qualitative section of the questionnaire addressed some of these issues.

Understanding Acceptance of Uncontrollable, Traumatic Situations

Procedures Followed for Data Analysis

The qualitative data consisted of written responses to three questions included in the questionnaire. The grounded theory method for identifying themes was adopted (Strauss & Corbin, 1990). This involved careful reading and re-reading of the text to identify different meanings. From this open coding, a codebook listing and describing each theme was produced following Miles and Huberman (1994). Themes were then compared and contrasted, and superordinate and subordinate themes identified. As a reliability check, four coders independently coded a random sample of 40 responses to each question using the codebook. Interrater reliability was 0.84, calculated using Cohen's kappa (1960). Capozzoli, McSweeney, and Sinha (1999) report that reliability values above 0.75 indicate excellent levels of agreement.

Question 1: Incidence of and Explanations for Irrational Attribution of Blame Participants rated how common they thought it was for individuals to try to attribute blame in situations such as natural disasters, like tsunamis and hurricanes, and to say why individuals attribute blame. Table 3.1 summarizes the ratings obtained. A Chi-square Test of Association indicated that there were no sex differences in the patterns of response. Overall, 80% of the sample suggested that it was "very common" or "common" to try to attribute blame in situations such as natural disasters. Various reasons were given by respondents to explain why individuals attribute blame. Most respondents only gave one reason; the overall mean number of responses per person was 1.15 ($SD = 0.32$).

The superordinate themes identified were blaming as a coping strategy, blaming to facilitate understanding of why it had occurred, blaming as a necessary part of the healing process, and blaming to bring about closure. The superordinate theme of coping contained 62.81% of the responses provided but, unlike the other categories, it included some distinct themes and subordinate themes within it. Table 3.2 summarizes the superordinate themes, themes, and subordinate themes, and the numbers of participants producing each.

Emotional Coping

Within the superordinate coping category (47.16% of all responses), results suggested that blaming was an emotional coping strategy. There were three subordinate themes within emotional coping. The

Table 3.1 Ratings of Perceptions of How Common It Is to Try to Attribute Blame in Situations Such as Natural Disasters

	RATINGS					
Sex	Very common	Common	Neither common nor uncommon	Uncommon	Very uncommon	Total
Men	26 (13.7%)	30 (15.8%)	5 (2.6%)	6 (3.2%)	0 (0%)	67 (35.3%)
Women	48 (25.3%)	48 (25.3%)	9 (4.7%)	13 (6.8%)	5 (2.6%)	123 (64.7%)
Total	74 (38.9%)	78 (41.1%)	14 (7.4%)	19 (10%)	5 (2.6%)	190 (100%)

Table 3.2 Why Individuals Try to Attribute Blame: Superordinate Themes, Themes, and Subordinate Themes Identified and Number of Responses

SUPERORDINATE THEMES	THEMES AND SUBORDINATE THEMES	*N*	% OF TOTAL
Coping	Emotional coping Emotional relief Guilt reduction and comfort Anger and pain release	108	47.16
	Turning to God	13	5.94
	Reassurance and safety needs	10	4.37
	Distraction	7	3.06
	Acknowledging evil	5	2.28
Understanding		44	19.21
Healing		36	15.72
Closure		6	2.62
Total		229	100

most popular (24% of all the responses) conceptualized blaming as a coping strategy that makes individuals feel better about a situation by bringing *emotional relief.* For example, one respondent wrote that "people feel better when they can blame someone." Another suggested that "it really helps to feel that someone is to blame; it brings a sense of relief, knowing that someone or something can be blamed. You feel better."

A second subordinate theme within emotional coping was focused on *guilt reduction and the provision of emotional comfort* that came from having a target to blame. This constituted 15.74% of the total responses to the question. This was expressed in statements such as "blaming reassures us that it is not our fault and grief is easier to bear if we can blame someone or something." A second respondent suggested, "It eases our conscience to blame the State or God and reassures us that it is not our fault; it removes all personal responsibility."

The third subordinate theme within emotional coping simply focused on the *release of anger and other painful emotions* and accounted for 7.42% of the responses. This was expressed in the following typical statements by respondents: "Blaming releases our anger and we forget the pain for a while when we are blaming someone" and "It gives us a target to vent our anger on even though we know really that it is not their fault."

Turning to God

This theme involved respondents turning to God and putting their faith in the occurrence as being part of God's plan (5.94%). Respondents indicated that it was inappropriate to blame God, with one respondent saying, "It is not God's fault, we cannot blame God." Everything was seen to be part of a greater plan and good would ultimately result from disasters. It was suggested that these tragic situations often brought out the best qualities in people as they would offer help, donate money, or show that they cared in other ways. This feeling of something positive ultimately being possible because of the event, helped individuals cope with the horror. As one individual put it, "It helps me to cope knowing that God has a plan and that good is his ultimate intention and good comes from these events in a roundabout way with aid and things."

Reassurance and Safety Needs

Within the superordinate theme of coping, there was a distinct category describing reassurance and safety needs (4.37%). There was an acknowledgment that the world is unpredictable but that we need to believe that this is not the case in order to feel safe. For example, one respondent said:

> The world does not feel safe when these things happen, so someone must be to blame. We like to think that we are in control of the world, so we blame people when unpredictable things happen to pretend that we have control and the future is safe.

By implication, if someone is culpable, then in the future such events can be prevented or dealt with more effectively.

Distraction

Within the superordinate theme of coping, individuals suggested that the effort that went into finding someone to blame actually served to distract individuals from the horror of what had happened. One respondent wrote:

> Looking for someone to blame takes us away from the reality of the situation and we cope better as we are focused on something else. You think about who might have done it rather than dwelling on how awful it was.

Individuals moved their focus from the actual event and this brought some sense of relief.

Acknowledging Evil

Within this final theme of coping, acknowledging evil, there were the fewest respondents (2.28%). Respondents attributed the cause to external evil forces or the devil, but felt that these messages had a purpose. For example, one respondent said, "The devil is responsible for such things, it sends a message to people to turn to God, and that is good." This was ultimately a personally reassuring message, as they perceived that there could be a positive outcome.

Understanding

The next superordinate theme, identified by 19.21%, was about what was perceived as a human need to understand why things happen. One respondent wrote that "people need to believe that there is a reason for everything. They need to understand why. Finding a scapegoat to blame helps make sense of the situation." Having a target to blame was a way of creating some understanding of why something had occurred. The feeling was that it was part of our nature to seek explanations and blaming was part of this process. As another participant put it, "It is hard to justify things when there is no real cause or fault so you try to apportion blame, even although it is not always rational to do so."

Healing

This superordinate theme represented 15.72% of the responses and was the only one in which forgiveness was actually mentioned. Individuals suggested that finding someone to blame actually facilitated acceptance of the situation. Acceptance of the situation was seen as beginning the healing process, as described by one respondent, "To forgive and accept you must first blame, even though it is not always rational to blame." Several respondents also mentioned that the need to blame was part of the human psyche and suggested that it was why litigation is common when something goes wrong, as we believe that someone must pay, even in the case of accidents. One respondent exemplified this, saying, "Someone always has to pay or be responsible, and then we can accept it and forgive." Finding someone to blame seems to help the healing process begin.

Closure

There were only six responses in this category and they referred to the uncertainty that remains when a target to blame in situations cannot be identified. One individual said:

> You are left with an unsatisfactory feeling of why did it happen and where do we go from here, whereas if someone is blamed you can take steps to make sure it doesn't happen again and move on with your life.

It is as if the situation cannot be satisfactorily resolved, and plans made for the future, until blaming occurs.

Question 2: Personal Attributions of Cause in Natural Disasters There was a wide range of responses to the question about why the respondents themselves thought that natural disasters like hurricanes and tsunamis occurred, with respondents producing a mean of 1.64 ($SD = 0.41$) reasons each. The themes and examples of quotes from individual respondents within each theme are included in Table 3.3. The examples included in the table are very typical of the responses received and give a clear understanding of what was meant in each theme, with the exception of the religious explanations theme, which, because it included subordinate themes, will be discussed in more detail.

The largest subordinate theme within the religious explanations simply stated that God was responsible ($n = 20$, 6.4% of total sample), saying things like, "It's down to God, only he knows." The next most popular religious subordinate theme was the assertion that God has a reason and that good ultimately comes from it ($n = 15$, 4.82% of total sample). An example of this way of thinking came from one respondent who wrote, "Everything has a reason with God and good comes out of things that are unjust and seem downright bad." The next subordinate theme suggested that such events are a warning from God

Table 3.3 Themes Identified in Response to Questions of Why Participants Thought That Natural Disasters Occurred: Typical Responses and Number of Responses in Each Category

THEMES	*N*	% OF TOTAL	TYPICAL RESPONSES
Natural order	84	27	It's just the way the world is—unpredictable.
Religious explanations	55	17.69	It's down to God.
Blaming human species for global warming	48	15.43	Ultimately, it is down to mankind exploiting the Earth.
Human powerlessness	38	12.22	Shows us that we have no control over nature.
Luck, fate, karma	31	9.96	People are in the wrong place at the wrong time.
Scientific explanations	29	9.33	Movement of tectonic plates and the like.
Ultimately, a force for good	11	3.52	They cause good things to happen with aid and so on.
Governments are blamed	10	3.22	Governments make bad decisions and don't cooperate.
Exceptions to natural justice	3	1	These are exceptions to the rule that people are treated fairly.
Warning to human species	2	.63	It is a wake-up call from nature about the environment.
Total	311	100	

to the human species ($n = 6$, 1.93% of total sample). Typical of these responses was the individual who wrote that "God is warning us, he wants us to know that he is all powerful, not human beings." The penultimate religious subordinate theme was that of punishment by God ($n = 3$, 1% of total sample). All respondents in this category also believed that good would ultimately result, responding, "It is a way of being punished by God, but good then comes out of it as it brings people together." The final subordinate religious theme asserted that such events are caused by the devil ($n = 2$, 0.64% of total sample), with one respondent exemplifying this by writing, "It is not God punishing us but the devil showing his power."

Question 3: The Logic of Blaming The final question required participants to say whether they thought it was logical to look for someone to blame for natural disasters. The majority (79.5%) suggested that it was not logical to blame. One respondent wrote, "As human beings, we are sort of flawed, and we don't think clearly always or behave consistently." Just under half of these respondents qualified their responses. The typical response referred to individuals not always being rational beings or to the lack of consistency in much of human behavior, as this quotation from a participant illustrates, "Human beings can be logical but they can also do very illogical things and not even be aware that they are being illogical. Blaming politicians for the tsunami is a case in point. It's crazy but comforting."

Concluding Reflections

The qualitative study confirmed that it is common for individuals to attribute blame in situations such as natural disasters despite the majority view that it is illogical to do so. This irrational attribution of blame seems to be what is encapsulated within the Thompson and Snyder (2003) concept of situational forgiveness. If blaming is irrational, then, logically, forgiving as a response must be equally irrational, as I have previously argued. The individuals who evoked religious coping strategies or mentioned God in their explanations all felt that blaming God was inappropriate, as did the respondents in Exline and Martin (2005). The data suggest that blaming is a helpful process as part of the adjustment to the situation and fits within the conceptual cognitive therapy models of Beck et al. (1995) and Ellis and Dryden (1997). The response to this irrational blaming within cognitive therapy would be for individuals to recognize the irrationality of blaming, see it as a coping strategy, and work to reduce their feelings of distress generated by the situation. Forgiveness is not really part of this process; instead, I propose that what is actually occurring is acceptance, not forgiveness, of uncontrollable, traumatic situations.

The reasons that individuals give for the occurrence of natural disasters gives some insight into their schemas about the world. The unpredictability of the natural world is the most common schema, followed by religious models. There was evidence of blaming occurring in the responses given—namely, blaming human beings and governments for exploiting the Earth. Scientific reasons were relatively low in the order of explanations that respondents gave for natural disasters, despite these being students studying for a Bachelor of Science degree. Participants did not appear to have any difficulty dealing with this concept and all generated meaningful responses, providing further evidence that irrational blaming is not a rare phenomenon.

This research involved a student sample and should be replicated in a general population sample with wider age groups and a better balance of men and women. Education may also be a significant factor as the participants were all studying at a university degree level. Participants' religious beliefs were not recorded but these may be relevant. The effects of different world schemas should also be explored. The participants' responses reflect the views of observers of natural disasters, and very different processes may apply to individuals who are actually involved in such situations.

Despite these limitations, some interesting findings have emerged that require further investigation. Cognitive schemas about the nature of the world, like belief in a just or unjust world, have been shown to have relevance for understanding the process of forgiveness. For men and women, the only significant predictor of forgiveness of others and self-forgiveness was unjust-world beliefs, accounting for a significant proportion of the variance in forgiveness scores. For acceptance of situations, unjust-world beliefs were a positive predictor and just-world beliefs a negative predictor for both men and women. Men had higher levels of unjust-world beliefs and the proportion of variance in forgiveness scores accounted for by the just- and unjust-world measures was different for men and women, stressing the importance of considering sex when undertaking forgiveness research.

Irrational blaming was common in situations like tsunamis and hurricanes. It is recognized to be an irrational response, but employed as a useful coping strategy for dealing with the anxieties that such natural disasters evoke. This research suggests that while Thompson and Snyder's measure of "situational forgiveness" provides useful data, the term forgiveness is inappropriate. Rather, I would suggest that the adjustments made following such situations involve the reduction of negative emotions associated with irrational blaming, so what is being measured by this scale is the degree of acceptance of uncontrollable, traumatic situations. The concept of irrational blaming is located within the cognitive therapy literature and this association with just-world beliefs is likely to have clinical relevance when helping clients deal with such situations.

References

Beck, A. T., Rush, A. J., Shaw, B. F., & Emery, G. (1995). *Cognitive therapy of depression*. New York: Guilford.

Bierhoff, H., Klein, R., & Kramp, P. (1991). Evidence of the altruistic personality from data on accident research. *Journal of Personality, 31*, 1096–1109.

Cantor, N. (1990). From thought to behavior. *American Psychologist, 45*, 735–750.

Capozzoli, M., McSweeney, L., & Sinha, D. (1999). Beyond kappa: A review of interrater agreement. *The Canadian Journal of Statistics, 27*, 3–23.

Cohen, J. (1960). A coefficient of agreement for nominal scales. *Education and Psychological Measurement, 20*, 37–48.

Dalbert, C. (1999). The world is more just for me than generally: About the personal belief in a just world scale's validity. *Social Justice Research, 12*, 79–98.

Dalbert, C., Lipkus, I. M., Sallay, H., & Goch, I. (2001). A just and an unjust world: Structure and validity of different world beliefs. *Personality and Individual Differences, 30*, 561–577.

Dalbert, C., Montada, L., & Schmitt, M. (1987). *Reports of the research group: Responsibility, justice, morality, 24*. University of Trier: FBI Psychologie.

De Judicibus, M., & McCabe, M. (2001). Blaming the target of sexual harassment. *Sex Roles, 44*, 401–407.

Ellis, A., & Dryden, W. (1997). *The practice of rational-emotive therapy* (2nd ed.). New York: Springer.

Enright, R. D., & North, R. F. (1998). *Exploring forgiveness*. Madison: University of Wisconsin Press.

Epstein, S. (1990). Cognitive–experiential self-theory. In L. A. Pervin (Ed.), *Handbook of personality, theory and research* (pp. 165–192). New York: Guilford Press.

Exline, J. J., & Martin, A. (2005). Anger toward God: A new frontier in forgiveness research. In E. L Worthington, Jr. (Ed.), *Handbook of forgiveness* (pp. 73–88). New York: Routledge.

Furnham, A., (1985). Just world beliefs in an unjust society: A cross-cultural comparison. *European Journal of Social Psychology, 15*, 363–366.

Furnham, A. (2003). Belief in a just world: Research progress over the past decade. *Personality and Individual Differences, 34*, 795–817.

Furnham, A., & Proctor, E., (1989). Belief in a just world: Review and critique of the individual difference literature. *British Journal of Social Psychology, 28*, 365–384.

Heaven, P., & Connors, J. (1998). Personality, gender, and just world beliefs. *Australian Journal of Psychology, 40,* 261–266.

Kline, P. (2000). *A psychometric primer.* London: Free Association Books.

Lerner, M. J. (1965). Evaluation of performance as a function of performer's reward and attractiveness. *Journal of Personality and Social Psychology, 1,* 355–360.

Lerner, M. J. (1977). The justice motive: Some hypotheses as to its origins and forms. *Journal of Personality, 45,* 1–32.

Lerner, M. J. (1997). What does the belief in a just world protect us from: The dread of death or the fear of undeserved suffering? *Psychological Inquiry, 8,* 29–32.

Lerner, M. J. (1980). *The belief in a just world: A fundamental delusion.* New York: Plenum.

Lerner, M. J. (1997). What does the belief in a just world protect us from? The dread of death or the fear of understanding suffering. *Psychological Inquiry, 8,* 29–32.ß

Lerner, M. J., & Miller, D. T. (1978). Just world research and the attribution process: Looking back and looking ahead. *Psychological Bulletin, 85,* 1030–1051.

Macaskill, A. (2005). Defining forgiveness: Christian clergy and general population perspectives. *Journal of Personality, 73,* 1237–1265.

Macaskill, A. (2007). Exploring religious involvement, forgiveness, trust, and cynicism. *Mental Health, Religion and Culture, 10,* 1–16.

Maltby, J., Macaskill, A., & Day, L. (2001). Failure to forgive self and others: A replication and extension of the relationship between forgiveness, personality, social desirability, and traditional health. *Personality and Individual Differences, 29,* 1–6.

McCullough, M. E., & Hoyt, W. T. (2002). Transgression-related motivational dispositions: Personality substrates of forgiveness and their links to the Big Five. *Personality and Social Psychology Bulletin, 28,* 1556–1573.

Miles, M. B., & Huberman, A. M. (1994). *Qualitative data analysis: An expanded sourcebook* (2nd ed.). Thousand Oaks, CA: Sage.

Mullet, E., Neto, F., & Riviére, S. (2005). Personality and its effects on resentment, revenge, forgiveness, and self-forgiveness. In E. L. Worthington, Jr. (Ed.), *Handbook of forgiveness* (pp. 159–181). New York: Routledge.

Neto, F., & Mullet, E. (2004). Personality, self-esteem, and self-construal as correlates of forgiveness. *European Journal of Personality, 18,* 15–30.

Rubin, Z., & Peplau, L. A. (1973). Belief in a just world and reactions to another's lot: A study of participants in the national draft lottery. *Journal of Social Issues, 29,* 73–93.

Rubin, Z., & Peplau, L. A. (1975). Who believes in a just world? *Journal of Social Issues, 31,* 65–89.

Schmitt, M. (1998). Methodological strategies in research to validate measures of belief in a just world. In L. Montada & M. Lerner (Eds.), *Responses to victimization and belief in the just world* (pp. 163–173). New York: Plenum.

Snyder, C. R. (2003, October). *The Heartland Forgiveness Scale: Measuring dispositional forgiveness of self, others, and situations.* Paper presented at the Scientific Findings About Forgiveness Conference, A Campaign for Forgiveness Research, Atlanta, GA.

Strauss, A. L., & Corbin, J. (1990). *Basics of qualitative research: Grounded theory procedures and techniques.* Newbury Park, CA: Sage.

Thompson, L. Y., & Snyder, C. R. (2003). Heartland Forgiveness Scale. In S. L. Lopez & C. R. Snyder (Eds.), *Positive psychological assessment: A handbook of models and measures* (p. 310). Washington, DC: American Psychological Association.

Worthington, E. L., Jr. (2005). Initial questions about the art and science of forgiving. In E. L. Worthington, Jr. (Ed.), *Handbook of forgiveness* (pp. 1–13). New York: Routledge.

4

Self-Forgiveness

An Empowering and Therapeutic Tool for Working With Women in Recovery

MARJORIE E. BAKER

Introduction

> Our capacity to make peace with another person and with the world depends very much on our capacity to make peace with ourselves.
>
> **Thich Nhat Hanh**

My main research interest is in the area of empowerment and how forgiveness and self-forgiveness, particularly as they relate to women's issues, help foster empowerment among women. This chapter details a focus group approach to examining the perceptions of women in recovery from alcohol and/or drug addiction, regarding the utility and importance of self-forgiveness in their treatment, their rehabilitation, and their recovery experiences.

Information about women in treatment programs and in recovery has been well documented. It has also been well documented that men and women in substance abuse treatment differ in their treatment program needs. For example, research shows that women entering treatment for substance abuse tend to have lower incomes and less education than men, tend to have more mental and physical health problems than men, have greater concerns about child care, and generally report more stressful life events than do their male counterparts (Green, 2006). Moreover, these and other noted differences have given rise to the discussion of need for and the debate over the value of treatment programs designed specifically for women (Reed, 1985). Some findings (Green) show that co-ed treatment programs are as effective with women as with men, and some even report outcomes that suggest that women in such programs sometimes do better than their male counterparts. By contrast, the results of one study that examined the role of sex of participant in the recovery process from alcohol dependence showed that among the men and women who completed a 30-day co-ed treatment program, women had higher relapse rates than men (Greenfield, 2002). While there are similar factors related to recovery and relapse for both sexes, those women who relapsed were found to have strong associations and ties with the men in their lives who are substance abusers (Grella, Scott, Foss, Joshi, & Hser, 2003).

Sex-related bias in treatment program planning is evident in the design of most treatment programs that were originally designed by men with a male population in mind. While some 30-day co-ed treatment programs have made adjustments for women, particularly around issues such as child-care needs, most continue to fall short in addressing the unique and complex needs and mental health issues of women seeking assistance with alcohol and substance abuse problems.

The past few decades have witnessed a host of studies examining the experiences of women in recovery from substance abuse. However, none of these studies has examined the value of self-forgiveness in the recovery process for women. Similarly, studies that have explored the construct of self-forgiveness have examined the offender's approach to self-forgiveness when the offense was committed against another person. In the case of women in recovery from alcohol or drug abuse, the greatest abuse and harm, in some cases, is arguably against the women themselves. However, research is lacking that examines the construct of self-forgiveness in cases where the offender has caused, in some instances, irreparable harm to the self. Investigative efforts have also consistently affirmed that guilt and shame are issues of grave concern among female substance abusers. Despite this fact, issues related to self-forgiveness for shameful acts are rarely discussed in treatment programs in a direct way and are generally underutilized as a therapeutic tool in the treatment and recovery processes for women.

In spite of these shortcomings, alcohol and substance abuse treatment programs are extremely valuable in helping those who seek to obtain and maintain sobriety. They are respectably known for introducing participants to the 12-step program and for guiding them through the steps. Because a significant part of the guilt felt by persons in recovery often centers around the alienation from family and friends resulting from past behaviors related to their addiction, treatment programs sometimes also provide help to participants seeking forgiveness from those whom they have hurt while abusing alcohol and/or drugs. While the importance of making amends to those who have been hurt by the alcohol or drug abuser's behavior is likely to emerge during the working of the 12 steps, issues related specifically to *self-forgiveness,* for harm done to the self and to others, are rarely addressed in treatment programs.

While much has been written about interpersonal forgiveness in the past two decades, little has been written about the restorative benefits of self-forgiveness (Snow, 1993), particularly as it relates to women in recovery from alcohol or drug abuse. Interventions designed to assess clients' readiness and need for self-forgiveness and then encourage and guide participants who are ready to work through the process of self-forgiveness in treatment programs are rarely utilized. This chapter introduces the inclusion of self-forgiveness as an innovative and therapeutic treatment approach that can enhance clients' personal empowerment as well as the quality, effectiveness, and overall benefits of the addiction treatment and recovery process.

Self-Forgiveness Defined

> Forgiving ourselves for a wrongdoing "allows for a future that is not determined by the past...." (Bauer et al., 1992, p. 150)

Self-forgiveness is the internal process of releasing resentment, loathing, and negative reproach toward the self by compassionately choosing to regard the self as a fallible but remorseful human being, capable of change, committed to personal growth, and worthy of forgiveness. In essence, "self-forgiveness is the process by which we make good to ourselves for our failing" (Snow, 1993, p. 75). Enright and the Human Development Study Group (1996) define self-forgiveness as "a willingness to abandon self-resentment in the face of one's own acknowledged objective wrong, while fostering compassion, generosity and love toward oneself" (p. 116). Enright points out that, in some cases, the offender must forgive himself or herself in order to be open to receiving forgiveness from the person who was injured. In other instances, feeling forgiven by the injured party can serve as a catalyst in helping the offender move to a stance of internal self-forgiveness. There are also situations in which the offender makes the choice to move through the self-forgiveness process even though the injured party refuses to forgive him or her (Enright & the Human Development Study Group). Pioneer authors of a phenomenological study of the experience of self-forgiveness describe it "not as an achievement, but rather as a gift where one moves from estrangement and 'brokenness' to a sense of at-homeness" (Bauer et al., 1992, p. 149).

Differences and Similarities Between Forgiveness and Self-Forgiveness

The process of forgiving oneself is different from seeking forgiveness for wrongs committed against others or wrongs committed against us by others. Similar to forgiveness, self-forgiveness is a choice and an internal process that involves an emotional and cognitive decision to release feelings of hate and loathing toward the self.

There are many similarities, but also a few differences between forgiveness and self-forgiveness. The main difference is that forgiveness does not require us to reconcile with the party who broke our trust. Reconciliation is great when it can happen, especially when family or close friends are involved, but sometimes, as in the case when the offender is not remorseful or is still offending, it may not be possible. A common misperception about forgiveness is that it is not possible to forgive someone who is not remorseful or repentant, but this need not be true, as is the case when reconciliation is not part of the process.

Genuine self-forgiveness, on the other hand, *does* require remorse for wrongdoing and for unwarranted harm caused to others, as well as a desire for self-reunification. Because one must, of necessity, reconcile with oneself if one is to forgive oneself, remorse and self-reunification are critical to the process of self-forgiveness and constitute the main difference between forgiving the self and forgiving others.

Critical Elements and Core Controversies about Self-Forgiveness

Research findings on studies that have been conducted on self-forgiveness have been mixed. Some scholars who have studied clients and self-forgiveness caution practitioners about promoting self-forgiveness too quickly (Fisher & Exline, 2006; Holmgren, 1998; Tangney, Boone, & Dearing, 2005). For example, Fisher and Exline, in their work on self-forgiveness, raised the question as to whether self-forgiveness was merely a means of easily pardoning one's own injurious offenses. In concert with that work, Tangney et al. found a positive linkage between self-forgiveness and narcissism.

According to Holmgren (2002), clients who would seek to forgive themselves without first fully and responsibly acknowledging the nature and impact of their wrongdoing: (1) are rationalizing the behavior in an effort to avoid taking responsibility for their wrongful actions, or (2) simply have no ill feelings toward the self despite the wrongdoing on their part. In these instances, the clients are deceiving themselves by condoning the wrong as opposed to honestly recognizing and taking responsibility for their wrongdoing and seeking to forgive themselves for the commission of it (Holmgren). The hasty pursuit of self-forgiveness is disingenuous, premature, and possibly indicative of narcissism, unless the client first acknowledges and owns the commission of the wrong, is truly remorseful, and has sought to make appropriate amends to those unjustly injured by the wrongful behavior.

Because behavior-related transgressions associated with substance abuse are, without question, intimately tied to the offender, women in treatment for substance abuse are less likely to deny wrongdoing. It has been my experience in working with women in treatment that even when entering a treatment program, they want to blame the "substance" for their behavior, these women must be encouraged to come to grips with the fact that for whatever reason, they made the poor choice to use the harmful substance repeatedly. Their sobriety is dependent on their acknowledging and taking responsibility for having chosen the substance over their children, other family members, and themselves. If sobriety is to be a lasting reality, women in recovery must be encouraged, while in therapy, to become empowered enough to recognize their ability to choose differently in the future.

Unlike many situations in which the wrongdoing is subject to debate, women in recovery from substance abuse have clearly been involved in undesirable behavior that was harmful to them and, in most cases, to others. While empirical evidence that has specifically included acceptance of responsibility for wrongdoing as a prerequisite for self-forgiveness is lacking in the literature (Tangney et al., 2005), for women in recovery, an acknowledgment of having behaved irresponsibly while under the influence and of having hurt others as well as themselves, is generally a given. Acknowledgment of transgressions, as well as a clear and obvious acceptance of responsibility for inappropriate overindulgence in their substance of choice is, in most cases, a prerequisite and a primary motivator for seeking treatment for their addiction.

Utilizing Self-Forgiveness in Treatment Programs for Women

The concept of self-forgiveness is an emerging issue that has far reaching utility in the addiction and substance abuse treatment milieu. Yet, despite its importance, issues related to self-forgiveness are rarely discussed in treatment programs and generally underutilized as a therapeutic benefit in the recovery process. Instead, in addition to the many informative and empowering lessons generally available for participants in both inpatient and outpatient treatment programs related to sobriety maintenance, treatment programs have focused mainly on helping participants seek forgiveness from, and make amends to, those they hurt while abusing alcohol or drugs. In helping clients to heal and to remain substance free, it is imperative that therapists and other mental health professionals working in treatment facilities understand the importance of addressing issues of self-forgiveness when indicated, particularly when working with women in recovery.

Given the societal stigma attached to women who abuse alcohol and/or other substances, the resulting feelings of shame and guilt are understandable. These feelings must be acknowledged, addressed, and worked through in treatment. Recognition of the benefits of self-forgiveness is particularly important for therapists who provide guidance and treatment to women in recovery programs.

Moreover, therapists working with women in recovery must feel a level of comfort and competence in working with this population and must be knowledgeable about addiction and recovery in terms of women's unique and complex needs. It is also important that they believe in the women's potential for growth and change. They should be prepared to incorporate teachings on the subject of self-forgiveness and to facilitate discussions about the value of self-forgiveness in treatment programs for women in recovery. Finally, they must understand the many benefits of self-forgiveness as it relates to self awareness, enhanced self-esteem, personal empowerment, and ultimately, relapse prevention and sobriety maintenance.

The Goal of Self-Forgiveness for Women in Recovery

My interest in the concept of self-forgiveness began several years ago upon realizing that many clients with alcohol and substance abuse problems—most particularly female clients in treatment—often hold on to deep-seated, very personal, unresolved issues that seemed rooted in shame and guilt and that these have often resulted in self-loathing. In my opinion, the goal of self-forgiveness is not solely to exonerate the self from a past gone bad, but to resolve and get beyond the deep-seated self-loathing to which female substance abusers in treatment for addiction can be prone. Self-forgiveness could lay the groundwork for getting reacquainted with, and resurrecting the long buried positive aspects of, the self. I have worked with women in recovery who have been remorseful and repentant (both core elements of self-forgiveness), but who still professed to hate themselves and still felt gut-wrenching shame at the core of their being. In these cases, the inner motivation to remain substance free is likely to be undermined. The goal of self-forgiveness for these women, therefore, centers mainly around self-reunification and the pursuit of self-respect, which I believe are critical for sobriety maintenance.

I think that for some, self-forgiveness might well be aligned with a spiritual connectedness of sorts in that it entails deep inward reflection and learning to identify and appreciate unique qualities that many women in recovery may never have thought about in relation to themselves. As I encountered women in recovery (in the focus groups I conducted) who were doing well, staying sober, and leading productive lives, I saw women who have learned to like themselves. I saw women who feel worthy to be doing well. I do not think that is likely to happen for women who are in recovery until some measure of self-forgiveness for their past behavior has taken place.

Method

The main purposes of the research effort were to (1) determine if, and to what extent, discussions of self-forgiveness had been part of the treatment process experienced by women who had been in a formal treatment program for alcohol and/or substance abuse; and (2) hear their perceptions, based on their personal experiences, of the importance, relevance, and overall utility of self-forgiveness in the recovery process and in relapse prevention. The goal of the focus groups was to have participants reflect on and discuss their experience in the treatment facility. They were asked to include in their reflections their thoughts about forgiving themselves for harm done to themselves as well as to others. In summary, they were asked to reflect on the extent to which self-forgiveness, as a topic, was addressed in individual counseling or in groups in which they had participated while in their treatment programs. They also discussed their perception about if and why working through issues of self-forgiveness should be an important part of the treatment process for women in recovery.

Two focus groups were conducted with 19 women in recovery who had had prior personal experience as participants in drug and/or alcohol treatment programs. All of the women were gainfully employed at the time of the focus group experience and reported a nonuse period ranging from 7 weeks to 19 years, with the majority having several years of sobriety. The education level ranged from GED to a 4-year college degree, with the majority having a high school education. They ranged in age from 31 to 55 years of age.

Participants described their experiences in treatment, including the interventions that were most and least helpful in maintaining sobriety. The focus groups were tape-recorded, after which the tapes were transcribed and emergent themes categorized for analysis.

Results

Emergent Themes From Women's Reflections on Their Treatment Programs

As participants reflected on their various treatment programs, their experiences with addiction, and their thoughts about self-forgiveness, four major themes emerged.

Sexual Molestation in Childhood and/or Young Adult Years

Almost all of the women in the focus groups reported having been sexually molested as children or young women, in many cases by a parent, a stepparent another relative, or a friend of a parent. Some reported feeling that their mothers knew, but did nothing. Issues of shame and guilt, but particularly guilt, often arose in connection with their discussion about molestation. Most of the participants discussed feeling guilty about the sexual abuse rather than being aware of feelings of anger. They felt they were to blame. Some verbalized feeling that the way they dressed had brought the abuse on. One participant, who was gang raped while partially intoxicated, thought it was her fault because she had been under the influence of alcohol. Possibly due to low self-esteem, some of the women seemed to "own" or take personal responsibility for the wrongs perpetrated against them. It was clear not only that self-forgiveness was a problem with which most of them struggled, but also that the majority had deep-seated and unresolved forgiveness issues related to themselves as victims of abuse.

Guilt, Loss, and Bereavement

A discussion about guilt, loss, and bereavement emerged in both groups. This discussion was particularly emotional for some participants whose deceased parents had been alcohol and drugs abusers. They reported that getting high or intoxicated was, at the time, a means of escape for them: "It is harder to forgive yourself because you knew that getting drunk was the wrong thing to do and that you would do crazy things, but you did it anyway."

Some participants discussed deep, unresolved anger against their parents and having tremendous guilt feelings, thinking, for instance, that their mother's death was caused by their incorrigibility as a teenager or because they stole from their mother. One participant wondered if her mother may have actually died from a broken heart because she was still using at the time of her mother's death. She commented, "I am working on forgiving myself, but when I think about my past behavior, I feel guilty all over again."

The Value of Treatment Programs

Participants verbalized that at the beginning of treatment, issues of self-forgiveness did not come up and, at that point, were not relevant. They unanimously shared that upon entry into their treatment programs, they were just happy to be there and finally doing something positive about their addiction. They were optimistic about just being in a treatment program and beginning the sobriety maintenance journey:

> I think it would be important to think about self-forgiveness, but you just don't think about that when you are in treatment. You just want to stay sober, stop hurting people you love, and get your life back on track.

It was the consensus that all issues related to forgiveness, whether seeking forgiveness from others or self-forgiveness, had roots in their substance use. That is, initially, these women blamed everything on their usage. The thinking was that if they could just remain sober, all of the bad feelings they had and the terrible things they did would cease. The entire focus in the beginning phase of treatment was necessarily on abstinence and remaining substance free.

A number of statements that were made reflected feelings of gratitude for having access to a treatment program. They reported that being in a treatment program with other addicted persons allowed them to discuss their wrongdoings in the presence of others who had committed similar offenses, stolen from family and friends, robbed, assaulted, and committed a host of other negative acts to obtain their drug of choice. It was helpful for them to discuss these terrible things without feeling isolated. They reported feeling good about "fitting in" in an environment that was positive, for the first time since beginning their history of substance abuse: "I feel I have forgiven myself, but it took a long time and a lot of therapy."

They shared that in their treatment groups, they often talked about and attempted to examine the root causes of their usage. Many said that they blamed God for having had a "bad childhood" and felt unloved by God and their parents. This was particularly so in cases where participants' parents were drug and/or alcohol abusers themselves and in cases where their parents were abusive to them physically, verbally, and/or sexually.

The insightfulness and skill of a caring therapist was reflected upon as being very critical when these deep emotional issues began to surface in the treatment process. This is where self-forgiveness comes in and can be a key factor in effective treatment:

> I relapsed over and over again before I realized I needed to forgive myself to move on. My therapist really helped me with this. My therapist had me write letters, and one of them was to myself. That helped me a lot.

Another participant said that the best and most positive experience in her entire treatment process was when a therapist had her write letters to her deceased parents, who had been abusive toward her. In the focus group, she said that her mother had been physically abusive and was aware of, but did nothing about, the stepfather's sexual abuse of her. She reported that over a period of several months, her therapist encouraged her to write letters to both her mother and her stepfather detailing why she was so angry and how her anger manifested itself in guilt, self-loathing, and ultimately, a host of negative, self-destructive behaviors, including alcohol and drug abuse. She was also instructed by her therapist to write letters to herself, acknowledging her pain and expressing why she was so angry at herself, encouraging insight into her usage, and then compassionately offering herself the very personalized gift of self-forgiveness.

The Need for Self-Forgiveness Intervention

While a few participants said that they had had a therapist who played a valuable role in helping them forgive themselves, the majority of participants indicated feeling that assistance with self-forgiveness would have been helpful, but the words were never mentioned in their treatment programs:

> I never heard the word self-forgiveness mentioned in my program.
>
> So many other things are so important, like just being there in a program, getting some help. I really didn't think much about forgiving myself, but at some point, we really need to.

It should definitely be a part of what we learn about, but it's not.

It was a good program and I learned a lot of things about myself, but I still needed to try to actually forgive myself and I didn't think about that. And, it wasn't mentioned.

I know I need to forgive myself, but I don't know how. I still need help with that because it is really hard. I need help. We all do.

Treatment programs focus on understanding addiction and then seeking forgiveness from others who have been harmed by your behavior.

I wish I could forgive myself, but I can't.

I want to forgive myself, but don't know how.

Summary of Focus Group Discussions

Overall, the content of the focus group discussion suggested that self-forgiveness could be a critical component in successful recovery and the relapse prevention process. While the subject of self-forgiveness was discussed and dealt with by a few individual therapists, issues related specifically to forgiving the self were rarely discussed in their addiction treatment programs. The group dialogue suggested that feelings of guilt and shame have a lingering impact and, if not addressed, can contribute to relapse. Some participants shared that they relapsed again and again—until they recognized the importance of forgiving themselves. Others in the group reported that while family and friends have forgiven them, they continue to struggle in their ability to forgive themselves.

Among all of the women in these focus groups, those who had worked through issues of self-forgiveness did so only as a result of a good and insightful therapist who assessed the appropriateness and need for them to forgive themselves and encouraged it. In helping women heal emotionally and remain substance free, it is imperative that professionals providing treatment in alcohol and substance abuse facilities understand the importance of introducing the topic of self-forgiveness, where appropriate, and assisting clients, particularly women, in addressing this critically important issue in the recovery and relapse prevention process.

Conclusion

Scholars using different methodologies, studying different populations, and researching different questions under different conditions have been led to differing conclusions regarding the moral appropriateness of self-forgiveness. I think, however, that most would agree that the importance of offenders taking honest and forthright responsibility for their misdeeds before seeking to forgive themselves is an essential component of healthy self-forgiveness. While it has been my experience in working with women in recovery that self-forgiveness can serve as a valuable therapeutic tool in the restoration of self-respect and self-esteem and in the prevention of relapse, I would caution practitioners to guard against routinely or prematurely promoting and encouraging self-forgiveness with clients. It is important for therapists to recognize and assess the difference between self-forgiveness following remorseful and honest ownership of a wrongdoing, and a client's simply excusing himself or herself for a misdeed without demonstrating genuinely the core elements of remorse, making amends, and taking personal responsibility for future behavior.

References

Bauer, L., Duffy, J., Fountain, E., Halling, S., Holzer, M., Jones, E., et al. (1992). Exploring self-forgiveness. *Journal of Religion and Health, 31,* 149–160.

Enright, R., & the Human Development Study Group (1996). Counseling within the forgiveness triad: On forgiving, receiving forgiveness, and self-forgiveness. *Counseling and Values, 40,* 107–126.

Fisher, M. L., & Exline, J. J. (2006). Self-forgiveness versus excusing: The roles of remorse, effort, and acceptance of responsibility. *Self and Identity: The Journal of the International Society for Self and Identity, 5,* 127–146.

Green, C. (2006). Gender and use of substance abuse treatment services. *Alcohol Research & Health, 29*(1), 55–62.

Greenfield, S. (2002). Women and alcohol use disorders. *Harvard Review of Psychiatry, 10,* 76–85.

Grella, C., Scott, C., Foss, M., Joshi, V., & Hser, Y. (2003). Gender differences in drug treatment outcomes among participants in the Chicago target cities study. *Evaluation and Program Planning, 26,* 297–310.

Hodgins, D., el-Guebaly, N., & Addington, J. (1997). Treatment of substance abusers: Single or mixed gender programs? *Addiction, 92,* 805–812.

Holmgren, M. R. (1998). Self-forgiveness and responsible moral agency. *The Journal of Value Inquiry, 32,* 71–91.

Holmgren, M. R. (2002). Forgiveness and self-forgiveness in psychotherapy. In S. Lamb & J. G. Murphy (Eds.), *Before forgiving: Cautionary views of forgiveness in psychotherapy* (pp. 112–135). New York: Oxford University Press.

Reed, B. G. (1985). Drug misuse and dependency in women: The meaning and implications of being considered a special population or minority group. *The International Journal of the Addictions, 20,* 13–62.

Snow, N. (1993). Self-forgiveness. *The Journal of Value Inquiry, 27,* 75–80.

Tangney, J. P., Boone, A. L., & Dearing, R. (2005). Forgiving the self: Conceptual issues and empirical findings. In E. L. Worthington, Jr. (Ed.), *Handbook of forgiveness* (pp. 143–158). New York: Routledge.

O'Connor, & Wade, 2001), a questionnaire that employs scenes to which subjects respond with their likelihood of forgiving, and with the Trait Unforgiveness Scale designed for that study. Statistical analyses revealed that higher levels of forgiveness were positively related to mental health status, while greater levels of unforgiveness were related to higher baseline cortisol, postimagery cortisol, and poorer mental health status.

Witvliet, Ludwig, and Vander Laan (2001) used an experimental design to explore the physiology of forgiveness and unforgiveness in male and female college students. Individuals imagined four responses to a person whom they blamed for mistreating, offending, or hurting them. During individual, two-hour sessions, participants engaged in thirty-two imagery periods, where each of the four conditions were imagined eight times for sixteen second durations (orders counterbalanced). Tones signaled the participant to think about two forgiving responses (empathizing with the offender's humanity, granting forgiveness) and two unforgiving responses (rehearsing the hurt, harboring a grudge), or relax. During the unforgiving imagery trials, participants showed greater brow muscle tension, skin conductance, heart rate, and blood pressure responses compared to forgiving trials. These results provided support for the idea that physiological responses could serve as mediators of the relationship between forgiveness and health.

Current Studies

Since 2001 we have conducted four studies examining the physiological correlates of forgiveness. With the exception of Study 4, our samples have included both male and female participants (see Edmondson, 2005; Lawler et al., 2003, 2005; Lawler-Row & Piferi, 2006, for details). The relationships between forgiveness and health were similar for men and women, but for the purpose of this chapter, we have described these data for only the female participants. The primary goal of these studies was to determine whether forgiveness has physiological correlates, or a clear expression in the body. In all but the third study, we examined physiological correlates of both state and trait forgiveness. State (situation-specific) forgiveness refers to the degree of forgiveness reported in response to a particular offense and offender, while trait (general) forgiveness refers to a stable characteristic or personality trait. In the third study, we explored only trait forgiveness as it related to physical health and successful aging in a sample of older adults.

Study 1: Forgiveness as a Change of Heart

Our first study (Lawler et al., 2003) of the physiological correlates of forgiveness included 64 college-age women. They completed a packet of questionnaires and came to the laboratory for an individual testing session. The laboratory session consisted of a 10-minute resting baseline, during which the participant watched a relaxing video of tropical fish. Next, two interviews were administered, each followed by a 5-minute recovery period, during which the state measures of forgiveness were completed. In counterbalanced order, each participant described a time when she was deeply hurt or upset by a parent and by a friend or relationship partner. During these sessions, periodic measures of heart rate and blood pressure were taken.

Trait forgiveness was measured with the Forgiving Personality Inventory (Kamat, Jones & Row, 2006). This measure assesses self-report of general forgiveness, defined as a readiness to forgive others when victimized by moral and interpersonal transgressions. State forgiveness was measured with the Acts of Forgiveness scale (Drinnon & Jones, 1998), a 45-item measure that includes a description of a specific event, as well as current thoughts and feelings toward the offender. Forgiveness groups were created by dividing the sample at the medians: There were high ($n = 35$) and low ($n = 29$) trait forgiveness groups and high ($n = 29$) and low ($n = 35$) state forgiveness groups.

In this study, we compared the groups of high and low state and trait forgivers at five time periods: rest; the first, third, and last minutes of the interview period; and minute 2 of the recovery period. Blood pressure responses, averaged across the two interviews, are shown in Figures 5.1 and 5.2 for high and low trait and state groups, respectively.

There were clear group differences in blood pressure: high trait forgivers had lower systolic, diastolic, and mean arterial pressure than low trait forgivers at all time periods. In addition, low trait forgivers

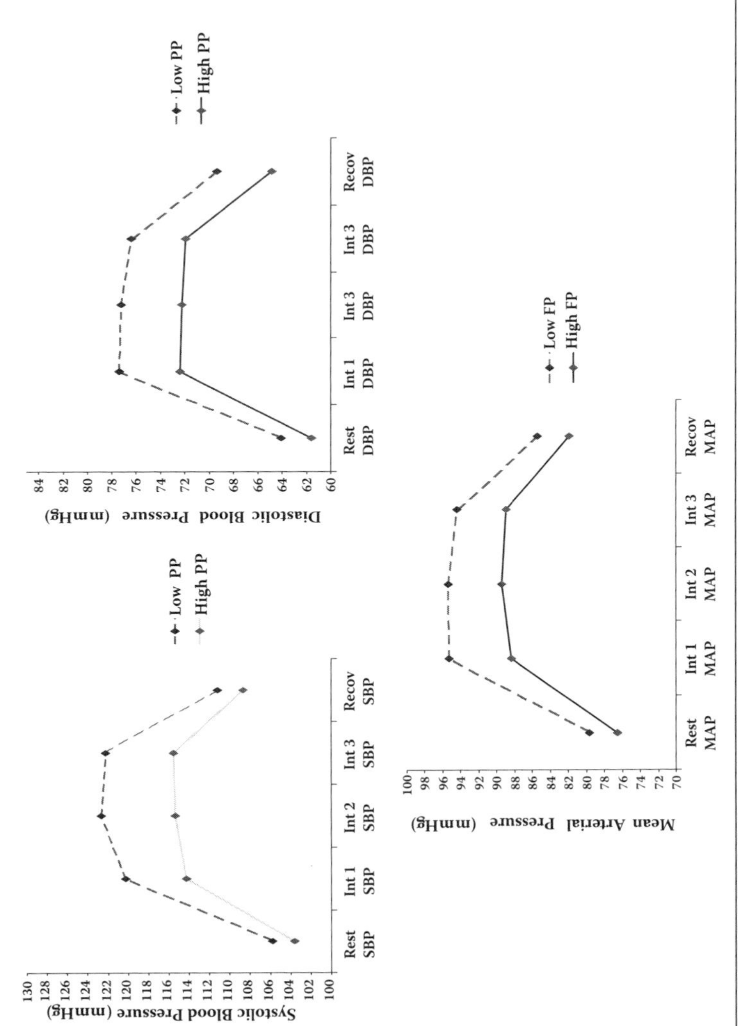

Figure 5.1 Blood pressure responses for high and low trait forgiveness groups.

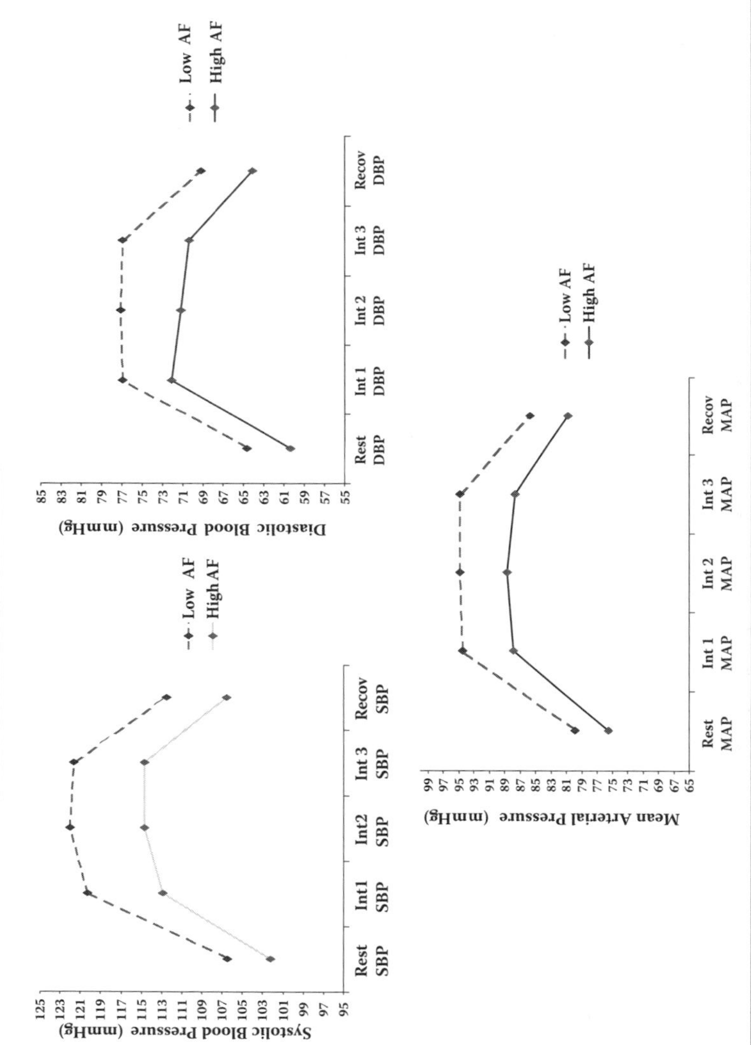

Figure 5.2 Blood pressure responses for high and low state forgiveness groups.

were more reactive than the high trait forgivers, showing a greater stress-related increase from rest to interview. Similarly, for the state forgiveness groups, the low state forgivers had higher blood pressure across all measurement intervals than high state forgivers. While there was a significant correlation between state and trait forgiveness ($r = .52$, $p < .0001$), there were no interactions between state and trait forgiveness groups in the physiological responses. Thus, one can assume that the effects of state and trait forgiveness on physiological responses are additive.

Examining self-reported health data, we compared both state and trait forgiveness with measures for physical symptoms, stress, and number of medications taken. As shown in Table 5.1, individuals with forgiving personalities reported less stress; those who were more forgiving of a particular recalled betrayal had fewer physical symptoms of illness.

Thus, this first study with college-age women indicated that both specific and general forgiveness had clear physiological correlates. Highly forgiving women had lower levels of blood pressure and were less reactive while relating a time of betrayal. In addition, those women who had forgiven in two particular instances had lower levels of blood pressure throughout the rest, interview, and recovery periods. Finally, both state and trait forgiveness scores were associated with stress, physical symptoms, and number of medications taken. These were intriguing findings, linking forgiveness to acute physiological responses and to health outcomes, and led us to consider whether we could generalize these findings beyond this young-adult, college-educated sample.

Table 5.1 Associations Between Forgiveness and Health Outcome Measures

	2	3	4	5
1. Forgiving personality	.52[a]	–.17	–.33[b]	.21
2. Specific forgiveness		–.25[c]	–.19	–.21
3. Physical symptoms			.41[a]	.26[c]
4. Stress				.07
5. Number of medications				

[a] $p<.001$
[b] $p<.01$
[c] $p<.05$

Study 2: Pathways From Forgiveness to Health

In the second study (Lawler et al., 2005), we employed the same procedure, with the exception of including only one betrayal narration rather than two. In this case, the sample included 62 women, ranging in age from 27 to 72 years ($M = 42$, $SD = 10.1$). The differences in acute physiological responses were much more modest: Only a derivative measure of heart rate and systolic blood pressure (rate-pressure product) differed between groups, reflecting sympathetic drive to the heart. In this case, as with the college-age women, women with a more forgiving personality were less reactive during the interview.

In addition to physical symptoms, several measures of health status were included: quality of sleep, symptoms of fatigue, and somatic complaints, as well as physical symptoms, stress, and number of medications. The relationships between both state and trait forgiveness and these health measures are shown in Table 5.2. All but one correlation (trait forgiveness and fatigue) reached statistical significance. Forgiveness was related to fewer physical symptoms of illness and to a smaller number of medications. In addition, forgiveness was associated with better quality of sleep, fewer stress-related bodily somatic symptoms, less stress, and fewer symptoms of fatigue. Thus, having a forgiving personality and being able to forgive specific offenses, even when those events occurred long in the past, are related to a variety of health measures.

Knowing that forgiveness is associated with health just describes a statistical association. The next step in this research was to explore

Table 5.2 Associations Between Forgiveness and Health Measures

	TRAIT (GENERAL)	STATE (SPECIFIC)
1. Quality of sleep	.44[a]	.54[a]
2. Somatic symptoms	–.28[c]	–.47[a]
3. Fatigue	–.23	–.44[b]
4. Physical symptoms	–.32[b]	–.51[a]
5. Stress	–.39[b]	–.47[a]
6. Number of medications	–.48[a]	–.53[a]

[a] $p < .0001$
[b] $p < .01$
[c] $p < .05$

pathways that might explain how forgiveness could lead to better health. Three potential pathways were considered: stress, conflict management, and spirituality. If forgiveness leads to less stress, then better health may result due to decreased stress. Similarly, if forgiveness is associated with better conflict management, then one's relationships may be of better quality and that may improve health. Finally, if forgiveness is a marker for spirituality, then the finding that religion and health are associated (Koenig, McCullough, & Larson, 2001) may underlie the effects of forgiveness.

In each case, the potential pathway explained part of the association between forgiveness and health, but not all of it. When we included all three pathways simultaneously (stress, conflict management, and spirituality), the relationship between having a forgiving personality and better health was fully captured. More forgiving individuals had better health because of the relationship of forgiveness to less stress, better ways of dealing with conflict, and higher existential well-being. However, the influence of a specific, important betrayal and how much forgiveness of that offense predicts health are only partially captured by these pathways. Being able to forgive an important betrayal has a unique effect on health, above and beyond the proposed pathways.

Study 3: Forgiveness and Successful Aging in Older Adults

Recently, we examined trait forgiveness in a large group of older adults and assessed its relationship to measures of successful aging (Lawler-Row & Piferi, 2006). Toussaint, Williams, Musick, and Everson (2001) have found that older people are more forgiving than younger, and that women have higher trait forgiveness scores than men. Thus, forgiveness may become more salient with age as a value or an interpersonal skill. Is it equally related to health? Carol Ryff (1989) has explored quality of life in the elderly, indicating that life satisfaction reflects much more than the absence of illness. Thus, we employed her Scales of Psychological Well-Being (Ryff, 1989) and a single measure of positive well-being (Pavot & Diener, 1993) to assess this construct more broadly.

The sample included 239 women, from more than 20 states, who completed a questionnaire packet measuring trait forgiveness,

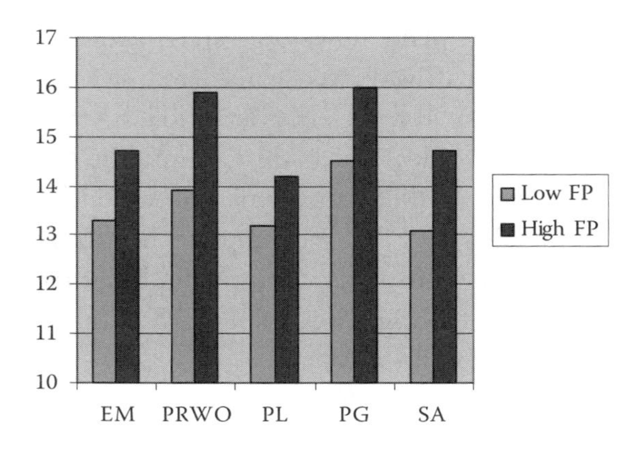

Figure 5.3 Highly forgiving (High FP) women differ from low forgiving (Low FP) on five measures of successful aging: environmental mastery (EM), personal relations with others (PRWO), purpose in life (PL), personal growth (PG) and self acceptance (SA).

physical symptoms, and subjective and psychological well-being. These women ranged in age from 52 to 95 ($M = 64.3$, $SD = 9.3$). As shown in Figure 5.3, highly forgiving women had higher levels on five of the six measures of successful aging: environmental mastery, personal relations with others, purpose in life, personal growth, and self acceptance. They also differed on subjective well-being ($p < .02$), but not on physical symptoms. As noted by Vaillant (2002) in the study of adult development, "Objective good physical health was less important to successful aging than subjective good health" (p. 13). Thus, among older women, having a forgiving personality was associated with all but one of the components of successful aging, as well as with higher subjective well-being.

Given that forgiveness and health have been related across three different age cohorts, we again explored pathways that might account for this relationship in older women. In this case, three factors were considered: healthy behaviors, spirituality, and social support. According to George, Larson, Koenig, and McCullough (2000), these factors may be particularly relevant mechanisms for health in older adults. First, all three were clearly linked to having a forgiving personality: Highly forgiving women took better care of themselves (healthy behaviors), had more social support, and reported superior levels of both religious and existential well-being. As with the middle-aged women, the effect of forgiveness on positive health was partly explained by these pathways, but not completely. Thus, having a forgiving personality has clear relevance for the psychological well-being of older women and adds some unique predictive power, over and above that contributed by healthy behaviors, social support, and spirituality.

Study 4: Forgiveness, Rumination, and Health in College-Age Women

In this last experiment (Edmondson, 2005), we returned to the college student sample and a laboratory-based study. This time we examined the relationship of forgiveness to rumination, depression, and loneliness, as well as examining both cardiovascular and neuroendocrine physiological responses. Because forgiveness is positively associated with health, we tested an additional means by which this association might be carried: the lack of rumination. Previous research has shown that rumination is associated with depression; women who ruminate or obsessively think about past interpersonal conflicts do not seem to benefit from this reflection. At the same time, lack of forgiveness has been linked to the tendency to ruminate over past offenses (McCullough, Bellah, Kilpatrick, & Johnson, 2001). Thus, it seemed that these factors should be examined together and in the context of physiological health or outcome variables.

Ranging in age from 18 to 49 years ($M = 21.1$, $SD = 4.7$ years), 60 college women participated in the study. The design involved a 20-minute baseline period, a 5-minute betrayal interview, followed by a 5-minute rumination period, and then a 10-minute recovery period. Blood pressure was measured every 2 or 3 minutes throughout, while saliva was collected for cortisol assessment following the baseline and the rumination periods.

Both trait and state forgiveness were assessed for their relationships to depression, anxiety, physical symptoms, body mass index, frequency of smoking, and number of medications taken. These factors and their relationships are shown in Table 5.3. Having a forgiving personality was associated with lower levels of depression and anxiety, and a higher use of cigarettes, while specific, event-related

Table 5.3 Associations Between Forgiveness and Health Measures

	TRAIT (FORGIVENESS)	STATE (FORGIVENESS)
Rumination	–.10	–.25[a]
Depression	–.28[a]	–.28[a]
Anxiety	–.43[b]	–.29[a]
Physical symptoms	–.01	–.18
Smoking	–.39[b]	–.25[a]
Medications	–.13	–.09

[a] $p<.05$
[b] $p<.01$

forgiveness was linked to less rumination, depression, anxiety, and smoking. There were no significant relationships between forgiveness and either physical symptoms or medications in this young, healthy female sample.

With regard to cardiovascular reactivity to the interview, specific forgiveness was associated with decreased reactivity in mean arterial pressure, repeating the finding of the first study. With regard to cortisol, mean levels decreased across the session for all participants. However, these decreases were not significant for the low state forgivers; for the high forgivers, cortisol decreased after the rumination period, compared with baseline. Thus, women who forgave their offender recalled the betrayal event with less blood pressure arousal and exhibited greater stress hormone recovery.

In this study, we also examined the relationship between forgiveness, anger response styles, and empathy. While specific forgiveness was unrelated to any typical style of anger response, having a forgiving personality was linked to three styles: greater assertiveness, fewer angry outbursts, and higher social support seeking or talking with friends. Finally, trait forgiveness was also positively associated with both emotional empathy and cognitive perspective taking. Thus, having a personality tendency to forgive predicts both better perspective-taking skills and more skillful expression of angry feelings. Understanding the offender and being able to communicate one's own perspective are critical to the forgiveness process.

Discussion

There are three general conclusions that we draw from these data. First, having a forgiving personality, whether at 22 or 92 years of age, is associated with a life well lived. These individuals have better levels of health, show more moderate physiological responses when recalling interpersonal conflict, have better relationships with others, and exhibit less stress and higher levels of spirituality. Forgiving women embody a way of being in the world that helps them move through life more easily, with more support and less wear and tear. Whether these individuals actually have fewer stressful experiences, perceive the same stress as less intense, or both is unknown. However, given the findings that depressed individuals seem to generate more stress, it may well be the case that unforgiving women, who are also more depressed, also experience more stress (Joiner, Wingate, Gencoz, & Gencoz, 2005). There is already a wealth of information on the dangers of hostility for health, from increased cardiovascular reactivity to higher mortality rates. The opposite of hostility is not simply low hostility, however, but a positive way of being in the world. This way of being in the world has been described as successful aging, comprising several dimensions such as autonomy, personal growth, and acceptance. Thus, a forgiving personality has been linked to better health outcomes in four separate studies that examined women across the life span.

The second conclusion is that those women who have been able to forgive a specific past betrayal show significantly better health, whether we are looking at concurrent physiological responses or self-reports of physical symptoms, stress, sleep, or medication use. Interviews with 62 women in Lawler et al. (2005) revealed that some of these women came to forgiveness fairly quickly while others followed a path that took many years. Some called on their religious or spiritual communities to assist them in finding forgiveness, and some responded to apologies and attempts to become a better person on the part of the offenders. Our sense, after listening to these interviews, is that forgiveness is a craft, as Jones (1995) described—one that takes patience, practice, and effort. Women who were able to forgive demonstrated a better sense of the offender's perspective, even when they disagreed completely with his or her actions. They were also able to communicate their own experience better. Forgiveness is not something to be taken on as an additional burden, out of guilt. Sometimes, women seek to forgive in order to find a way out of the strain of carrying the anger and resentment. However, it is our belief that forgiveness has its own timetable: When sufficient healing has taken place, the heart can begin to mend. Forgiveness clearly reflects a change of heart, both philosophically and physiologically.

Finally, there are several potential pathways, all of which explain part of the association between forgiveness and health, but not all of it. When we included three pathways simultaneously (stress, conflict management, and spirituality), the relationship between having a forgiving personality and fewer symptoms of physical illness in younger, adult women was fully captured. More forgiving individuals had better health because of the relationship of forgiveness to less stress, better ways of dealing with conflict, and higher existential well-being. However, the influence of a specific important betrayal and how much forgiveness of that offense predicts health is only partially captured by these pathways. Being able to forgive an important betrayal has a unique effect on health, above and beyond the proposed pathways. Similarly, among older adult women, more forgiving women had better health through three pathways: healthy behaviors, social support, and spirituality. However, forgiveness also added unique predictive power to measures of positive health. Future studies will explore additional pathways, such as cognitive flexibility and a sense of humility, which may well explain additional variance.

According to Rowe et al. (1989), social injury elicits a need to reestablish the self outside the context of the relationship that was damaged. As individuals accept the reality of the transgression, they give up trying to change the other person or undo the past and move toward a revision of their bedrock assumptions (Flanigan, 1998). When this process has moved through the stages of forgiveness and has not been adopted too quickly or without sufficient acceptance of reality, then conflict can become an opportunity to create, as well as to lose, one's sense of identity (Buber, 1924/1987). Face-to-face conflict has the power to create and transform the meanings, beliefs, and relationships that serve as an essential ground for our experiences in human life. But that potential power is only achieved when one has found a successful resolution to the conflict: Forgiveness provides a window into that possibility, one that provides clear mental and physical benefits as well as existential ones.

References

Berry, J. W., & Worthington, E. L., Jr. (2001). Forgivingness, relationship quality, stress while imagining relationship events, and physical and mental health. *Journal of Counseling Psychology, 48,* 447–455.

Berry, J. W., Worthington, E. L., Jr., Parrott, L., O'Connor, L. E., & Wade, N. G. (2001). Dispositional forgivingness: Development and construct validity of the transgression narrative test of forgivingness (TNTF). *Personality and Social Behavior, 27,* 1277–1290.

Buber, M. (1924/1987). *I and thou.* New York: Charles Scribner and Sons.

Drinnon, J. R., & Jones, W. H. (1998, March). *Measuring an act of forgiveness.* Paper presented at Southeastern Psychological Association, Mobile, AL.

Edmondson, K. A. (2005). Forgiveness and rumination: Their relationship and effects on psychological and physical health. *Dissertation Abstracts, 65,* 6694.

Enright, R. D., & North, J. (1998). *Exploring forgiveness.* Madison: University of Wisconsin Press.

Fitzgibbons, R. (1998). Anger and the healing power of forgiveness: A psychiatrist's view. In R. D. Enright & J. North (Eds.), *Exploring forgiveness* (pp. 63–74). Madison: University of Wisconsin Press.

Flanigan, B. (1998). Forgivers and the unforgivable. In R. D. Enright & J. North (Eds.), *Exploring forgiveness* (pp. 95–105). Madison: University of Wisconsin Press.

Friedman, M., Thoresen, C., Gill, J., Ulmer, D., Powell, L. H., Price, V. A., et al. (1986). Alterations of type A behavior and its effects on cardiac recurrence in post-myocardial infarction patients: Summary results of the coronary prevention recurrence project. *American Heart Journal, 112,* 653–665.

George, L. K., Larson, D. B., Koenig, H. G., & McCullough, M. E. (2000). Spirituality and health: What we know, what we need to know. *Journal of Social and Clinical Psychology, 19,* 102–116.

Huang, S. T. T., & Enright, R. D. (2000). Forgiveness and anger-related emotions in Taiwan: Implications for therapy. *Psychotherapy, 37,* 71–79.

Joiner, T. E., Wingate, L. R., Gencoz, T., & Gencoz, F. (2005). Stress generation in depression: Three studies on its resilience, possible mechanism, and symptom specificity. *Journal of Social and Clinical Psychology, 24,* 236–253.

Jones, L. G. (1995). *Embodying forgiveness: A theological analysis.* Grand Rapids, MI: Erdmann Publishing Company.
Kamat, V. I., Jones, W. H., & Lawler-Row, K. (2006). Assessing forgiveness as a dimension of personality. *Individual Differences Research, 4,* 322–330.
Koenig, H. G., McCullough, M. E., & Larson, D. B. (2001). *Handbook of religion and health.* Oxford, UK: Oxford University Press.
Lawler, K. A., Younger, J. W., Piferi, R. L., Billington, E., Jobe, R., Edmondson, K., et al. (2003). A change of heart: Cardiovascular correlates of forgiveness in response to interpersonal conflict. *Journal of Behavioral Medicine, 26,* 373–393.
Lawler, K. A., Younger, J. W., Piferi, R. L., Jobe, R. L., Edmondson, K. A., & Jones, W. H. (2005). The unique effects of forgiveness on health: An exploration of pathways. *Journal of Behavioral Medicine, 28,* 157–167.
Lawler-Row, K. A., & Piferi, R. L. (2006). The forgiving personality: Describing a life well lived? *Personality and Individual Difference, 41,* 1009–1020.
McCullough, M. E., Bellah, C. G., Kilpatrick, S. D., & Johnson, J. L. (2001). Vengefulness: Relationships with forgiveness, rumination, well-being, and the Big Five. *Personality and Social Psychology Bulletin, 27,* 601–610.
McCullough, M. E., Pargament, K. I., & Thoresen, C. E. (2000). *Forgiveness: Theory, research, and practice.* New York: Guilford Press.
Murphy, J. G. (1988). Forgiveness and resentment. In J. G. Murphy & J. Hampton (Eds.), *Forgiveness and mercy* (pp. 14–34). Cambridge, UK: Cambridge University Press.
Pavot, W., & Diener, E. (1993). Review of the satisfaction with life scale. *Psychological Assessment, 5,* 164–172.
Rowe, J. O., Halling, S., Davies, E., Leifer, M., Powers, D., & von Bronkhurst, J. (1989). The psychology of forgiving another: A dialogal research approach. In R. S. Valle & S. Halling (Eds.), *Existential-phenomenological perspectives in psychology: Exploring the breadth of human experience* (pp. 233–244). New York: Plenum Press.
Ryff, C. D. (1989). Happiness is everything, or is it? Explorations on the meaning of psychological well-being. *Journal of Personality and Social Psychology, 57,* 1069–1081.
Seybold, K. S., Hill, P. C., Neumann, J. K., & Chi, D. S. (2001). Physiological and psychological correlates of forgiveness. *Journal of Psychology and Christianity, 20,* 250–259.
Spiegel, D., Bloom, J. R., Kraemer, H. D., & Gottheil, E. (1989). Effect of psychosocial treatment on survival of metastatic breast cancer. *Lancet, 14,* 888–891.
Toussaint, L. L., Williams, D. R., Musick, M. A., & Everson, S. A. (2001). Forgiveness and health: Age differences in a U.S. probability sample. *Journal of Adult Development, 8,* 249–257.
Vaillant, G. E. (2002). *Aging well.* Boston: Little, Brown and Company.

Witvliet, C. V. O., Ludwig, T. E., & Vander Laan, K. L. (2001). Granting forgiveness or harboring grudges: Implications for emotion, physiology, and health. *Psychological Science, 12,* 117–123.

Worthington, E. L., Jr. (1998). *Dimensions of forgiveness: Psychological research and theological perspectives.* Philadelphia: Templeton Foundation Press.

6

Forgiveness Education With At-Risk Adolescents

A Case Study Analysis

SUZANNE FREEDMAN

Introduction

> We reenact our past everywhere—at home, at school, at the workplace, on the playground, in the streets. We cue each other to play roles in our personal dramas, secretly hoping that someone will give us a different script, a different outcome to the drama. (Bloom, 1999, p. 10)

At first glance, the notion of forgiveness may seem straightforward: An offense occurs, an apology is offered, and a relationship is mended. A deeper look, however, reveals a much more complex philosophical system of hurt and healing. In practice, the idea of forgiveness is one that varies greatly in both definition and philosophy from researcher to researcher and person to person. Further, as forgiveness has emerged as a powerful healing tool for victims (Enright & Fitzgibbons, 2000; Worthington, 2005), the need for forgiveness education and counseling has increased. In order to broaden the outreach of forgiveness ideas, it is first necessary to explore and describe individuals' experiences with forgiveness education. By focusing on real-life experiences, forgiveness knowledge will move beyond theory or ideals to include a picture of what forgiveness education and the forgiveness process look like for individuals in the real world.

This chapter reports a case study of the use of forgiveness education with an at-risk female adolescent who was part of a forgiveness education research project. It is important to describe how forgiveness education can be used with adolescents in a school setting so that it can be applied more frequently. The recent increase in school violence by both children and adolescents illustrates that there is a real need for education that could help students cope with their hurt and angry feelings. This chapter may be helpful to clinicians working with at-risk adolescents or other populations who have been deeply, personally, and unfairly hurt and carry around anger related to that hurt, as well as to educators who want to include forgiveness education in their curriculum. Misunderstanding and confusion associated with forgiveness result from a lack of knowledge. More information available about what forgiveness is and is not, how to forgive, and how forgiveness can be healing for individuals will increase its use in a variety of settings, both educational and therapeutic.

When we think of at-risk adolescents, what often comes to mind is delinquency, alcohol and drug use, poverty, conduct disorders, academic failure, teenage pregnancy, dysfunctional families, and difficulty with interpersonal relationships. What is often missing from the description of at-risk adolescents is the fact that the majority of them have experienced deep, personal, and unfair hurts. These adolescents have been deeply betrayed by parents, siblings, significant others, relatives, peers, and/or strangers—some more than once.

Adolescents who have experienced deep, personal, and unfair hurts carry around a great deal of anger, resentment, and negative feelings (Parrott, 1993). When discussing interventions, professionals and researchers would do well to recognize how much of an impact being hurt has on these adolescents. It is often the unresolved feelings related to being hurt that cause an adolescent to be identified as at-risk as well as being a potential danger to himself or herself and others. As Fitzgibbons (1986) states "Anger is a natural response to the failure of others to meet one's need for love, praise, and acceptance" (p. 629) and is often a reaction to unbearable pain. It is also true that chronic anger interferes with adolescents' ability to learn and form long-lasting healthy relationships (Dill & Haberman, 1995). Adolescents with anger problems are often a danger to themselves as well as others, as anger affects nearly every aspect of their lives (Fuller & Sabatino, 1996). Enright (2001) gives the example of the adolescent from Jonesboro, Arkansas, who shot and killed students, teachers, and himself, and asks, "What if ...?" We can also ask, "What if ...?" in regard to the tragic school shootings in Pennsylvania of the Amish girls, as the shooter was said to have carried a grudge for over 20 years (Scolforo, 2006).

Unfortunately, if anger is not effectively dealt with, revenge behaviors take over, with adolescents living an "eye for an eye" philosophy. Teenagers frequently practice revenge because they know of no other way to deal with their angry and negative feelings. As Dill and Haberman (1995) explain, "This defend or die mentality results from utter terror in the absence of options" (p. 69).

If we are aware that adolescents have anger and resentment related to past hurts, it is important to provide them with resources they can use to cope with their intense, negative feelings. It is also important to tell adolescents that they have a right to be angry when bad things happen to them and that they be given opportunities to express their feelings. As Witkin (2005) states, "What's tragic about teens who kill is not only that so many could be rehabilitated but that their crimes might have been prevented in the first place if someone had paid attention to the early distress signals" (p. 209). In addition, if we want to decrease revenge behaviors among at-risk adolescents, they need to be exposed to alternative ways of coping, such as behaviors and ways of thinking and feeling that they might not have seen at home or in their neighborhood. Revenge behavior will be passed on from generation to generation unless adolescents learn other ways of dealing with their pain (Bergin, 1988). According to Dill and Haberman (1995), when we increase the capacity of students for moral reasoning and empathy when making decisions, juvenile delinquency is reduced. For example, one correctional facility in the Midwest uses a combination of moral reasoning, anger management, and social-skills training to rehabilitate young offenders (Witkin). Helping adolescents manage their anger more effectively is a critical component of healthy development (Enright & Fitzgibbons, 2000; Fitzgibbons, 1986).

Interpersonal forgiveness is one alternative to seeking revenge that is gaining more attention in the areas of psychology, counseling, and education. Specifically, the past 20 years have seen a great increase in interest in the topic of forgiveness from a psychological perspective

(Freedman, Enright, & Knutson, 2005). Although typically associated with religion and philosophy, the concept of forgiveness has most recently been explored by psychologists as a way to help people heal emotionally and physically after a deep hurt (Freedman et al., 2005). Unfortunately, forgiveness as a psychological construct is frequently misunderstood and confused with forgetting, pardoning, reconciling, excusing, condoning, and accepting (Enright, Freedman, & Rique, 1998). As Ransley (2004) explains, people use expressions such as "letting go," "forgive and forget," and "reconciliation" interchangeably. Although forgiveness can lead to reconciliation, it does not have to, and forgiveness is not synonymous with any of the preceding terms (Freedman, 1998; see Enright & Fitzgibbons, 2000, for a more thorough description of what forgiveness is and is not). A definition that is easily understood and applied constitutes forgiveness as overcoming negative thoughts, feelings, and behaviors toward an offender and, perhaps, over time, developing more positive thoughts, feelings, and behaviors toward him or her (Enright & Fitzgibbons, p. 23). In fact, one does not have to experience a feeling of love toward the offender to engage in true forgiveness.

Based on this definition, as well as a thorough review of the literature, Enright and the Human Development Study Group (1991) developed a 20-unit model of interpersonal forgiveness as their best estimate of the process people go through when trying to forgive (see Table 6.1). The model is to be viewed as "a flexible set of processes with feedback and feed-forward loops" (Enright et al., 1998, p. 12) and is divided into four different phases. The first phase is the *uncovering* phase (units 1–8), which refers to awareness of the problem and emotional pain following an offense. This includes anger, shame, guilt, insight, and most importantly, willingness to deal with the pain. The *decision* phase (units 9–11) includes recognizing the need for an alternate resolution and exploring forgiveness as one possible solution before making the commitment to forgive. The *work* phase (units 12–15) includes processes such as reframing, developing feelings of empathy and compassion, and accepting and absorbing the pain, which make up the active working through of the forgiveness process after the commitment to forgive has been made. The *outcome* phase includes the last five units (units 16–20), which help the injured realize

Table 6.1 Psychological Variables That May Be Involved When We Forgive

VARIABLE	REFERENCE
Uncovering phase	
1. Examination of psychological defenses	Kiel, 1986
2. Confrontation of anger; the point is to release, not harbor, the anger	Trainer, 1981
3. Admittance of shame, when this is appropriate	Patton, 1985
4. Awareness of cathexis	Droll, 1984
5. Awareness of cognitive rehearsal of the offense	Droll, 1984
6. Insight that the injured party may be comparing self with the injurer	Kiel, 1986
7. Realization that oneself may be permanently and adversely changed by the injury	Close, 1970
8. Insight into a possibly altered "just world" view	Flanigan, 1987
Decision phase	
9. A change of heart, conversion, new insights that old resolution strategies are not working	North, 1987
10. Willingness to consider forgiveness as an option	
11. Commitment to forgive the offender	Neblett, 1974
Work phase	
12. Reframing, through role taking, who the wrongdoer is by viewing him or her in context	Smith, 1981
13. Empathy toward the offender	Cunningham, 1985
14. Awareness of compassion, as it emerges, toward the offender	Droll, 1984
15. Acceptance and absorption of the pain	Bergin, 1988
Deepening phase	
16. Finding meaning for self and others in the suffering and in the forgiveness process	Frankl, 1959
17. Realization that self has needed others' forgiveness in the past	Cunningham, 1985
18. Insight that one is not alone (universality, support)	
19. Realization that self may have a new purpose in life because of the injury	
20. Awareness of decreased negative affect and, perhaps, increased positive affect, if this begins to emerge, toward the injurer; awareness of internal, emotional release	Smedes, 1984

Note: This table is an extension of Enright and the Human Development Study Group's (1991) work. The references shown here at the end of each unit are prototypical examples of discussions of that unit.

that as she or he gives the gift of forgiveness to the offender, she or he is healed. As a person completes the process of forgiveness, she or he may experience positive changes in relationships and the self, including improved physical and psychological health and well-being.

The 20 units in the model will be explained in more detail throughout the case study. Enright and colleagues' process model illustrates that forgiveness does not occur overnight. It involves hard work and a willingness to admit to having been hurt and requires the courage to deal with the associated feelings of anger and resentment. This model has been used and found to be effective for increasing forgiveness and psychological well-being among various populations, including elderly women who have hurts of various types (Hebl & Enright, 1993), incest survivors (Freedman & Enright, 1996), men who have been hurt by their partners' decision to have an abortion (Coyle & Enright, 1997), patients with substance abuse dependence (Lin, Mack, Enright, Krahn, & Baskin, 2004), terminally ill cancer patients (Hansen, 2002), and married couples (Knutson, 2003).

Most of the research using Enright's (2001) process model of forgiveness has been conducted with adults, and according to Sim (2003), literature on forgiveness in the adolescent population is limited and inadequate. However, the forgiveness education and research that has been conducted with children and adolescents illustrates positive outcomes associated with forgiveness in these populations as well. For example, Hepp-Dax (1996) studied fifth-grade inner-city school students and found that a 4-week forgiveness education program increased experimental group participants' willingness to forgive at post intervention. At 7-month follow-up, a significant increase in self-esteem was also illustrated even though it had not been illustrated immediately following the intervention (Hepp-Dax). Freedman and Knupp (2003) examined the effects of forgiveness education with junior high school students who experienced hurt related to parental divorce. Results illustrated significant increases in forgiveness and hope for the experimental participants compared with the control group.

Gambaro (2002) implemented a forgiveness intervention with adolescents with higher than average levels of anger and results illustrated increases in positive attitude toward school and family, enhanced quality of relationships with friends and family, improved school grades, and decreases in detention. Park (2003) assessed the impact of a forgiveness intervention on female adolescents who had been victimized by a peer and had, in turn, become aggressors themselves. At post-test the group that participated in the forgiveness intervention demonstrated greater increases in forgiveness and greater decreases in anger, self-reported delinquency, self-reported aggression, and hostile attributions than the other groups, which did not differ from one another.

Clearly, existing research demonstrates that adolescents can greatly benefit from forgiveness education. Research also illustrates that adolescents are able to understand the nuanced definition of forgiveness and have the skills necessary to be able to forgive. According to Piaget (1932), developmental implications must be considered when discussing moral development and forgiveness. For forgiveness to occur, individuals must be able to move beyond egocentrism and acknowledge the perspectives of others. Developmentally, this begins to happen during adolescence and thus adolescents are cognitively and morally mature enough to understand forgiveness. Specifically, progression through the forgiveness stages involves decreasing self-centeredness and an increasing ability to see others in a different way or from another perspective—both of which are essential elements of successful forgiveness.

Although adolescents are developmentally prepared to give and receive forgiveness, this population sorely needs education about what it really means to forgive and how to forgive. Further supporting this, Enright, Santos, and Al-Mabuk (1989) developed a model of forgiveness and found that adolescents were in Stage 3, labeled Expectational Forgiveness. According to Enright et al., a specific theme that appeared in adolescent responses included the impact of external factors on adolescents' willingness to forgive, such as being pressured to forgive or feeling that it was expected by others. Teachers, religious leaders, authority figures, and peers may greatly impact teenagers' willingness and/or ability to forgive. Gaughf (2002) points out the importance of providing opportunities for adolescents to interact with individuals who encourage the use of forgiveness and act as positive role models. According to Enright et al., "If adolescents will ever develop a sense of forgiveness that is more internally influenced, they need an atmosphere that consistently challenges them to use forgiveness as a strategy to resolve deep hurts" (p. 108).

One environment that offers an ideal setting for educating adolescents about forgiveness is the school. As Dill and Haberman (1995) point out:

> Schools are not the cause of youth violence; however, they can provide attractive options to violent behavior and give students a pattern for social behavior. Schools that don't take advantage of this opportunity waste what may be the only chance to help many students succeed productively in society and avoid a life of crime. (p. 71)

According to Fuller and Sabatino (1996), to be most effective, alternative high schools should include intensive group counseling in their curriculum, with a focus on self-esteem, self-concept, personal responsibility, and appropriate expression of feelings. Also to be included are drug and alcohol prevention, and career exploration and preparation. Forgiveness education has the potential to address all of these issues.

Because of the increase in school violence among children and adolescents and the potential for forgiveness to be healing, a forgiveness education intervention was conducted with at-risk adolescents attending an alternative school as described next.

Intervention Procedure

Students in 10th, 11th, and 12th grades were initially asked if they would like to participate in a class that would help them cope with a deep, personal, and unfair hurt. The participants ranged in age from 15 to 19 with an average age of 17.3 years. Almost all had a parent, relative, or significant other in jail; were pregnant or had a child; had a parent or stepparent who was a drug user, drug dealer, recovering alcoholic, or drug addict; were physically, sexually, or emotionally abused by a parental figure; were still experiencing some type of deep hurt or betrayal by a parent or significant other; and, if female, were or had been involved in an abusive relationship with a male. After screening to make sure all interested students were still experiencing negative effects related to their deep hurt, the 7-week group education began. Class met daily for a total of 31 sessions and approximately 23 hours of education consisting of instruction, discussion, group exercises, reflective writing, and case studies read aloud in class. Videos with a forgiveness theme were also shown. All participants were asked to read *Forgiveness Is a Choice* (Enright, 2001). However, the majority of participants did not read the book outside class or complete any work at home due to their chaotic family lives and other responsibilities.

Given the short duration of the educational intervention and the deep hurt experienced by participants, the purpose of the group ultimately became one of making the decision to consider forgiveness as an alternative to revenge and making the commitment to forgive one's offender eventually. Some participants were able to progress further in the model based on their injuries and developmental level. The following case study provides a qualitative description of how one at-risk adolescent benefited from forgiveness education, and highlights how the forgiveness intervention program acknowledges the severity of the hurt, its impact on the individual, the various processes one must go through to truly forgive, and the obstacles this adolescent experienced during her forgiveness journey.

Case Study

Mindy (a pseudonym) is a Caucasian female and one of 22 participants in the educational intervention. She was 16 at the time of the intervention and a junior attending the alternative high school. When asked to describe whom she wanted to forgive, Mindy described several offenders and two different situations. Mindy first talked about her experience of being raped by three men she did not know at a graduation party on her last day in ninth grade. She was 14, became pregnant from the rapes, and had a baby at the age of 15. Mindy did not tell anyone about the rapes and only told people about the pregnancy when she was 7½ months pregnant. She felt ashamed about what had happened and had a deep hatred for the men who had raped her.

The second deep hurt that Mindy talked about was the ongoing abuse she received from her mother. In Mindy's words:

> I can't talk about a specific hurt from my mother because it is ongoing. My mother is totally unsupportive of me. She constantly nags me and is

> verbally and emotionally abusive. She calls me ugly and fat all the time and says that she wished she never had me and that she doesn't love me. (initial individual interview)

Most individuals are encouraged to try to forgive one offender at a time, but Mindy could not choose between the rapists and her mother and decided to apply the forgiveness education and process to both. As illustrated throughout the case study, forgiving an offender when the abuse is still occurring is very difficult. Complete forgiveness might not occur until the individual is no longer being hurt by the offender and some time has passed since the last offense.

When asked how her injuries affected her life, Mindy reported that she had been depressed since age 7 and had very low self-esteem. She tells herself, "I can't do it. It won't work, and I am no good." She described herself as mentally scarred by all the abuse from her mother and from being raped. She had seen a counselor at school but stated that counseling was not helping her.

Mindy was in her first year of the alternative school during the intervention and reported that she liked school now because people at school treated her as an equal. She said that she was doing well in her classes and had made the honor roll in the first semester. Part of the reason Mindy had "flunked out" of the traditional high school was because of her drug use. When asked about this, Mindy said that she had been heavily into methadone when she found out she was pregnant. One month into her pregnancy, she stopped drinking and using drugs. Before then, she had been too strung out on drugs to recognize, or even care, what she was doing with her life. In addition to using meth, Mindy smoked crack and drank a lot. Before having her son, Mindy said that she had nothing to live for and that she did not care about anything, including herself.

Introduction to Forgiveness

Mindy had not thought about forgiveness as a way of dealing with her pain and was not exactly sure what was meant by the term or what was involved in forgiving. This reaction was similar to that expressed by the other students in the forgiveness education class. Mindy initially defined forgiveness as "disregarding the bad things that another person has done to you and putting the wrong behind you." Mindy was not sure where she learned the definition but guessed the dictionary. Her score on the knowledge of forgiveness pretest was 10 out of 16, which was better than many of the other students, but showed that Mindy still had some misunderstanding regarding forgiveness. Specifically, Mindy mistakenly thought that forgiveness involved absolving the offender of responsibility, involved reconciling with the offender, and was something that should be practiced by everyone. She thought that anger was not part of the process and that forgiveness was primarily a self-help approach. Although interested in learning more about forgiveness, Mindy was initially skeptical because of her misconceptions about forgiveness—a skepticism shared by other students in the class. Gassin (1998) explains that given the moral betrayal involved in the types of offenses adolescents experience, along with the adolescents' developing concept of justice, it is not surprising that adolescents express a lot of anger and hurt toward their offender and feel ambivalent about the idea of forgiveness.

Defense Mechanisms—Unit 1 Psychological defenses are methods of self-protection used to shield oneself from the pain and hurt experienced after an injury of any kind. When asked to think about ways she used defense mechanisms, Mindy said that she used school as an outlet because she had to block out things when at school in order to concentrate. Although school is a healthy outlet, Mindy engaged in some suppression in which she would consciously try to push the painful events and feelings out of her mind. This is necessary to function at times, but if used too much will not allow her to effectively deal with her injury.

Mindy also reported that she often held her anger in until it exploded, which resulted in yelling matches with her mother, threatening her mother's life, and getting physical with her brother. Mindy said that she had a horrible temper and would displace her anger toward her mother and the rapists on her brother. Mindy wanted to learn healthy ways to express her anger rather than ignore it until she burst. Mindy said that she often became extremely angry in an "out of the blue" way and could be very mean for no reason.

In class we discussed how expressing our feelings is very important. We also discussed the consequences of displacing negative feelings or withholding feelings. One reason so many adolescents either hold their anger and hurt feelings in or take their anger out on others is because they do not know how to express their anger in a healthy and safe way. As Fitzgibbons (1986) explains, "Significant numbers of people in our society do not know how to deal appropriately with their anger" (p. 629). Their feelings may be too powerful for them to handle alone, which was true for many of the at-risk adolescents in this class.

The first step in breaking down defenses is to admit to having been hurt and to begin feeling the pain associated with the hurt. Mindy was willing to do this knowing that she was part of the class and had someone to help her process her negative emotions. One exercise that helped Mindy get in touch with her sadness, disappointment, and anger was describing the hurt by brainstorming the feelings associated with what she had experienced and how she had been coping thus far. Mindy listed the following when asked to describe her hurts: "horrified, disgusted, screams, crying, mental, physical, put downs, anger, depressed, small, and yelling." Mindy, like the other adolescents, used defenses to protect herself from getting hurt again. For example, it took her awhile to feel comfortable in the class and to disclose her personal experiences. As she had been hurt before, she did not know how much she could trust the leader and the other students in the class.

Feelings of Anger—Unit 2 The lesson on anger involved identifying the destructive nature of prolonged anger and encouraging participants to learn to make the pain constructive. Students spent a lot of time discussing anger and its important role in the forgiveness process. We discussed how to release anger in healthy ways and how holding onto anger for a long time is damaging. It was very freeing for Mindy to learn that she had a right to be angry with her mother and the rapists. The fact that she could express her anger helped Mindy to have fewer outbursts at home. As Mindy discussed in class, one of the misconceptions she had about forgiveness was that anger was not part of the process. Understanding that getting angry was acceptable and even encouraged helped Mindy get in touch with her feelings and let go of her anger. She wrote down the following in an exercise that asked about the perceived benefits of holding onto anger, resentment, and other negative feelings: "because you love to hate them" and "so, no one else can hurt you." Thus, Mindy used anger to feel powerful and to protect herself from being hurt. Mindy also listed the following as advantages of giving up anger and other negative feelings: improved mood, physical well-being and basic outlook on life, better relationships, increased inner peace, emotional maturity, low blood pressure, and decreased anxiety and fear. Mindy wanted to give her anger up after realizing the toll it had taken on her and agreed that being a good mother to her son and doing well in school were more adaptive ways to feel powerful. Mindy benefited by learning, as one student expressed it, how to "take care of her anger."

Guilt and Shame—Unit 3 Feelings of guilt and shame are the third unit in the forgiveness model, although they may not be experienced by all individuals who have experienced a deep hurt. Mindy did feel a certain amount of shame as a result of being raped. However, it was difficult for Mindy to talk about these feelings in the group setting. When she brought up the fact that she felt shame, we talked about how Mindy did nothing to cause the rape and how she was defined by more than just being a survivor of rape. Mindy did not feel guilty about the rape but struggled with low self-esteem as a result of years of abuse from her mother, indicating that it was hard to care about herself. She was overweight, wore very baggy clothes, and did not seem to care about her appearance. Helping Mindy recognize her assets was effective in decreasing her feelings of shame and increasing her self-esteem. Mindy wrote down the following in an exercise that had students think about their positive features: "good mother, good grades, good attendance, good personality and fun to be around." Seeing that people accepted her even after they knew she had been raped helped Mindy feel less shame about what had happened and better about herself as a person. Behaviorally, Mindy seemed more outgoing and more willing to share her feelings at the end of the intervention, compared with the beginning. At the end, one of Mindy's teachers took her to Wal-Mart and helped her pick out some new clothes. The fact that she was willing to go shopping for herself suggested that her self-esteem was increasing.

Preoccupation With Pain and Awareness of Cognitive Rehearsal—Units 4 and 5 One needs to become aware of his or her emotional pain before he or she can forgive. It is often the case that pain is a motivator for the decision to forgive. However, sometimes one can invest too much emotional energy feeling the pain associated with an injury. During this unit, Mindy was able to recognize that she spent a lot of energy being angry and feeling hurt because of the way her mother treated her. Mindy also realized that her situation was especially difficult as the pain from her mother's abuse was ongoing as a result of continuing to live with her mother. It was helpful for Mindy to recognize her mother's limitations and set realistic expectations. Prior to the beginning of the forgiveness education program, Mindy had hoped her mother would change. Accepting that this might not happen helped Mindy find a healthy balance between feeling the pain from her hurt and releasing the pain so that she could move on.

We also discussed safe places Mindy could go when she needed to escape or get some distance from her mother. One misconception of forgiveness is that it perpetuates abuse. Before forgiving, one needs to be in a safe place and know the difference between forgiveness and reconciliation. Unfortunately, children and adolescents often have no choice but to remain with their abuser, unless the abuse is life threatening, and sometimes even *when* the abuse is life threatening. Mindy wanted to forgive her mother but stated that the process was blocked with each new hurt she received from her. She knew that true reconciliation was not possible until her mother changed her abusive behavior.

Mindy also admitted that she had not really allowed herself to feel much pain from being raped. She tried to numb herself as much as possible and to block any feelings associated with the rape. Thus, before Mindy could forgive her rapists, she needed to release her negative feelings without letting them take over. A writing exercise helped Mindy express her feelings, and talking about her feelings in class helped her process them without becoming overwhelmed. Mindy remarked how good it felt to let go of her negative feelings. She described the process as a wall that had been built around her gradually coming down brick by brick.

The fifth unit in the process is cognitive rehearsal, which focuses on how the injured person may spend a lot of time thinking about the injury and the unfairness of it all by playing the event over and over in her or his mind. As with feeling the pain, it is normal and healthy to think about the injury and how one was hurt, but one should not spend too much time thinking or becoming fixated on the hurt. In an individual interview postintervention, Mindy reported that she was close to forgiving the rapists and said:

> I have moved on and don't spend a lot of time thinking about the event. When I was pregnant I prayed to God that the pregnancy would go away. I prayed and prayed but I knew it would not and now I just think about my son and how much I love him. I just wish I had him when I was older.

Mindy was better at not allowing the pain from her mother's abuse to control her actions. When she found herself thinking about her mother too much she distracted herself and thought about something more positive. In class we talked about how sometimes it is helpful to have a specific time of day and a specific amount of time (such as 30 minutes) that one will allow oneself to think about the injury and then not again.

Insight That Injured Party May Be Comparing Self With the Injurer—Unit 6 It is often the case that the one hurt compares his or her unhappy state with the emotional and physical state of the offender and believes that the offender is much better off. This type of comparison can lead to increased anger, emotional outpouring, and cognitive rehearsal. Mindy did not really know anything about the men who raped her, so she did not engage in much comparison with them. However, Mindy *did* compare herself with her mother and believed her mother to be better off. She questioned why her mother did not want to have a close relationship with her daughter. Recognizing that she was a much better mother to her son than her mother was to her helped Mindy realize that she was better off than her mother in several ways. She acknowledged that her mother must have a lot of anger and hurt feelings to be so mean to her own children. Mindy also felt good about her success in school and plans for the future, and wondered if her mother's lack of goals contributed to her mother's low self-esteem and unhappy life.

Realization That Self May Have Been Permanently Changed by the Injury—Unit 7 Mindy realized that she had been permanently changed in both good and bad ways as a result of being raped and emotionally abused by her mother. She now has a son she loves and she also knows how important it is to be a good mother. Mindy came to realize that some of the changes she experienced were permanent (her son) and some were temporary (negative attitude and constant anger). Mindy remarked that working on the process of forgiveness gave her hope for a better life than her mother had had. Mindy knew that her life experiences had affected her negatively, but after our discussion, she was able to identify the positive changes she had made as well.

Insight Into a Possibly Altered "Just-World" View—Unit 8 The focus in this unit involves the individual taking on new assumptions and views about the fairness of the world (Flanigan, 1992). An exercise that had students identify who "can and should change" helped Mindy realize what she did and did not have control over. We talked about how, although we cannot control who our parents are, we *can* control how we react to our experiences. After having her son, Mindy was forced to change the way she had been coping with her mother's abuse. She realized that she could not stop her mother from calling her names or putting her down and could not force her mother to care more, but she could do something to change they way she coped with the abuse. Specifically, Mindy said that she could spend as little time as possible around her mother and, when able, try to find somewhere else to live so that she did not have to see her mother. After discussing this unit, Mindy recognized that although she was not responsible for her mother's abuse, the way she coped with it was *her* choice and responsibility. By seeing things in a different way Mindy came to realize that life was not always fair and bad things can happen to good people. Hearing the other students' experiences helped Mindy see that she was not the only one to experience unfairness in her life. Mindy felt that learning to forgive was a positive way to cope and deal with the unfairness she experienced.

Decision Phase: Change of Heart, Willingness to Consider Forgiveness as an Option, and Commitment to Forgive the Offender—Units 9–11 Realizing that her old ways of coping were not working and that she was angry all the time helped Mindy make the decision to try to forgive. It was important to emphasize to the students that making the commitment to forgive did not mean that they had to forgive at the moment. It just meant that they were choosing to work on the forgiveness process as a way to deal with their pain. According to Neblett (1974), the commitment to forgive one's offender is the crux of the entire process. Mindy was more easily able to make the decision to forgive as a result of knowing exactly what forgiveness is and is not and that forgiveness is not only a gift to the offender but also a gift to the injured. According to Mindy:

> [Forgiveness is] good for you, raises your self-esteem, lets you feel more free, and vital in the healing process. It also allows you to let go of the anger, accept what the person did, is difficult to do, takes time, and includes many steps. (intervention notes)

During the discussion of this unit, Mindy stated that forgiveness is not, "saying it is okay, forgetting, reconciliation, revenge, easy, dependent upon an apology from the person, telling the person you have forgiven, stuffing it or denying the hurt, a sign of weakness, or an invitation to be hurt again." Mindy said that she chose to forgive because she wanted to give up her feelings of anger, bitterness, and resentment, and realized that doing so would enable her "to move on, find peace, and live a healthier life in which everyone around you benefits." Mindy also recognized that her old ways of coping were not effective.

The discussion about the decision to forgive included the insight that when one is angry with someone, forgiving that person helps oneself and others. The fact that the injury will always be remembered and that the offender is still responsible was emphasized, as was the idea that if one commits to forgive, she or he does not get even or force the offender to make it up. Mindy made the commitment to forgive knowing that it involved hard work and time. Although Mindy did not feel forgiveness toward her offenders at the time she made the commitment, she hoped that by working on the units in the work phase, the feelings of forgiveness would develop. This lesson also called for the forswearing of revenge that was problematic at first for students who live by the motto "an eye for an eye." Emphasizing the fact that anger is not fully resolved until a conscious decision is made to let go of the desire for revenge or to forgive helped students make the commitment to forgive (Fitzgibbons, 1986). Focusing on the effectiveness of students' current coping mechanisms also helped students make the decision to try forgiving.

Work Phase: Reframing, Feelings of Empathy, Awareness of Compassion, and Acceptance and Absorption of Pain—Units 12–15 The 12th unit in the process is referred to as reframing or "seeing with new eyes" and is the first unit to make up the active working part of forgiveness. Reframing can be defined as a new perspective taken by the injured not to minimize the hurt but to begin to view the other in a larger context and to think about how certain vulnerabilities in the offender may have led to the offense (Enright, Gassin, & Wu, 1992). Reframing also involves broadening one's perception of the offender as a human being rather than simply the person who committed the offense. Reframing does not mean excusing, as one still holds the offender responsible for the injury while trying to understand more about the offender's past and what led up to the injury.

According to Mindy, her mother's family "is a bunch of drunks and weirdos" and her dad's family tries to pretend that they are the "ideal family and cover up their craziness." Thinking about the way her mother was raised and what type of abuse her mother may have experienced helped Mindy begin to feel some empathy and compassion for her mother. Mindy realized that as long as her mother was drinking, she was not going to change her abusive behavior. Mindy said that she felt sorry for her mother and hoped that one day her mother would realize how much she was hurting herself as well as those around her. Although she knew more about her mother's past than the rapists' pasts, it was easier for Mindy to recognize that the men who raped her must have been in pain in order to do what they did to her. Imagining what their lives were like and beginning to understand their pain helped Mindy develop empathy for them. It was harder for Mindy to feel empathy and compassion for her mother because her mother was supposed to love and care for her, while the men who had raped her were strangers. As Hope (1987) states, "If one looks at the individual's network of connections, it is clear that those who hurt the person the most are often those who are most clearly connected—parents, siblings, friends, spouse, and children" (p. 242). Mindy also thought that her mother could choose to stop drinking if she wanted.

Introducing the concepts of "unconditionality" and "inherent worth" helped students begin to realize that all persons are equal and have inherent worth at some level, regardless of personal characteristics (e.g., skin color, personal values, socioeconomic status) and behavior. The Dr. Seuss book, *Horton Hears a Who,* was read aloud in class to help students realize that no matter one's size, appearance, etc., she or he still has worth. Thus, even though their offenders had hurt them, they were human beings who have inherent worth because they existed.

These concepts were difficult for most students to grasp. They condemned their offenders because of their actions and could not understand how the offenders' actions did not affect their worthiness as human beings. Mindy knew that her mother and the rapists were human beings but had trouble admitting that they were "worthwhile regardless of their behavior" (Enright & the Human Development Study Group, 1994). It is true that developing feelings of empathy and compassion are some of the most difficult units in the process model and often take the longest time (Freedman, 1999).

Mindy found it easier to think about her mother in a compassionate way when she learned that she could feel compassion and still be angry with her mother's behavior. Mindy wondered if the men who raped her had raped any other women. These thoughts were obstacles to her feeling more empathy and compassion toward them as she hoped that they had stopped their abusive behavior. Mindy stated that while she used to wish that her offenders had a horrible life, during the intervention those thoughts gradually decreased and she was almost able to wish them a good life.

Unit 15 refers to one's ability to accept the pain, both one's own and that of the injurer, and the first step in doing this is accepting what happened (Bergin, 1988). Prior to beginning this class, Mindy stated that she took her pain out on her brother, her mother, and others. She realized that by absorbing the pain she could stop the hurt from negatively affecting others. Mindy liked the analogy of a sponge soaking up water as she soaked up the pain. She knew how important it was to be a good parent and thus she had already made the decision not to take out her pain on her son. As an adolescent, Mindy often acted impulsively and she knew that absorbing her anger would require her to consciously not act on her impulses.

Outcome Phase The class was almost over by the time we had finished discussing Unit 15 and we were only briefly able to discuss the last five units in the model. Students were asked to think about what *meaning they had made and discovered from experiencing their injury and from working on the forgiveness process* (Unit 16). For Mindy, the meaning the rape had for her was that she now had a son who had helped her turn her life around. She felt that if she had not become pregnant, she would not be doing as well in school or have goals for the future. The meaning she had discovered from her mother's abuse was that she knew how important it was to be a good mother, and having her son gave her the opportunity to put that meaning into practice. Mindy also said that the meaning she made from working on the forgiveness process was that she now knew she did not have to live a life filled with anger and hatred.

The idea that Mindy had *needed others' forgiveness in the past* (Unit 17) was easy for her to understand. She knew that she had hurt other people as a reaction to feeling hurt and recognized that if she wanted the people she had hurt to forgive her, she had to be willing to forgive her offenders. Mindy knew that she was not perfect and applied that idea to her offenders. Mindy felt good about her forgiveness, as she was being a positive role model to her son and younger brother.

The *insight that she was not alone in her pain and suffering* (Unit 18) was very apparent to Mindy when she heard the injuries that the other students had experienced. According to Mindy, some students had it worse than she did and some had it better. Although there were students whose negative stance toward the idea of forgiveness influenced others' attitudes, knowing that others were also working on the forgiveness process helped Mindy want to progress and continue. Thus, knowing that others also experienced deep and unfair pain and were trying to forgive helped Mindy feel less alone, less shame about her experiences, and more willing to commit to forgiveness.

The *realization that self may have a new purpose in life because of the injury* (Unit 19) had already occurred for Mindy. She took her role as a mother seriously and realized how much her actions would influence her son. Graduating from high school was Mindy's immediate goal and she also listed being able to forgive her mother and the rapists as another goal. Having goals and a purpose in life gave Mindy hope for the future.

The last unit in the model, *awareness of decrease in negative affect and, perhaps, increased positive affect as well as internal emotional release* (Unit 20), was beginning to occur for Mindy as the class finished. The fact that her negative feelings toward the rapists had decreased was a sign that Mindy was very close to forgiving. Although some people believe that forgiveness has to involve the addition of positive thoughts, feelings, and behavior, it is this author's opinion that the cessation of negative thoughts, feelings, and/or behaviors can define forgiveness. Mindy had replaced her negative thoughts with more neutral ones and even some positive thoughts. She no longer wished the rapists or her mother a horrible life and she was even hoping that the men who had raped her could get help to deal with their pain. Her fantasies of revenge as well as her anger, hatred, and bitterness had all decreased. Mindy was no longer consumed by the injury and by her anger. In her words, "I am really close to forgiving the guys but not as close to forgiving my mother because she still hurts me."

Mindy found it very helpful knowing that one can forgive someone even if the person does not apologize. She accurately stated the differences between forgiveness and reconciliation and understood that reconciliation was not necessary for healing and moving forward. Mindy was going to continue to work toward forgiving her mother, but realized that reconciliation might not be possible unless her mother changed her behavior. When asked how she had changed since the start of the course, Mindy replied that her negative energy had been replaced by more positive energy. Mindy felt more peaceful and less angry and stressed as a result of the release she experienced from forgiving.

Guidelines for Educating Adolescents About Forgiveness

Parrott (1993) states that parents are influential in their children's willingness to forgive. If parents refuse to forgive, children will come to believe that this response is normal and appropriate. Children who are violent have often been the victims of violence and bullying (Dill & Haberman, 1995). Children and adolescents who seek revenge learn that aggression is the way to get what they want and the way to deal with their negative feelings. Considering these statements, it is surprising that more information related to educating adolescents about forgiveness does not exist.

Adolescents may best respond to discussion that focuses on the social benefits of forgiving and the principles that underlie forgiveness such as compassion and empathy (Gassin, 1998). According to Gassin, it is important to allow adolescents to express the negative emotions related to being hurt. Expression of all emotions can help adolescents with identity development as they process their pain and realize they can cope with the hurt. Like adults, children and adolescents learn more deeply when challenged and encouraged. We must talk to adolescents about forgiveness so that they know it is an option. According to Enright (1998), one way we can do this is by weaving forgiveness into discussions about current events and happenings in the world. It is important to make the topic real for adolescents so that they can see the advantages of forgiveness and releasing anger in contrast to their ideas about the necessity and benefits of revenge.

We must also give children and adolescents opportunities to think about forgiveness. Reflection will allow a deeper understanding of forgiveness to develop. Enright (1998) emphasizes the importance of parents and teachers modeling forgiveness.

Discussion and Conclusions

Mindy is an example of a student who moved more quickly through the model compared with some of the other students. As Enright and the Human Development Study Group (1991) emphasize, the helping professional who uses the forgiveness model to help educate others about forgiveness must be willing to invest as much time as it takes for the person to forgive. Although Mindy was successful in her efforts to forgive the men who raped her and was in the process of trying to forgive her mother, there were some limitations related to conducting a forgiveness intervention with a population of at-risk adolescents in a school setting using a group format. Specifically, the students needed more individual sessions with the researcher. While group education was helpful for sharing and seeing that one was not alone in his or her feelings, trust could have been developed more easily with more individual sessions. In addition, more time for trust-building exercises at the beginning of the intervention would have made it easier for students to share personal information.

Another problem with the group format was that some students negatively influenced others. Specifically, some were not as willing to show interest in learning about forgiveness when other students were strongly critical of the concept. In addition, several students had difficulty with certain units while others were ready to move on. However, students were also positively influenced by each other. For example, sometimes the students could explain an idea better than the researcher, which made comprehension easier.

Another limitation was that some adolescents were still being hurt by the offender they were trying to forgive or by another offender, as was the case for Mindy. It is a lot easier to forgive when one is safe and not being hurt and, ideally, when some time has passed since the last abusive incident. This was not the case for some of the adolescents in the forgiveness intervention. Another limitation had to do with the time of day when the intervention occurred, as students did not have time to process their feelings after the class. For example, many students went to math class after talking about being raped or Mom's drug use and neglect, and did not get as intensely involved because of the timing and structure of the forgiveness education. Having the education every day rather than once a week was too intense for some students. One student dropped out of the forgiveness class because she was not ready to deal with her feelings. Finally, the intervention duration was too short. The class did not make it through all the units in the model, and students definitely needed more time to process their feelings and understand the concepts related to forgiveness.

According to Freedman et al. (2005), those who do forgiveness research and education do so because they are interested in whether forgiveness can help people heal. As clearly illustrated in this case study, forgiveness education did help Mindy heal and had an overall positive impact on her psychological well-being. Considering these limitations, the overall results of this forgiveness intervention with at-risk adolescents are even more noteworthy. Specifically, students who received the forgiveness education increased significantly in forgiveness toward their offender, self-esteem, and hope, and decreased significantly in both state and trait anxiety and depression compared with the control group. Future researchers, educators, and helping professionals interested in examining the effects of forgiveness education with at-risk adolescents may want to take the limitations described into consideration when developing the specifics of their interventions, curriculum, and therapy. Although much progress has been made in the study and practice of forgiveness, as illustrated in this chapter, there is still a great need for more research to be conducted with adolescents, especially, at-risk adolescents. Further work in this area will make it possible to apply new findings about forgiveness to the lives of individuals who are seeking the powerful healing benefits forgiveness can offer.

References

Bergin, A. E. (1988). Three contributions of a spiritual perspective to counseling, psychotherapy, and behavior change. *Counseling and Values, 33,* 21–31.

Bloom, S. L. (1999, October). Final action plan: A coordinated community-based response to family violence. *Attorney General of Pennsylvania's Family Violence Task Force.*

Close, H. T. (1970). Forgiveness and responsibility: A case study. *Pastoral Psychology, 21,* 19–25.

Coyle, C. T., & Enright, R. D. (1997). Forgiveness intervention with post-abortion men. *Journal of Consulting and Clinical Psychology, 65,* 1042–1046.

Cunningham, B. B. (1985). The will to forgive: A pastoral theological view of forgiving. *The Journal of Pastoral Care, 39,* 141–149.

Dill, V. S., & Haberman, M. (1995). Building a gentler school. *Educational Leadership, 52,* 69–71.

Droll, D. M. (1984). Forgiveness: Theory and research. (Doctoral dissertation, University of Nevada–Reno, 1984). *Dissertation Abstracts International, 45,* 2732.

Enright, R. D. (1998). Helping El Nino to forgive. *The World of Forgiveness, 2,* 1–4.

Enright, R. D. (2001). *Forgiveness is a choice.* Washington, DC: APA Books.

Enright, R. D., & Fitzgibbons, R. P. (2000). *Helping clients forgive: An empirical guide for resolving anger and restoring hope.* Washington, DC: American Psychological Association.

Enright, R. D., Freedman, S., & Rique, J. (1998). The psychology of interpersonal forgiveness. In R. D. Enright & J. North (Eds.), *Exploring forgiveness* (pp. 46–62). Madison: University of Wisconsin Press.

Enright, R. D., Gassin, E. A., & Wu, C. (1992). Forgiveness: A developmental view. *Journal of Moral Education, 21,* 99–114.

Enright, R. D., & Human Development Study Group. (1991). The moral development of forgiveness. In W. Kurtines & J. Gewirtz (Eds.), *Handbook of moral behavior and development* (Vol. 1, pp. 123–152). Hillsdale, NJ: Erlbaum.

Enright, R. D., & Human Development Study Group. (1994). Piaget on the moral development of forgiveness: Identity or reciprocity? *Human Development, 37,* 63–80.

Enright, R. D., Santos, M. J., & Al-Mabuk, R. (1989). The adolescent as forgiver. *Journal of Adolescence, 12,* 95–110.

Fitzgibbons, R. P. (1986). The cognitive and emotional uses of forgiveness in the treatment of anger. *Psychotherapy, 23,* 629–633.

Flanigan, B. (1987). Shame and forgiving in alcoholism. *Alcoholism Treatment Quarterly, 4,* 181–195.

Flanigan, B. (1992). *Forgiving the unforgivable: Overcoming the bitter legacy of intimate wounds.* New York: Macmillan.

Frankl, W. E. (1959). *The will to meaning: Foundations and applications of logotherapy.* New York: World Publishing House.

Freedman, S. R. (1998). Forgiveness and reconciliation: The importance of understanding how they differ. *Counseling and Values, 42,* 200–216.

Freedman, S. R. (1999). A voice of forgiveness: One incest survivor's experience forgiving her father. *Journal of Family Psychotherapy, 10*(4), 37–61.

Freedman, S. R., & Enright, R. D. (1996). Forgiveness as an intervention goal with incest survivors. *Journal of Consulting and Clinical Psychology, 64,* 983–992.

Freedman, S., Enright, R. D., & Knutson, J. (2005). A progress report on the process model of forgiveness. In E. L. Worthington, Jr. (Ed.), *Handbook of forgiveness* (pp. 393–406). New York: Routledge.

Freedman, S. R., & Knupp, A. (2003). The impact of forgiveness on adolescent adjustment to parental divorce. *Journal of Divorce and Remarriage, 39,* 135–165.

Fuller, C. G., & Sabatino, D. A. (1996, May/April). Who attends alternative high schools? *The High School Journal,* 293–297.

Gambaro, M. E. (2002). *School-based forgiveness education in the management of trait anger in early adolescents.* Unpublished doctoral dissertation, University of Wisconsin, Madison.

Gassin, E. (1998) Children, adolescents, and forgiveness. *The World of Forgiveness, 2,* 4–8.

Gaughf, N. B. (2002). *The developmental aspects of forgiveness.* Unpublished doctoral dissertation, The University of Southern Mississippi, Hattiesburg.

Hansen, M. J. (2002). *Forgiveness as an educational intervention goal for persons at the end of life.* Unpublished doctoral dissertation, University of Wisconsin, Madison.

Hebl, J. H., & Enright, R. D. (1993). Forgiveness as a psychotherapeutic goal with elderly females. *Psychotherapy, 30,* 658–667.

Hepp-Dax, S. H. (1996). *Forgiveness as an educational goal with fifth-grade inner-city children.* Unpublished doctoral dissertation, Fordham University, New York.

Hope, D. (1987). The healing paradox of forgiveness. *Psychotherapy, 24,* 240–244.

Kiel, D. V. (1986, February). I'm learning how to forgive. *Decisions,* 12–13.

Knutson, J. A. (2003). *Strengthening marriages through the practice of forgiveness.* Unpublished doctoral dissertation, University of Wisconsin, Madison.

Lin, W., Mack, D., Enright, R. D., Krahn, D., & Baskin, T. (2004). Effects of forgiveness therapy on anger, mood, and vulnerability to substance use among inpatient substance-dependent clients. *Journal of Consulting and Clinical Psychology, 72,* 1114–1121.

Neblett, W. (1974). Forgiveness and ideals. *Mind, 83,* 269–275.

North, J. (1987). Wrongdoing and forgiveness. *Philosophy, 42,* 336–352.

Park, J. H. (2003). *Validating a forgiveness education program for adolescent female aggressive victims in Korea.* Unpublished doctoral dissertation, University of Wisconsin, Madison.

Parrott, L. (1993). Forgiveness. In L. Parrott (Ed.), *Helping the struggling adolescent: A guide to thirty common problems for parents, counselors, & youth workers* (pp. 119–124). Grand Rapids, MI: Zondervan Publishing House.

Patton, J. (1985). *Is human forgiveness possible?* Nashville, TN: Abingdon.

Piaget, J. (1932). *The moral judgment of the child.* London: Routledge.

Ransley, C. (2004). Be cautious about forgiveness. In C. Ransley & T. Spy (Eds.), *Forgiveness and the healing process: A central therapeutic concern* (pp. 51–68). New York: Brunner–Routledge.

Scolforo, M. (2006, October 3). Details emerge about shooter in Amish school tragedy. *Time Magazine.*

Sim, J. L. (2003). *A forgiveness protocol for externalizing adolescents: Efficacy and religious commitment.* Unpublished doctoral dissertation, Regent University, Virginia Beach.

Smedes, L. B. (1984). *Forgive and forget: Healing the hurt we don't deserve.* New York: Harper & Row.

Smith, M. (1981). The psychology of forgiveness. *The Month, 14,* 301-307.

Trainer, M. F. (1981) *Forgiveness: Intrinsic, role-expected, expedient, in the context of divorce.* Unpublished doctoral dissertation, Boston University, Boston.

U.S. Department of Justice. (1994, March). *Urban Delinquency and Substance Abuse, Initial Findings.* NCJ 143454. Washington, DC: U.S. Department of Justice Office of Justice Programs, 22-27.

Witkin, C. (2005, July). Too young to kill. *O, the Oprah magazine, 6,* 188–209.

Worthington, E. L., Jr. (2005). Initial questions about the art and science of forgiving. In E. L. Worthington, Jr. (Ed.), *Handbook of forgiveness* (pp. 1–13). New York: Routledge.

7

Forgiveness as an Outcome in Emotion-Focused Trauma Therapy

HELEN CHAGIGIORGIS
AND SANDRA PAIVIO

Introduction

In the past decade, forgiveness theory and research have gained increased attention in the field of psychology (Scobie & Scobie, 1998). Particular attention has focused on examining the processes involved in forgiveness and the psychological benefits of forgiveness-oriented interventions or strategies within the therapeutic context. However, the concept of forgiveness in psychological treatment is controversial, particularly when applied to issues of childhood abuse. This chapter examines forgiveness as a possible outcome in emotion-focused trauma therapy (EFTT; Paivio & Nieuwenhuis, 2001) for adult survivors of childhood abuse. Our position is that forgiveness could represent one type of outcome among others.

Emotion-focused trauma therapy is an individual trauma-focused therapy for resolving emotional, physical, and sexual child abuse issues that does not explicitly promote forgiveness. Rather, the goal is to resolve issues stemming from abuse and with perpetrators. As such, resolution is characterized as a reduction in negative feelings, increases in self-empowerment and self-esteem (*resolving issues stemming from abuse*), and a more differentiated perspective of abusive or neglectful others (*resolving issues with perpetrators*; Paivio & Nieuwenhuis, 2001). In this chapter, we report results from a study examining whether forgiveness afforded particular benefits in EFTT. First, a brief review of the prevalence and long-term consequences of child abuse and available treatments for adult survivors of childhood abuse will be provided. Second, issues with the controversy concerning forgiveness with abuse survivors will be presented. Third, the EFTT approach will be outlined, and theory and research findings related to forgiveness in EFTT will be reviewed. Finally, results from an exploratory study examining forgiveness in EFTT will be reported followed by a discussion of the implications concerning forgiveness in EFTT.

Prevalence of, Effects of, and Treatments for Child Abuse

Research indicates that 25 to 30% of women (Bagley, 1991) and 15% of men in the general population report having been sexually abused as children (Elliot & Briere, 1995), and 10 to 20% of women and men report having been physically abused as children (Briere, 1997). It is also estimated that as many as one third of the general adult population of the United States has been emotionally abused as children (Binggeli, Hart, & Brassard, 2001). Experiences of childhood abuse are associated with numerous long-term disturbances, including depression, anxiety, post-traumatic stress disorder (American Psychiatric Association, 2000), feelings of guilt and shame about the abuse, negative self-esteem, under-regulation or overcontrol of emotions, issues of distrust, powerlessness, difficulties with intimacy, and maladaptive interpersonal patterns (Herman, 1992; Paivio, Hall, Holowaty, Jellis, & Tran, 2001; van der Kolk, 1996).

Several treatment approaches have been used to address the long-term effects of childhood abuse. Herman's (1992) recommendations have been adapted as the "gold standard" treatment for most approaches: The "fundamental stages of recovery are establishing safety, reconstructing the trauma story, and restoring connection between survivors and their community" (p. 3). Resolution, in this therapy, is accomplished through restructuring abuse memories and integrating them into the client's life story, and a good therapy outcome is defined as one in which clients no longer feel alienated but are able to reconnect with individuals in their community. Briere (2002) incorporates exposure of abuse memories in his treatment for clients with severe abuse histories in order to restructure abuse memories. A good outcome in his treatment model is when clients become desensitized to emotional pain and are able to integrate painful emotions and previously avoided or repressed memories into current meaning systems.

Wolfsdorf and Zlotnik's (2001) group treatment for female sexual abuse survivors focuses on changing trauma-related cognitive distortions, such as emotional reasoning and overgeneralization, and increasing clients' ability to tolerate stress. The primary focus of affect regulation is anger management skills. Clients are informed regarding the role and experience of anger in response to abuse, helped to identify anger, and taught various coping skills as a replacement for their angry reactions. Thus, the ability to regulate emotions, particularly anger, defines a good outcome in this therapy.

Forgiveness-oriented therapies recently have been considered for treating child abuse issues. The goal of treatment (Freedman & Enright, 1996) is for the client to begin viewing offenders as more complete individuals, rather than as people who simply committed the injury, and thus come to a stance of forgiveness. A good outcome in these therapies is defined as one in which clients come to a stance of forgiving their offenders.

Emotion-focused trauma therapy is one of the few empirically supported, individual psychological therapies for men and women dealing with different types of abuse (emotional, physical, sexual, emotional neglect). The therapy focuses on resolving child abuse issues through empathic exploration and exposure. As indicated previously, resolution is defined as reduced negative feelings, increased self-empowerment and self-esteem, and a more differentiated perspective of abusive or neglectful others. Unlike other treatments that focus exclusively on changing a client's self-concept, EFTT also focuses on helping clients resolve issues with past abusive or neglectful others. However, forgiveness of offenders is not explicitly advocated as a treatment goal. Rather, forgiveness represents one possible good outcome, among others and is a function of multiple factors, including individual client values and goals, relationships to and perceptions of perpetrators, and client stage in the process of resolving abuse issues. Forgiveness is not synonymous with resolution or good outcome. In fact, in some instances, promoting forgiveness could have deleterious effects and would not be part of the therapy process at all.

Controversy Concerning Forgiveness With Abuse Survivors

There is controversy about the appropriateness of interpersonal forgiveness in the area of child abuse and other trauma. Advocates believe that interpersonal forgiveness is a necessary aspect of growth (Davenport, 1991). They perceive forgiveness as a choice and thus choosing not to forgive is seen as a refusal to let go (DiBlasio, 1998). However, advocates also agree that the traumatic event and negative feelings, including anger resulting from that event, must be acknowledged prior to forgiving. Acknowledging and expressing anger are crucial because anger signals to the self that an offense has taken place and that something must be done to correct it (Davenport). Only when the anger and hatred toward the offender have been explored, understood, and validated as legitimate can clients begin the process of letting go of anger and forgiving. Thus, forgiveness is seen as the final stage in a larger process.

Freedman (2000) advocates forgiveness as an important part of the process of resolving child abuse issues. Accordingly, forgiveness involves expanding or shifting victims' view of offenders such that they begin viewing them not only as people who committed the injury, but also as individuals with personal and developmental histories (Freedman & Enright, 1996). In so doing, clients begin to view perpetrators in a more compassionate manner. In circumstances where the traumatic event is extremely painful, such as rape, incest, murder, or abuse, it may be difficult for clients to expand their view of offenders beyond that of rapist, murderer, or abuser. In such cases, the role of the therapist is to support clients as they voice negative feelings and thoughts about offenders and, at the same time, help them expand their view of offenders. Here, again, changed perceptions of offenders lead to interpersonal forgiveness, which is the desired outcome.

Other experts dispute the appropriateness of interpersonal forgiveness in cases such as childhood sexual abuse. Forgiving perpetrators in these cases could be equated with overlooking the offense and thus could retraumatize victims (Katz, Street, & Arias, 1997). Forgiveness also could foster denial of the abuse, validate actions of perpetrators, or be forced upon victims (Bass & Davis, 1994; Olio, 1992). Bass and Davis are strong opponents of forgiveness, believing that victims need to come to "some resolution, that is, to make peace with the past and move on. Whether or not this resolution encompasses forgiveness is a personal matter, and in fact if you never reach an attitude of forgiveness, it's perfectly alright [*sic*]" (p. 160). Similarly, Murphy (2002) suggests that in some cases, clients could exhibit more self-respect if they maintained a posture of resentment toward offenders; the offense may be so heinous that it is simply unforgivable. Murphy concludes that forgiveness is individual and situational. However, unlike Bass and Davis, he maintains that interpersonal forgiveness is always a morally appropriate and desirable goal of therapy for those who are willing and able to achieve it.

The EFTT perspective coincides most closely with Murphy's view. As previously stated, forgiveness is not advocated as a goal of therapy in EFTT. Rather, the goals are to resolve issues stemming from abuse and with perpetrators. Again, in EFTT, resolving issues stemming from abuse is characterized by reduced negative feelings and increased self-empowerment and self-esteem; resolving issues with perpetrators is characterized as clients having a more differentiated perspective of abusive or neglectful others (Paivio & Nieuwenhuis, 2001). When resolving issues with perpetrators, EFTT therapists elicit clients' perceptions of abusive or neglectful others and those perceptions typically change over the course of therapy. It is possible that this process is similar to the one described by Freedman (2000), in which clients expand or shift their view of offenders. In EFTT, this may lead to forgiveness as clients gain more compassion and understanding toward abusive or neglectful others. Alternatively, clients may become less enmeshed and more separate from perpetrators through this process, such that perpetrators no longer have a powerful effect over clients' lives, and yet clients may not reach a stance of forgiveness.

Emotion-Focused Trauma Therapy

Emotion-focused trauma therapy is an individual, trauma-focused therapy that is grounded in experiential therapy, theory, and research (Gendlin, 1996; Greenberg & Paivio, 1997; Greenberg, Rice, & Elliott, 1993; Paivio & Greenberg, 1995). It draws on emotion theory and research (e.g., Frijda, 1986), attachment theory (e.g., Bowlby, 1988), and the literature on trauma and child abuse (e.g., Herman, 1992; van der Kolk, 1996). One of the basic assumptions of experiential therapy is that clients are experts in their own experience and that their subjective internal experience, rather than skills training or interpretations, is the primary source of new information. Therapists help clients attend to, explore, and symbolize their moment-by-moment experience, thereby constructing new meaning and promoting healthy functioning (Greenberg & Paivio).

Furthermore, emotions are seen as playing a key role in the client's experience of self and others (Greenberg & Paivio, 1997). Emotions are important sources of adaptive information that help to organize thoughts and actions (Frijda, 1986) and are seen as having three adaptive functions. First, emotions are attentional because they influence the salience of information. For example, a client who feels angry and is able to articulate that she feels angry "because I never know when he's going to be there for me" can recognize that her concern is for support and predictability. Another client who feels angry and can articulate, "I feel angry because it's just so unfair," can begin to clarify that he feels unjustly treated and wishes for fair play (Greenberg & Paivio, p. 20). Second, emotions are motivational because they influence goal setting. For example, feeling sad motivates individuals to reach out to someone caring and supportive. Third, emotions function to communicate and regulate interpersonal interactions. For example, anger allows one to set up interpersonal boundaries or to assert the self (Greenberg & Paivio).

The fundamental assumption of attachment theory that is incorporated into EFTT is that early experiences with attachment figures are the basis for a sense of self and expectations of intimate others (Bowlby, 1988). Early violations of trust, security, and control are encoded in memory in the form of representations of self and others (Bowlby). Abused children can develop a sense of themselves as weak or bad and may view others as untrustworthy or dangerous. These internal representations of self and others serve as enduring prototypes that influence expectations and behaviors in subsequent intimate relationships (Paivio & Patterson, 1999). Emotion-focused trauma therapy focuses on changing maladaptive internal representations of self and significant others by helping clients resolve issues with primary attachment figures who were perpetrators of abuse and/or neglect.

EFTT Change Processes, Tasks, and Interventions

In EFTT the therapeutic relationship and memory work are viewed as the two primary and interrelated change processes (Paivio et al., 2001). There are three tasks. The first is to cultivate a safe and collaborative therapeutic relationship through empathic responding to clients' subjective experience. This allows for exploration of trauma material and helps to counteract early attachment injuries and empathic failures (Paivio et al.). The second task is to resolve self-related difficulties, such as self-blame and experiential avoidance. This is accomplished through the use of Gestalt-derived interventions and imagery techniques or empathic exploration. Strengthening the self allows clients to approach and explore abuse experiences and to hold abusive or neglectful others accountable for harm.

The third task is to resolve issues with abusive or neglectful others. This is accomplished by accessing and modifying trauma memories that generate maladaptive experiences, such as fear and shame, and accessing constricted adaptive emotion, such as anger and sadness. This information is used to modify maladaptive meaning (Paivio & Nieuwenhuis, 2001). For example, anger at the other counteracts fear and self-blame, whereas sadness accesses self-soothing and compassion for the self. The primary vehicle for accessing and exploring childhood abuse memories is an imaginal confrontation procedure, in which clients are encouraged to express previously constricted feelings and needs directly to imagined abusive or neglectful others in an empty chair (Paivio & Nieuwenhuis).

Resolution and Forgiveness in EFTT

The process of resolution in EFTT is based on an empirically verified model that identified steps in the process of resolving unfinished business with past others (Greenberg & Foerster, 1996). Briefly, the steps identified were an expression of intense emotion, a sense of entitlement to unmet needs, and a more positive view of the self and the other. Clients shift from self-blame and powerlessness to increased self-affiliation and self-empowerment. There is also an increase in their understanding of the other or of holding the other accountable for harm.

Changed perceptions of others result from a process that initially focuses on strengthening clients' sense of self. This includes reducing avoidance of feelings and memories related to the abuse, as well as guilt and self-blame for the abuse (Paivio & Nieuwenhuis, 2001). Emotion-focused trauma therapy therapists explicitly state that the goals of treatment include clients feeling better about themselves, no longer being plagued by feelings and memories of abuse, and moving on in their lives. Forgiveness could be a goal when particular clients want to achieve that goal. Nonetheless, EFTT is a process-oriented rather than goal-oriented model that begins with strengthening the client's sense of self. Working through self-related issues provides clients with a greater sense of self-empowerment, and it allows clients to confront perpetrators in the imaginal confrontation procedure.

Throughout this procedure, therapists explicitly elicit perceptions of how abusive others would respond to their feelings and needs. When the imaginal confrontation procedure is carried out in the early stages of therapy, the other initially is seen negatively and as defensive and nonresponsive. However, this can shift over the course of therapy, such that perpetrators are imagined as acknowledging the harm done and/or as being repentant. These changes in perceptions of perpetrators could lead to forgiveness, which could represent one type of good outcome in EFTT. On the other hand, if imagined others are seen as entrenched in their negative behaviors and clients do not forgive, but rather feel stronger and more detached and/or separated from abusive or neglectful others, this also represents a good outcome in EFTT.

Research on EFTT

Emotion-focused trauma therapy is based on more than 20 years of programmatic research on resolving interpersonal issues from the past. First, an empirically based model was developed that defined the steps in the resolution process using an empty-chair technique (Greenberg & Foerster, 1996). Second, Paivio and Greenberg (1995) demonstrated the efficacy of short-term (12 sessions) therapy based on this model with a general clinical sample. Results from this study revealed clinically and statistically significant improvements in multiple domains. Process analyses of sessions with a subset of clients in the Paivio and Greenberg study, who were dealing with child abuse issues, led to the further development of EFTT. Treatment was longer (16–20 sessions) to allow more time for dealing with avoidance and other self-related disturbances, and the empty-chair technique was reframed as imaginal confrontation to emphasize the focus on trauma work. Paivio and Nieuwenhuis (2001) tested the efficacy of EFTT and found significant improvements in multiple domains, including depression, anxiety, trauma symptoms, current target complaints, interpersonal problems, self-esteem, and resolution of issues with past abusive or neglectful others. Furthermore, clients maintained treatment gains at 6-month follow-up. More recently, Paivio, Hall, Chagigiorgis, Ralston, and Lee (2006) found two versions (imaginal confrontation and empathic exploration) of EFTT effective.

Research also supports two posited mechanisms of change in EFTT. Paivio and Patterson (1999) found improved alliance over time and contributions of alliance to outcome in EFTT. Paivio et al. (2001) examined the contribution of engagement in the imaginal confrontation procedure to outcome beyond the contributions made by alliance. Results indicated that alliance quality was associated with both post-treatment and follow-up change on measures of global self-esteem and resolution of abuse issues. Emotional engagement with trauma memories during imaginal confrontation was associated with resolution of abuse issues at both post-treatment and follow-up.

Results Concerning Forgiveness as an Outcome in EFTT

Research on EFTT has indirect implications for the concept of forgiveness. For example, in the Paivio and Greenberg (1995) study, clients dealing with nonabuse issues reported increased separation from and affiliation toward offenders, which is consistent with definitions of forgiveness. However, the subset of clients who were dealing with child abuse issues reported resolution of past interpersonal trauma and increased separation from perpetrators, but no increased affiliation. Indeed, those dealing with abuse issues reported increased hostility toward abusive others following therapy, which is inconsistent with forgiveness. This raised the issue of the appropriateness of forgiveness for this group.

Another study (Rice & Paivio, 1999) examined changes in clients' perceptions of past relationships with abusive or neglectful others following EFTT. Results indicated that on average, clients reported resolving issues and increased separation in both abusive and neglectful relationships, but they reported no reductions in hostility in either relationship. Again, it appeared that resolution of child abuse issues in EFTT was not synonymous with forgiveness. However, clinical observations indicated that a number of clients in the Paivio and Niewenhuis (2001) study forgave their offenders. A more recent study (Paivio, 2001) examined post-therapy interviews in which clients were asked about changes in their perceptions of self and others following EFTT. Results supported the observation that some clients forgave their offenders. Thus, it seems likely that the use of mean scores and statistical analyses employed in the Rice and Paivio study masked individual client outcomes on this dimension. This warranted a closer examination of forgiveness as an outcome in EFTT.

Exploratory Study Examining Forgiveness in EFTT

In this section, we report results from a study that examined the prevalence of forgiveness in EFTT and whether clients who forgave were distinct from those who did not forgive in terms of pretreatment characteristics, therapy processes, and outcome. Archival data from 23 clients who completed post-therapy interviews in the Paivio and Niewenhuis (2001) study were used. We examined changes in perception of self and others identified in the post-therapy interviews and individual items on two measures. Changes of client perceptions of the self and others were examined along dimensions of separation and affiliation.

Sample Characteristics

Most clients in the study were Caucasian women who were, on average, 40 years old, married, and employed, with a family income between $20,000 and $39,000 and a high school diploma. Approximately one third were diagnosed as having a personality disorder. Most clients also reported histories of severe childhood abuse and neglect and met the criteria for a diagnosis of post-traumatic stress disorder, with moderate symptoms. Clients reported multiple types of abuse but were asked to identify a primary focus for therapy. The most frequent type of abuse selected for therapy focus was sexual abuse, and these experiences ranged from a single episode of anal penetration to paternal incest over many years. The second most frequent focus was emotional abuse that ranged from chronic verbal derogation by a caregiver to repeated threats of harm or witnessing extreme family violence. The third most frequent focus was physical abuse that ranged from harsh physical discipline to severe beatings that resulted in injury.

Procedure

Specific criteria* were applied to the post-therapy interview and two measures that were administered at pre-, mid-, and post-treatment. These were used to categorize clients as forgivers or nonforgivers. Clients were categorized as forgivers or nonforgivers in terms of two relationships that were the focus of therapy. These were the relationship with the abusive other, who most frequently was a father or father figure, and the relationship with a secondary other, who most frequently was a neglectful mother. Because reduced self-blame is an important focus and outcome in EFTT, we also categorized clients as forgivers or nonforgivers of self. Last, clients were categorized as resolvers or nonresolvers.

Pretreatment measures assessed client characteristics in terms of abuse severity, the presence and current symptom severity of posttraumatic stress disorder, and the presence of personality disorder. Treatment outcome was evaluated using a battery of questionnaires that assessed global and trauma-specific symptom distress and interpersonal problems. Therapy processes were measured with postsession questionnaires that assessed alliance and client level of engagement with the imaginal confrontation procedure.

Results Concerning Number of Clients Who Reported Resolution and Forgiveness

Twenty-three clients focused on an *abusive other* in therapy. Most of these clients (65%) were categorized as resolvers, whereas only 22%

* Contact Helen Chagigiorgis (chagigi@uwindsor.ca) for further information on specific criteria for categorizing clients as forgivers of others, forgivers of selves, and resolvers.

were categorized as forgivers of abusive others. Approximately one third of these clients were categorized as both resolvers and forgivers of abusive others. Twenty-two clients also focused on a *neglectful other* in therapy. Most of these clients (70%) were categorized as resolvers and 30% were categorized as forgivers of neglectful others. Approximately half of these clients were categorized as both resolvers and forgivers of neglectful others. It should be noted that *all* clients categorized as forgivers of abusive or neglectful others also were categorized as resolvers; however, not all resolvers were categorized as forgivers. Last, most clients (70–99%) were categorized as self-forgivers in both abusive and neglectful relationships.

In sum, most clients in EFTT resolved issues with past abusive and neglectful others and most forgave themselves. However, less than one third of the clients forgave the abusive and neglectful others at the end of therapy. As well, more clients resolved and forgave neglectful compared with abusive others.

Results Comparing Forgivers and Nonforgivers in EFTT

The second objective of this study was to determine, among those who resolved, if there were any differences between clients who forgave the abusive or neglectful other ($n = 9$) compared to those who did not forgive in these relationships ($n = 9$). Clients who forgave abusive or neglectful others, compared to those who did not, reported a lesser extent of childhood abuse and neglect, higher levels of current trauma symptoms, and higher prevalence of post-traumatic stress disorder. Also, clients who forgave reported lower levels of emotional engagement with trauma memories during the imaginal confrontation task and higher alliance scores, compared to those who did not forgive. None of these observed differences achieved statistical significance.

Last, results indicated that on average, clients made large gains from pre- to post-treatment on several dimensions (regardless of forgiveness categorization). The average treatment gains across five dimensions (trauma-related symptoms, interpersonal problems, resolution, perceptions of others, and global distress) were well above the standards for successful therapy specified by the APA Task Force on the Promotion and Dissemination of Psychological Procedures (1995).

There were no observed differences in treatment outcomes between clients who forgave and those who did not.

Implication of Findings

Finding 1: Most Resolved and Few Forgave Abusive or Neglectful Others

The finding that more clients in EFTT reported resolving issues with abusive or neglectful others compared to forgiving them is consistent with the treatment approach. EFTT is based on an empirically verified model of resolving issues with past significant others, and treatment focuses more on steps in the process of resolution. Specifically, one of the steps in the process of resolution entails promoting client expression of feelings and needs, as well as exploring client perceptions of others, rather than advocating specific relationship goals per se. For example, EFTT therapists explicitly promote client expression of emotion and unmet needs to the imagined abusive or neglectful others during the imaginal confrontation procedure. As clients become better able to acknowledge and express their feelings and needs, perceptions of others shift. Thus, another step in the process of resolution is the exploration of shifting perceptions. This is done by asking clients to imagine how abusive or neglectful others would respond to their expressions.

In addition, therapy emphasizes client and therapist collaboration on treatment goals, and clients are viewed as experts in their own experience. The therapist's job is to facilitate exploration of that experience. Thus, if forgiveness is an important goal for particular clients, therapists will help clients to explore the meaning and value of forgiveness and to achieve that goal. Normally, forgiveness is an issue only if clients introduce it. In the present study, forgiveness was driven by clients' own processes or desires rather than the therapy protocol. It is possible that more clients would have reached a stance of forgiving abusive or neglectful others if EFTT had explicitly addressed the issue of forgiveness, but again, forgiveness is not explicitly advocated as a treatment goal. Such a process-oriented stance is characteristic of experiential, humanistic, and client-centered therapies, in general (Gendlin, 1996; Greenberg & Paivio, 1997; Rogers, 1961).

Another issue concerns increased affiliation as the critical distinction between forgiveness and other types of resolution as outcomes. Most clients in EFTT who resolved, but did not forgive, were more separate from, but still angry with, abusive or neglectful others, and expressed no desire to connect with abusive or neglectful others who had been the focus of therapy. The common conceptualization of forgiveness, however, includes increased separation from and reduced anger toward offenders, and involves viewing perpetrators as people with their own developmental history, releasing resentment toward perpetrators, and restoring relationships (Enright & Fitzgibbons, 2000; Freedman, 2000). For this sample, it appears that movement toward increased autonomy and interpersonal separation, rather than affiliation, was the critical aspect of good outcome.

From a process perspective, both advocates and opponents of interpersonal forgiveness believe that angry feelings resulting from traumatic events have to be acknowledged, validated, and expressed (Bass & Davis, 1994; Davenport, 1991; Freedman, 2000). The difference lies in what occurs next. Advocates view forgiving offenders as a desirable choice that clients make following expression of anger. For clients in EFTT, it appears that what was more important than choosing to forgive perpetrators was acknowledging and expressing their anger, so that it no longer dominated and interfered with their functioning. The following excerpt illustrates this point. This client resolved issues with the abusive other but did not report increased affiliation:

> I have been able to *get the anger at my sexual abuse out* ... I don't need to worry about it anymore. I don't need to feel dirty about it anymore ... You know I was an innocent child ... *getting rid of the hatred, getting rid of the anger*, learning who I really was ... voice how I felt ... I don't really feel that my view of my father has changed ... that is part of the past that I don't have to own.

According to EFTT and emotion theory, acknowledging anger about abuse is a healthy, adaptive response that is different from lingering hostility and resentment. Acknowledging and expressing legitimate anger about maltreatment is thought to access associated adaptive information. Furthermore, by definition, emotions such as anger are fleeting responses—in this case, to memories of abuse—that would be appropriately expressed and then pass. Good outcome thus involves increased self-empowerment, interpersonal separation, and reduced minimization of harm as well as increased speed with which angry feelings, once aroused, can be worked through and pass, rather than continue to eat away at the individual.

Finding 2: More Forgiveness in Neglectful Compared to Abusive Relationships

The finding that more clients forgave neglectful compared to abusive others suggests that forgiveness is partly a function of the type of relationship. The abusive other was usually a father or father figure, while the neglectful other was usually a mother who did not protect the client from the abuse. Attachment theory (Bowlby, 1988) would suggest that there is a greater need to heal relationships with primary attachment figures, such as a mother. The following excerpt illustrates how a client came to view her mother as a person with her own difficulties. This client forgave her mother, but at the same time, appropriately held her mother, rather than herself, accountable for the harm:

> Well I look at her [mother] as somebody that I really care for, that is my mom ... *I understand where she came from a lot better.* Which is something that I needed to go through. Understand what her role was in the abuse that happened in our family. And to also not just be accountable to myself but to hold her accountable for some of it. ... And I was able to *understand that and to accept that* that's the case but that's not me and that she is her own person with her own difficulties and struggles and that those are her things.

The fact that more clients forgave neglectful compared to abusive others could also be a function of time spent on task. Most clients in EFTT spent more sessions focused on neglectful rather than abusive others. Observations of clinical files indicated that 60% of therapy sessions focused on neglectful others, thus allowing for greater exploration and working through with issues related to neglectful others. Of course, more time spent on issues with a primary attachment figure such as a mother could also be related to our earlier point, which is the need to heal such relationships.

Finally, forgiveness could be a function of the offense such that it is easier to forgive sins of omission than sins of commission. Sins of omission could be perceived as less severe and only indirectly related to the abuse. Research has found that individuals often rate harmful omissions as less immoral than harmful commissions because omissions are not viewed as the direct cause of harm (Spranca, Minsk, & Baron, 1991). On the other hand, abusive others in this study were usually father figures who severely physically or sexually abused clients.

Finding 3: More Forgivers of Self Than Forgivers of Others

Most clients reported less self-blame and higher self-esteem, self-understanding, and self-empowerment by the end of therapy. This finding likely is a function of the EFTT treatment protocol that explicitly focuses on these self-related issues in the middle phase of treatment. This is seen as a necessary step in the process of resolving issues with offenders. Clients need to feel better about and stronger within themselves before they can fully confront offenders and unequivocally hold them responsible for harm. The following excerpt from a post-therapy interview, illustrates this point:

> Yeah, because I'd always, you know, I've always had that same memory for as long as I can remember. *But I've always looked at it as being my fault* ... We were the only two there. So in effect I was just a little girl who had been told and taught how to respect authority ... you know, it was *my fault* ... I'm getting to the point where ... I'm doing what I'm doing and whether it's O.K. or not *is really not my problem, it's theirs.*

In sum, it appears that key outcomes for this group of EFTT clients were reduced self-blame for the abuse, resolving issues with abusive or neglectful others, and increased self-empowerment and separation from others. Reduced anger and thus forgiveness of abusive or neglectful others were not integral to the healing process and not important outcomes for most individuals in EFTT.

Finding 4: No Observed Differences Between Forgivers and Nonforgivers

There were no statistically significant differences between forgivers and nonforgivers in terms of the pretreatment characteristics, therapy processes, and outcome dimensions that were measured. However, this was an exploratory study employing a small sample and, as such, the purpose was to examine potentially meaningful clinical findings that merit further investigation. Observed differences between forgivers and nonforgivers on pretreatment characteristics fulfill this criterion. For example, present findings suggest that forgiveness could be easier with less severe maltreatment, neglect, or failure to protect. Future research with larger samples and more power could detect small but real differences in these areas. It also is possible that client characteristics other than those measured in the present study could help to explain forgiveness of others in EFTT. Research has identified other client characteristics that distinguish forgivers from nonforgivers. Accordingly, forgivers tend to be more empathic and warm, to express more positive emotions towards others, and to be more in touch with their painful feelings (Lawler, 2000). Future research could determine with a larger sample whether these features characterize clients who forgave in EFTT.

With respect to therapy processes, results of the present study indicated that both forgivers and nonforgivers in EFTT reported equally strong alliances and were equally engaged in the process of exploring child abuse feelings and memories. Failure to find differences in alliance is consistent with expectations because, in EFTT, collaboration with clients on goals and tasks of therapy is central to alliance formation. Engagement with trauma material during the imaginal confrontation procedure was defined in terms of psychological contact with the others, degree of involvement with the imaginal confrontation process, and emotional expressiveness. It is possible that therapy processes other than these were more related to forgiveness as an outcome. Recall that during the imaginal confrontation procedure, clients are encouraged to express previously constricted feelings and needs to imagined others (Paivio & Nieuwenhuis, 2001). Clients also are asked to imagine how others would respond to their expressiveness. Initially, others typically are seen as defensive and nonresponsive to clients' feelings and needs. It is possible that over the course of therapy, clients who forgave imagined that the other was more responsive to them, acknowledged the harm done, and was repentant. This helped clients let go of anger toward others and come to a stance of forgiving (Greenberg & Paivio, 1997).

On the other hand, clients who did not forgive perceived others as remaining nonresponsive and refusing to acknowledge or take responsibility for the harm they had done. Findings from a recent study of key change events leading to forgiveness in individual and couples forgiveness-oriented EFTT support this view (Malcolm & Greenberg, 2005). The key change event was clients' perception that others were compassionate in response to their pain in individual therapy or were genuinely apologetic—that is, accepting responsibility for the harm that was done and expressing shame and guilt (Malcolm & Greenberg).

Finally, results indicated no differences in treatment outcome between forgivers and nonforgivers in EFTT. Thus, forgiving offenders did not afford additional benefits over and above the resolution of issues that involved forgiveness of self and separation from others. Again, this could be a function of method constraints, such as the measures used, the sample size, and definitions of forgiveness. However, this could also be due to a treatment model that does not explicitly advocate forgiveness as a desirable outcome of therapy.

Conclusions

Results of our research on EFTT indicate that overall, clients benefit from therapy and make large gains in multiple domains of disturbance. Results clearly support reduced symptom distress and self-forgiveness as key outcomes of therapy. Working through self-related difficulties, such as shame and guilt, and appropriately holding offenders, rather than self, accountable for harm are integral elements in the healing process. Also, resolving issues with perpetrators by developing a more differentiated perspective and becoming more separate from and powerful relative to neglectful or abusive others were key outcomes. Another outcome for some clients was forgiveness of perpetrators that included letting go of anger and increased compassion. Such findings support our position that forgiveness could represent one possible outcome among others.

Future research could compare forgivers and nonforgivers in EFTT with a larger sample, which would provide greater power to detect differences, if any exist. Future research also could develop a forgiveness-oriented EFTT and compare the two versions (FEFTT vs. EFTT) in order to assess the independent contribution of forgiving offenders to positive client outcome. Future research should investigate the process of therapy for clients who forgive offenders compared to those who do not. In particular, the types of emotions, such as anger and sadness, and frequency with which they are expressed during therapy could distinguish forgivers from nonforgivers. Additionally, one could examine differences between forgivers and nonforgivers in terms of changes in the perceptions of others during the therapy process. Finally, one could examine the therapist's role in forgiveness. Factors such as introducing the possibility of forgiveness, clients' level of empathy, and their ability to moderate emotional arousal during imaginal exposure exercises could influence the likelihood of forgiving offenders.

References

American Psychiatric Association. (2000). *Diagnostic and statistical manual of mental disorders* (4th ed.). Washington, DC: Author.

American Psychological Association. (1995). *Template for developing guidelines: Interventions for mental disorders and psychological aspects of physical disorders* (policy document). Washington, DC: Author.

Bagley, C. (1991). The prevalence and mental health sequels of child sexual abuse in a community sample of women aged 18 to 27. *Canadian Journal of Community Mental Health, 10,* 103–116.

Bass, E., & Davis, L. (1994). *The courage to heal: A guide for women survivors of child sexual abuse* (3rd ed.). New York: Harper Perennial.

Binggeli, N. J., Hart, S. N., & Brassard, M. R. (2001). *Psychological maltreatment of children.* Thousand Oaks, CA: Sage.

Bowlby, J. (1988). *A secure base.* New York: Basic Books.

Briere, J. (1997). *Psychological assessment of adult posttraumatic states.* Psychotherapy practitioners resource book series. Washington, DC: American Psychological Association.

Briere, J. N. (2002). Treating adult survivors of severe childhood abuse and neglect: Further development of an integrative model. In J. E. B. Myers, L. Berliner, J. N. Briere, C. T. Hendrix, C. Jenny, & T. A. Reid (Eds.), *The APSAC handbook on child maltreatment* (2nd ed., pp. 175–203). Thousand Oaks, CA: Sage.

Davenport, D. S. (1991). The functions of anger and forgiveness: Guidelines for psychotherapy with victims. *Psychotherapy Theory, Research and Practice, 28,* 140–144.

DiBlasio, F. A. (1998). The use of decision-based forgiveness intervention within intergenerational family therapy. *Journal of Family Therapy, 20,* 77–94.

Elliot, D. M., & Briere, J. (1995). Posttraumatic stress associated with delayed recall of sexual abuse: A general population study. *Journal of Traumatic Stress, 8,* 629–647.

Enright, R. D., & Fitzgibbons, R. P. (2000). *Helping clients forgive: An empirical guide for resolving anger and restoring hope.* Washington, DC: American Psychological Association.

Freedman, S. (2000). Creating an expanded view: How therapists can help their clients forgive. *Journal of Family Psychotherapy, 11,* 87–92.

Freedman, S., & Enright, R. D. (1996). Forgiveness as an intervention goal with incest survivors. *Journal of Consulting and Clinical Psychology, 64,* 983–992.

Frijda, N. H. (1986). *The emotions.* Cambridge, UK: Cambridge University Press.

Gendlin, E. T. (1996). *Focusing-oriented psychotherapy: A manual of the experiential method.* New York: Guilford Press.

Greenberg, L. S., & Foerster, F. S. (1996). Task analysis exemplified: The process of resolving unfinished business. *Journal of Consulting and Clinical Psychology, 64,* 439–446.

Greenberg, L. S., & Paivio, S. C. (1997). *Working with emotions in psychotherapy.* New York: Guilford Press.

Greenberg, L. S., Rice, L. N., & Elliott, R. (1993). *Facilitating emotional change.* New York: Basic Books.

Herman, J. L. (1992). *Trauma and recovery: The aftermath of violence—From domestic abuse to political terror.* New York: Basic Books.

Katz, J., Street, A., & Arias, I. (1997). Individual differences in self-appraisals and responses to dating violence scenarios. *Violence and Victims, 12,* 265–276.

Lawler, K. (2000, March). *UT study shows forgiveness linked to lower blood pressure.* Paper presented at the annual meeting of the American Psychosomatic Society, Savannah. GA.

Malcolm, W. M., & Greenberg, L. S. (2005, May). *The process of forgiveness in individuals and couples.* Paper presented at the annual meeting of the Society for the Exploration of Psychotherapy Integration, Toronto, Ontario, Canada.

Murphy, J. G. (2002). Forgiveness in counseling: A philosophical perspective. In S. Lamb & J. G. Murphy (Eds.), *Before forgiving: Cautionary views of forgiveness in psychotherapy.* London: Oxford University Press.

Olio, K. (1992). Recovery from sexual abuse: Is forgiveness mandatory? *Voices: The Art and Science of Psychotherapy, 28,* 73–79.

Paivio, S. (2001). Stability of retrospective self reports of child abuse and neglect before and after therapy for child abuse issues. *Child Abuse and Neglect, 25,* 1053–1068.

Paivio, S., Hall, I., Chagigiorgis, H., Ralston, M., & Lee, T. (2006, May). *Comparative outcome study for two different versions of emotion focused trauma therapy.* Paper presented at the Society for the Exploration of Psychotherapy Integration, LA.

Paivio, S. C., & Greenberg, L. S. (1995). Resolving "unfinished business": Efficacy of experiential therapy using empty-chair dialogue. *Journal of Consulting and Clinical Psychology, 63,* 419–425.
Paivio, S., Hall, I. E., Holowaty, K. A. M., Jellis, J. B., & Tran, N. (2001). Imaginal confrontation for resolving child abuse issues. *Psychotherapy Research, 11,* 443–453.
Paivio, S., & Nieuwenhuis, J. A. (2001). Efficacy of emotion focused therapy for adult survivors of childhood abuse: A preliminary study. *Journal of Traumatic Stress, 14,* 115–134.
Paivio, S. C., & Patterson, L. (1999). Alliance development in therapy for resolving child abuse issues. *Psychotherapy: Theory, Research, Practice, Training, 36,* 343–354.
Rice, K. M., & Paivio, S. C. (1999). *Change in perceptions of relationships with abusive and neglectful other following therapy for child abuse issues.* Unpublished master's thesis, University of Saskatchewan, Saskatoon, Saskatchewan, Canada.
Rogers, C. R., (1961). *On becoming a person.* Boston: Houghton Mifflin.
Scobie, E. D., & Scobie, G. E. W. (1998). Damaging events: The perceived need for forgiveness. *Journal for the Theory of Social Behaviour, 28,* 373–401.
Spranca, M., Minsk, E., & Baron, J. (1991). Omission and commission in judgment and choice. *Journal of Experimental Social Psychology, 27,* 76–105.
van der Kolk, B. A. (1996). The complexity of adaptation to trauma: Self-regulation, stimulus discrimination, and characterological development. In B. A. van der Kolk & A. C. McFarlane (Eds.), *Traumatic stress: The effects of overwhelming experience on mind, body and society.* New York: Guilford Press.
Wolfsdorf, B. A., & Zlotnik, C. (2001). Affect management in group therapy for men and women with posttraumatic stress disorder and histories of childhood sexual abuse. *Journal of Clinical Psychology, 57,* 169–181.

8

Forgiveness and Coping

RENATE YSSELDYK AND
KIMBERLY MATHESON*

Introduction

From minor conflicts and disagreements to more serious acts of betrayal and abuse, individuals often face the challenge of contending with interpersonal transgressions in their most valued relationships. The notion that forgiveness might facilitate the ability to cope with a range of interpersonal stressors is not new; indeed, numerous studies have found a positive relation between forgiveness and well-being in the context of dealing with personal relationship conflicts (Brown & Phillips, 2005; Lawler et al., 2003; Witvliet, Ludwig, & Vander Laan, 2001). The ubiquitous use of the term "forgiveness" suggests that there is a common understanding of what exactly constitutes forgiveness, including its form and function. Such consensus, however, is lacking (Macaskill, 2005; McCullough, Pargament, & Thoresen, 2000) and may contribute to inconsistencies regarding the mechanisms linking forgiveness and well-being, and the circumstances wherein it is likely to be effective.

Forgiveness can serve both *inter*personal (e.g., a positive change in attitudes or behavior toward another person; McCullough et al., 2000) as well as *intra*personal functions (e.g., an internal process of releasing resentment, irrespective of the offender; Denton & Martin, 1998). These forms of forgiveness are typically talked about in relation to specific transgressions and are often referred to as *state forgiveness*. However, forgiveness can also be viewed as a disposition or personality

* Our appreciation to Dr. Hymie Anisman for his contribution to and feedback regarding this project.

trait (e.g., Berry, Worthington, Parrott, O'Connor, & Wade, 2001; Brown, 2003; McCullough & Worthington, 1999; Mullet, Barros, Frongia, Usaie, & Shafighi, 2003), rather than (or in addition to) an act or process in response to a particular offense. *Dispositional forgiveness* refers to the general tendency to forgive transgressions across time, relationships, and situations (Berry et al.; Brown).

Additional variations in understanding what is meant by forgiveness are also evident in its measurement. Forgiveness has often been measured (at least in part) as the extent to which the individual expresses motivations to avoid or to seek revenge against the transgressor, frequently termed *unforgiveness* (Worthington & Wade, 1999). Yet, forgiveness should not be viewed simply as the absence of avoidance of the offender or a diminished desire for revenge, but ought to include more benevolent motivations as well (Brown, 2003; McCullough & Hoyt, 2002). For example, someone who takes revenge against another would clearly seem to be unforgiving, but a lack of vengeful feelings or behaviors does not necessarily imply forgiveness (Brown, 2003, 2004).

It should not be surprising that the psychological mechanisms linked to forgiveness vary depending on how forgiveness is defined. For example, our research has suggested that when forgiveness is measured as a prosocial interpersonal attitude (e.g., "I feel warmly toward this person"; Brown & Phillips, 2005), it is associated with an ability to limit the scope of the conflict in terms of its perceived threat or emotional consequences (Ysseldyk, Sudom, Skomorovsky, Matheson, & Anisman, 2005). In contrast, we and others (Barber, Maltby, & Macaskill, 2005; Berry, Worthington, O'Connor, Parrott, & Wade, 2005; McCullough, Bellah, Kilpatrick, & Johnson, 2001; Ysseldyk, Matheson, & Anisman, 2006) have observed that a desire for vengeance (reflecting unforgiveness) is linked to perceptions that the situation was out of the injured party's control and to increased rumination about the transgression. In effect, processes associated with forgiveness and the facets that comprise unforgiveness (e.g., vengeance and avoidance) may be distinct (Worthington & Wade, 1999). Clearly, in order to understand how forgiveness might come to promote well-being, it is important to define precisely what it entails. Curiously, there is limited research that permits a comparative evaluation of the implications of various definitions and measures.

Forgiveness as a Coping Strategy

It has been argued that forgiveness operates fundamentally as a coping strategy in itself or that it may elicit other coping strategies that buffer against the negative impacts of encountering interpersonal transgressions. Dominating this body of research is the notion that forgiveness may be a positive form of religious coping (Pargament, 1997; Pargament, Koenig, & Perez, 2000; Pargament, Smith, Koenig, & Perez, 1998; Webb, 2003). What separates it from the constellation of other religious coping methods is that while some may regard forgiveness to be a theological, spiritual act, it may be as much secular as it is religious (McCullough & Worthington, 1999; Pargament; Thoresen, Harris, & Luskin, 2000). In fact, forgiveness is not always found to be related to religious beliefs or faith, suggesting that other social or psychological factors are implicated (McCullough & Worthington; Ysseldyk et al., 2006).

Coping: a Brief Overview

In general, coping styles are often understood along two fundamental dimensions: problem-focused and emotion-focused styles (Folkman & Lazarus, 1980; Lazarus & Folkman, 1984; Parker & Endler, 1992). In addition to or subsumed under these two core categories is a wide range of coping strategies. Emotion-focused coping may encompass emotional expression, emotional containment, self- and other-blame, denial, or passive resignation; problem-focused coping may entail cognitive restructuring (reframing of the situation) or problem-solving techniques (Carver, Scheier, & Weintraub, 1989; Matheson & Anisman, 2003). In addition, individuals may turn to positive activities (e.g., constructive or recreational activities), social support seeking (as a buffer or venting outlet), humor, and/or rumination (Carver et al.; Endler & Parker, 1994; Nolen-Hoeksema, Parker, & Larson, 1994); all of which might serve in multiple capacities in terms of managing the stressor situation or regulating emotional reactions.

The research relating coping to psychological health has often indicated that problem-focused coping is associated with positive indices of well-being (e.g., Hynes, Callan, Terry, & Gallois, 1992) and is, therefore, considered to be of more adaptive value, whereas emotion-focused coping is primarily related to poor well-being and is, thus, regarded as less adaptive. For example, symptoms of depression have been associated with increased use of strategies that are regarded as emotion focused, especially rumination (Nolen-Hoeksema et al., 1994), emotional expression and containment (Matheson & Anisman, 2003; Ravindran, Matheson, Griffiths, Merali, & Anisman, 2002). However, particular coping efforts may be situation specific (DeLongis & Holtzman, 2005; Folkman & Lazarus, 1980; Mattlin, Wethington, & Kessler, 1990; Tennen, Affleck, Armeli, & Carney, 2000), may serve different functions (Snyder & Pulvers, 2001), or may operate in conjunction with other strategies (Matheson & Anisman) to influence well-being. Social support seeking, for instance, may provide a distraction from problems, may be a component of problem-solving, or may provide an outlet for emotional expression (Endler & Parker, 1994; Parker & Endler, 1992). Likewise, emotion-focused coping strategies—particularly those involving engagement with emotions (i.e., acknowledging, understanding, and expressing emotions)—may have some beneficial effects; however, the effectiveness of emotion-focused strategies likely depends to some extent on the individual and/or the circumstances (Austenfeld & Stanton, 2004).

Forgiveness and Emotion-Focused Coping

In line with the notion that people may use forgiveness as a coping strategy quite separate from religion, Worthington and Scherer (2004) argued that forgiveness is primarily an emotion-focused coping effort. In this regard, these authors suggest that there are two types of forgiveness: decisional and emotional. Decisional forgiveness is a form of interpersonal forgiveness involving "a behavioral intention statement that one will seek to behave toward the transgressor like one did prior to a transgression" (p. 386). In contrast, emotional forgiveness appears to be an intrapersonal form of forgiveness involving "an emotional juxtaposition of positive emotion against the negative emotions comprising unforgiveness" (p. 387). Within a stress and coping framework, the latter type of forgiveness entails an effort to manage emotions and hence may be regarded as an emotion-focused coping strategy, which might, in fact, be adaptive. However, the possible relations between forgiveness and coping are more often theorized about than empirically demonstrated (Maltby, Day, & Barber, 2004).

Of the few studies that have evaluated forgiveness in relation to emotion-focused coping, inconsistent results have been reported, in part emanating from, as noted earlier, inconsistencies in definitions and variations in the circumstances in which forgiveness is considered. For example, forgiveness of an offending other was associated with higher levels of emotion-focused coping (Konstam, Holmes, & Levine, 2003), whereas dispositional forgiveness was found to be associated with *low* levels of emotion-focused coping (Seybold, Hill, Neumann, & Chi, 2001). In our own research, both dispositional (Ysseldyk et al., 2006) and offense-specific (Ysseldyk et al., 2005) forgiveness (whether measured in prosocial terms or as a *lack* of vengeance and avoidance) were related to *lower* levels of emotion-focused coping. Likewise, the examination of several types of forgiveness (i.e., dispositional, transgression specific, self-forgiveness, and the absence of unforgiveness) within a personality-coping framework revealed negative associations between forgiveness and a neuroticism-coping factor reflecting the emotion-focused strategies of denial and both mental and behavioral disengagement (Maltby et al., 2004). In addition, the latter study demonstrated a positive association between prosocial forgiveness and an extraversion-coping factor (comprising coping through social support seeking). Thus, the few empirical studies that have been conducted suggest that forgiveness and emotion-focused coping are primarily negatively related, although there may be specific emotion-focused efforts that are more likely to be elicited in conjunction with forgiveness.

Although specific coping strategies are often assessed, for the sake of parsimony, they are typically combined to form two to three overarching coping categories. We have argued that an investigation of the unique properties of the multiple and diverse strategies that make up the various coping options available to individuals may provide a richer understanding of the coping responses within a given context (Matheson & Anisman, 2003). In this regard, it is possible that forgiveness may elicit particular emotion-focused strategies, producing different outcomes as a result of the combinations of strategies endorsed. Although our research did not yield notable differences in the relations between forgiveness and emotional-approach versus emotional-avoidance coping (Ysseldyk et al., 2005), different patterns may emerge when more specific strategies, or coping profiles, are considered. For example, forgiveness of a transgressor coupled specifically with self-blame may lead to reduced well-being, whereas forgiveness paired with problem-solving and emotional expression may lead to reconciliation between the offender and the victim, possibly resulting in positive outcomes. Moreover, even when reconciliation is not possible (or not appropriate, for example, in the context of a continuing abusive relationship; McCullough, 2000), forgiveness tied to the use of a coping strategy such as cognitive restructuring (e.g., looking for what one has learned from the situation) may still result in positive outcomes for the injured individual.

An Empirical Assessment of Coping Profiles in Relation to Forgiveness

Dispositional Versus State Forgiveness

To explore the coping processes that might be linked to various forms of forgiveness, we examined the specific coping profiles that corresponded to both dispositional forgiveness and forgiveness of a specific relationship transgression. To this end, 204 participants responded to Brown's (2003) Tendency to Forgive measure, which is intended to capture personality differences in the tendency to engage in forgiving thoughts or behaviors across situations. Individuals were considered to be either "forgiving" or "unforgiving," based on whether their average score was in the top half or in the bottom half of the sample, respectively. Coping profiles of people who tended to be forgiving versus unforgiving were then evaluated by having them complete the Survey of Coping Profile Endorsements (Matheson & Anisman, 2003). This measure of coping evaluates 14 coping dimensions, including a range of problem-focused strategies such as problem-solving, cognitive restructuring (learning from the situation), active distraction (engagement in constructive alternative activity), and social-support seeking, as well as emotion-focused coping methods (namely, cognitive avoidance, rumination, humor, emotional expression, other- and self-blame, emotional containment, passive resignation, wishful thinking) and finally, religious faith.

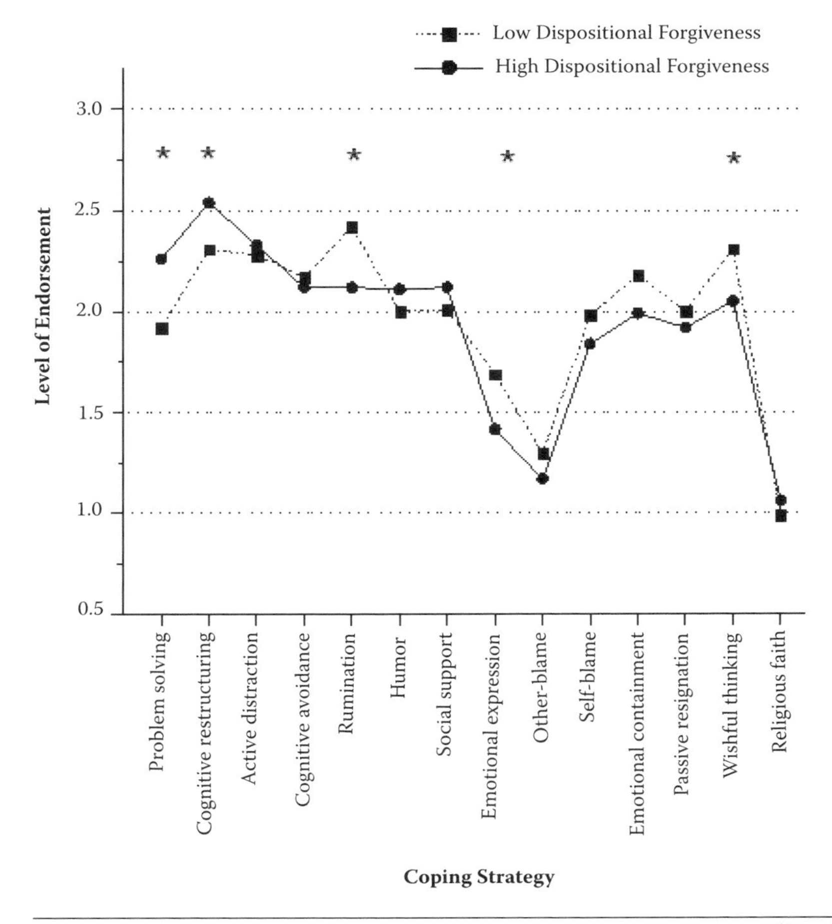

Figure 8.1 Coping profiles as a function of dispositional forgiveness (* = groups differed at $p < .05$).

As seen in Figure 8.1, the coping profiles differed between individuals who were high versus low in dispositional forgiveness, $F(13, 2327) = 2.17$, $p = .009$. It appeared that high dispositional forgivers were inclined to endorse coping strategies that are typically considered to be adaptive, such as problem solving and cognitive restructuring. In addition, in line with previous research (Seybold et al., 2001; Ysseldyk et al., 2006), participants who had highly forgiving dispositions indicated a reduced propensity to endorse those coping strategies that were emotional in nature, including rumination, emotional expression, and wishful thinking—a combination of strategies that is generally considered to be maladaptive.

In addition to having a forgiving disposition, people encounter specific situations in which they may be more or less forgiving, and their choice of response, in turn, might reflect different coping efforts. One of the most common situations in which forgiveness is likely to play a role is in response to transgressions from an intimate partner. Thus, to assess the coping profiles associated with transgression-specific forgiveness, we asked individuals in dating relationships to indicate their willingness to forgive their partners for a recent relationship transgression (measured in prosocial terms; Brown & Phillips, 2005), along with their coping responses in that situation. Once again, the coping profiles associated with individuals who were high versus low in their willingness to forgive their partner for a specific conflict differed, $F(13, 2600) = 2.45$, $p = .003$.

As seen in Figure 8.2, individuals who were highly forgiving of their partners did not appear to be significantly more inclined to use adaptive problem-focused coping strategies than their less forgiving counterparts, suggesting that forgiveness in this context was not necessarily aimed at finding a solution to the situation, per se. However, transgression-specific forgiveness was associated with lower endorsements of rumination, emotional expression, and wishful thinking, along with more limited reliance on other emotion-focused strategies, including cognitive avoidance, emotional containment, other-blame, and passive resignation. Thus, a willingness to forgive the partner appeared to stem from a desire to keep the emotional aspects of the situation from getting out of hand. Notably, these differences in the coping profiles of individuals who were more or less likely to forgive their partners remained evident even after dispositional tendencies toward forgiveness were taken into account.

Thus, it appears that there are variations in the coping processes linked to dispositional and transgression-specific forgiveness. However, it is certainly possible that the variations in problem-focused coping efforts that are associated with dispositional forgiveness represent a constellation of attitudinal responses to transgressions, rather than reflecting coping efforts that are elicited in a given situation. The finding that these coping strategies were not implicated in the

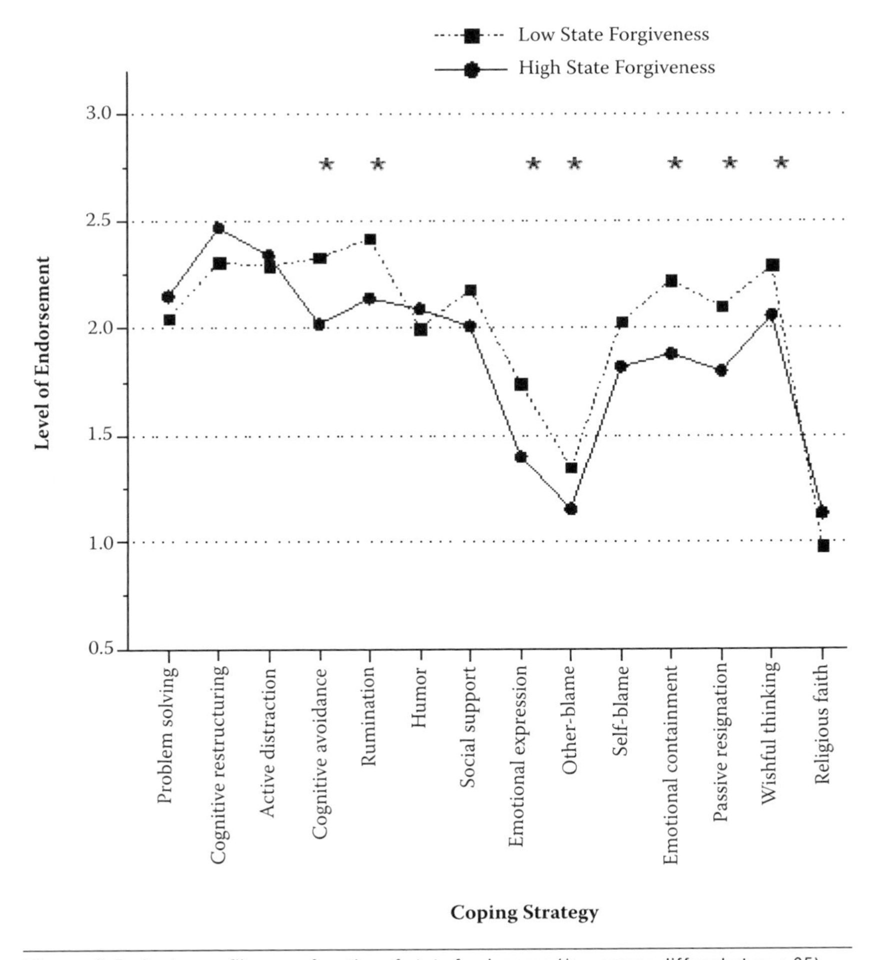

Figure 8.2 Coping profiles as a function of state forgiveness (* = groups differed at $p<.05$).

context of forgiving an intimate partner for a particular transgression would support this possibility, but it is also possible that if the transgression or nature of the relationship with the perpetrator had been different, these problem-oriented coping efforts might have come into play. Notably, both dispositional and state forgiveness were associated with the *diminished* reliance on a common set of emotion-focused coping efforts. However, individuals were disinclined to use an even broader array of emotional coping strategies in the context of forgiving a partner for a specific offense, suggesting that in this situation, particular efforts were made to avoid employing coping strategies that might exacerbate (e.g., blame) or prolong (e.g., cognitive avoidance, emotional containment, passive resignation) distress.

Forgiveness Versus Unforgiveness

As noted earlier, on occasion, conceptualizations of forgiveness and unforgiveness (including vengeance) have been regarded as simply the inverse of one another. However, it was also suggested that the mechanisms underlying forgiveness and unforgiveness might vary. In this regard, the coping profiles associated with dispositional vengeance (as measured by seven vengeance-related items from Mauger and colleagues' 1992 Forgiveness of Others Scale) and transgression-specific unforgiveness (i.e., motivations for vengeance and avoidance as measured by the Transgression Related Interpersonal Motivations Inventory, McCullough et al., 1998) might not simply yield the inverse pattern that was found to be associated with prosocial forgiveness, but ought to be linked to a particular coping profile, even after taking into account dispositional or state forgiveness, respectively. Indeed, the coping profiles associated with individuals who were high versus low in dispositional vengeance differed significantly, $F(13, 2327) = 2.50$, $p = .002$.

As seen in Figure 8.3, rather than exhibiting profiles that differed in levels of emotion-focused coping strategies, individuals with vengeance-seeking dispositions were less inclined to engage in traditionally adaptive coping styles, including problem solving, cognitive restructuring, and social support seeking, than were their less vengeful counterparts. This pattern remained even after taking into account variations due to dispositional forgiveness. Thus, it appears that the ostensible unforgiveness, implicated by a vengeful disposition, does not evoke the same emotion-focused efforts that are rejected by forgiving individuals.

When the coping profiles associated with transgression-specific unforgiveness were examined, as with transgression-specific forgiveness, differences were more evident among the emotional rather than the problem-focused coping strategies, $F(13, 2600) = 2.80$, $p = .001$. As seen in Figure 8.4, individuals who were high in motivations to seek vengeance and avoidance (i.e., unforgiveness) from their partner following a conflict were significantly more inclined to engage in a plethora of emotional coping styles, including

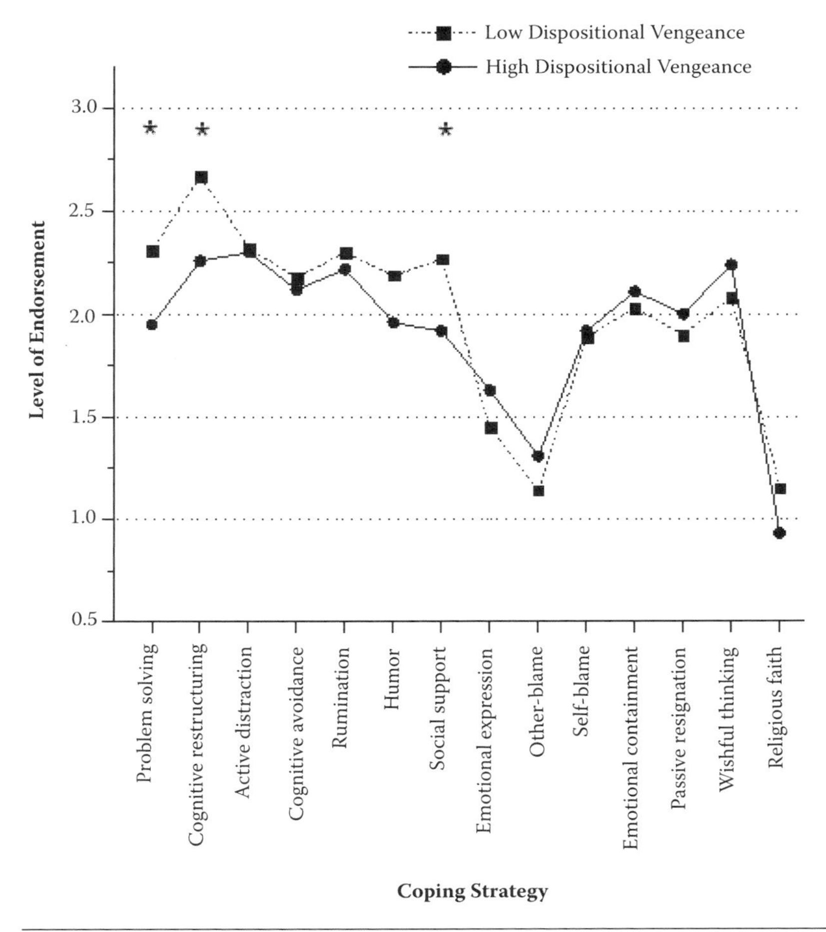

Figure 8.3 Coping profiles as a function of dispositional vengeance (* = groups differed at $p < .05$).

rumination, emotional expression, and wishful thinking, as well as self- and other-blame, emotional containment, and passive resignation. Although this pattern was similar to that noted for state forgiveness (in the reverse), it remained significant even after forgiveness was taken into account. Nonetheless, it appears that either forgiveness or unforgiveness in response to a specific partner transgression in a dating relationship was linked to the endorsement of a broad set of emotion-focused coping strategies, simply in the reverse direction from one another.

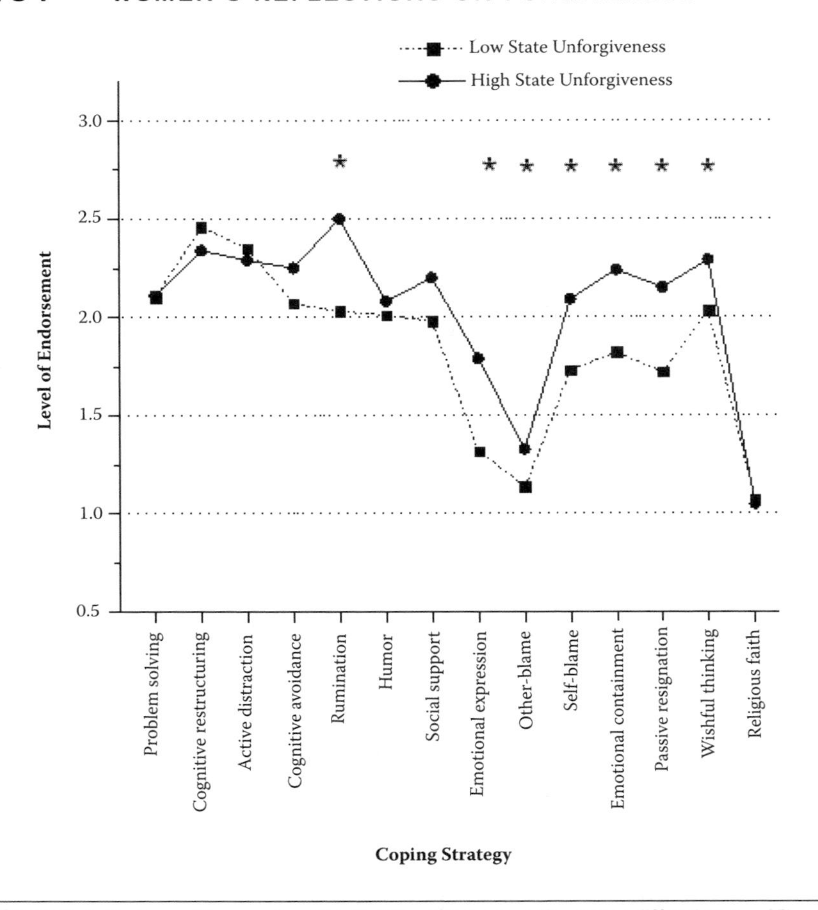

Figure 8.4 Coping profiles as a function of state unforgiveness (* = groups differed at $p < .05$).

Forgiveness and Coping Across Relationship Stressors

As suggested earlier, the coping profiles that are associated with forgiveness or unforgiveness in a particular situation might depend on the nature or severity of the transgression encountered (Scobie & Scobie, 1998). Indeed, it would seem that forgiveness comes more readily in the context of minor conflicts (e.g., Exline, Baumeister, Bushman, Campbell, & Finkel, 2004; Fincham, Jackson, & Beach, 2005; Zechmeister & Romero, 2002) than in the aftermath of more intrusive transgressions with long-term consequences, such as abuse (e.g., Freedman & Enright, 1996; Tracy, 1999; Ysseldyk et al., 2005) or torture (e.g., Vrba, 1964). Yet, the intricacies associated with the role of forgiveness in these various contexts are rarely explicitly considered.

The forgiveness (or lack thereof) of intimate partner abuse may be particularly complex, especially in the context of an ongoing abusive relationship. Given the expectation of an intimate partner to be loving and protective, abuse at the hands of that person might be viewed as an unpardonable betrayal. There are several issues that appear to influence forgiveness of abuse, including whether reconciliation is hoped for (which might motivate forgiveness, although this relation may be reciprocal; Worthington, Mazzeo, & Canter, 2005) or is even appropriate (Tracy, 1999), whether the abuser has been brought to justice (Casey, 1998), the severity of abuse and whether it was attributed to malicious intent (Gordon, Burton, & Porter, 2004), as well as the safety of the victim (e.g., McCullough, 2000). Indeed, McCullough proposes the notion of "forgiving as a red flag" (p. 51), in that the willingness to forgive an abuser might continue to put the victim's health and well-being at risk.

Thus, although forgiveness typically serves as a resilience factor that promotes well-being, in response to a currently abusive partner it may leave the woman vulnerable to further abuse and to an understanding of her situation (e.g., self-blame) that may render her more likely to develop pathology. On the one hand, abused women may forgive their partners in an effort to manage an ongoing situation by limiting the conflict (i.e., appeasing the transgressor); on the other hand, forgiveness in this context may be linked to emotion-focused coping styles that encourage women to deny their own feelings and reactions, which might itself leave them more vulnerable to continued abuse.

We compared the coping profile of 52 women who reported recent (within the past month) conflict behaviors in their current dating relationships that could be regarded as psychologically abusive to that of 186 women who did not report experiencing such abuse. Specifically, we were interested in whether the coping profile of the abused women who forgave their partners differed from the coping profile associated with forgiveness among nonabused women. Not surprisingly, the majority of women whose relationships were characterized by psychological abuse did not indicate that they were willing to forgive their partners' transgressions, in that 71% of these women indicated low levels of forgiveness (i.e., their scores were in the bottom half of the sample), compared to 44% of women in nonabusive relationships. Moreover, although the coping profile of psychologically abused women who were *not* willing to forgive their partners did not differ from that of unforgiving nonabused women, the profiles associated with *forgiveness* among abused and nonabused women did vary, $F(13, 1508) = 2.09$, $p = .012$.

In particular, as seen in Figure 8.5, psychologically abused women who chose to forgive their partners were less likely to seek active distractions to make themselves feel better (e.g., going to the gym or

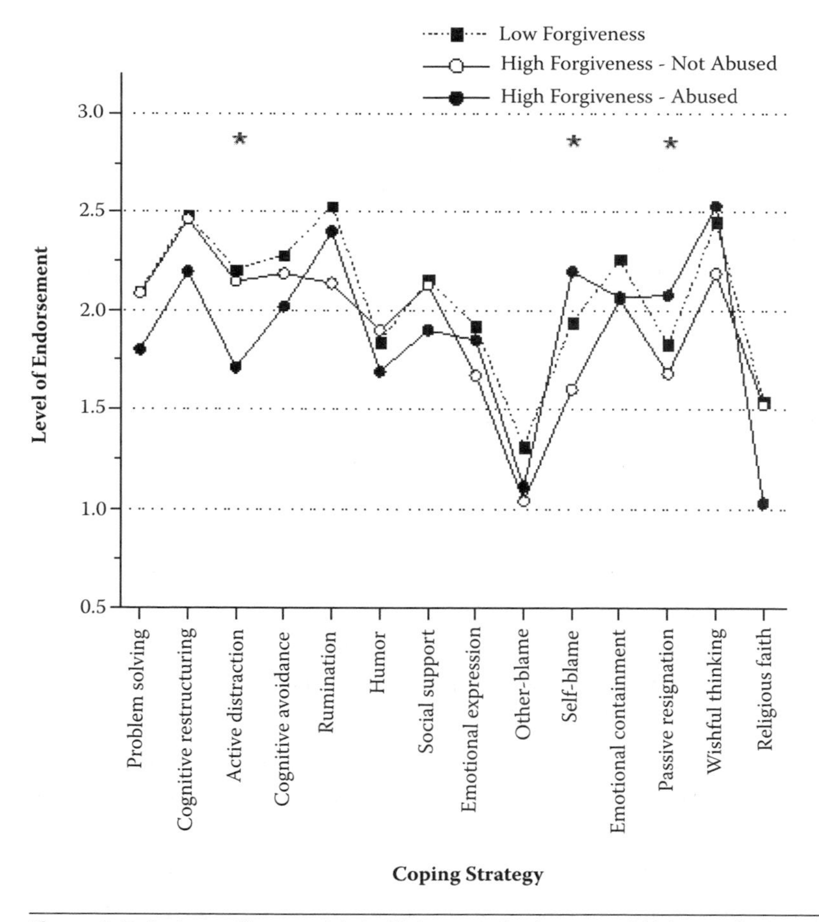

Figure 8.5 Coping profiles associated with low state forgiveness and high state forgiveness as a function of psychological abuse in a dating relationship (* = forgiving abused and nonabused women differed at $p < .05$).

to a movie) and were more likely to endo
resignation as strategies for coping with their s
use of these particular strategies among wom
their abusive relationships has been documented in
(Clements, Sabourin, & Spiby, 2004; Follingstad,
Vormbrock, 1988). Thus, although forgiveness is typical
with rejecting emotion-focused strategies, it appears that in
text of ongoing abuse, forgiveness was associated with malad
coping efforts that likely worked against women's ability to cha
their abusive situations. Incidentally, we further found in this stud
that forgiveness was most likely to be expressed by abused women who did not perceive control in relation to their abusive situation. Thus, rather than serving as a method to promote reconciliation, women's forgiveness within an abusive relationship might have represented an intrapersonal response that allowed them to endure situations they did not know how to resolve.

Conclusions and Caveats

Consistent with the suggestion that the way in which forgiveness is defined and measured might implicate different underlying coping processes, it appeared that dispositional and state forgiveness could be distinguished on the basis of the coping profiles endorsed to contend with relationship transgressions. The dispositional tendency to grant forgiveness appeared to be uniquely related to problem-focused coping efforts coupled with a disinclination to use a limited set of emotion-focused coping strategies—namely, rumination, emotional expression, and wishful thinking. Conversely, transgression-specific forgiveness was solely related to rejecting the use of emotion-focused coping strategies and went well beyond the specific strategies implicated by dispositional forgiveness to include a broad array of emotional coping efforts.

It will be recalled that problem-focused coping has typically been considered to be an adaptive coping approach, whereas emotion-focused coping is generally viewed as maladaptive. Thus, the inclination of individuals with an inherently forgiving nature to engage in constructive problem-focused strategies, combined with the rejection contribute to the positive n the forgiveness literature. notion-focused strategies in important, as avoiding an erve to attenuate negative bility to find constructive

elation to forgiveness and geance) also highlighted hese two constructs. Differ ation to the dispositional ..., although the processes ... these constructs did not differ substantially at the transgression-specific level. In particular, a vengeful disposition was associated with a disinclination to endorse problem-focused coping styles, including a tendency not to seek social support; however, vengefulness was *not* linked to an increased use of the emotion-focused efforts that were rejected by individuals with a more forgiving disposition. This discrepancy suggests that even though a vengeful disposition does not necessarily reflect a constructive approach to coping with transgressions, it is not rooted in an inability to manage emotions.

Certainly, there may be circumstances in which the effectiveness of both forgiveness and various coping efforts might vary; in particular, we considered this possibility in the context of an abusive relationship. It will be recalled that abused and nonabused women who did not forgive their partners demonstrated similar coping profiles; indeed, a lack of forgiveness in response to abuse could be regarded as a relatively "normal" reaction. In contrast, women in psychologically abusive relationships who were willing to forgive their partners were more likely to self-blame and to endorse passive resignation, and were less likely to employ healthy, active distractions to cope with their situations than were nonabused women who forgave their partners' transgressions.

Self-blame has frequently been found among abused women, and this especially appeared to be the case among women who were prepared to forgive their abusive partners. Clearly, this is a maladaptive coping strategy in this context; however, given the correlational nature of the data, it is uncertain whether forgiveness bred self-blame or self-blame prompted forgiveness. Alternatively, a third factor (e.g., low self-esteem, Clements et al., 2004; neurotic personality, McCullough & Hoyt, 2002) may be at work to influence both forgiveness and self-blame. Unfortunately, there is also reason to believe that women's forgiveness of abuse is related to increased rates of remaining in an abusive relationship (as coping by means of self-blame or passive resignation might encourage) or returning even after an attempt to leave (Gordon et al., 2004).

Overall, having clear conceptualizations and measures of both forgiveness and unforgiveness are important to the understanding of their underlying mechanisms and functions, including how they might relate to coping efforts and well-being. In this regard, the associations of forgiveness and vengeance to specific coping profiles suggested that these processes were not interchangeable, especially as they were reflected in dispositional propensities. Despite the comparability of the coping profiles associated with state forgiveness and unforgiveness, the coping processes associated with transgression-specific forgiveness depended on whether it was offered in response to a conflict entailing a relatively minor disagreement or one that reflected betrayal in the form of abuse. In this regard, the role of forgiveness in promoting well-being might be inconsistent and, at the very least, ought to be considered in relation to the transgression.

Indeed, even within the context of intimate relationship transgressions, the coping mechanisms linked to forgiveness appeared to be relatively complex. Consideration of other factors associated with interpersonal relationships (e.g., pre-offense intimacy, commitment) might continue to elucidate some of these complexities. In addition, successful replication of the associations found among forgiveness and coping here would provide further support to the relatively modest strength of our current findings, increasing our ability to assert confidently that these relations are stable. Further exploration of forgiveness, coupled with a greater understanding of the subtle distinctions found in its conceptualization and measurement, may clarify its role in promoting individuals' capacity to cope with the range of interpersonal stressors that inevitably occur in our lives.

References

Austenfeld, J. L., & Stanton, A. L. (2004). Coping through emotional approach: A new look at emotion, coping, and health-related outcomes. *Journal of Personality, 72,* 1335–1363.

Barber, L., Maltby, J., & Macaskill, A. (2005). Angry memories and thoughts of revenge: The relationship between forgiveness and anger rumination. *Personality and Individual Differences, 39,* 253–262.

Berry, J. W., Worthington, E. L., Jr., O'Connor, L. E., Parrott, L., & Wade, N. G. (2005). Forgivingness, vengeful rumination, and affective traits. *Journal of Personality, 73,* 183–225.

Berry, J. W., Worthington, E. L., Jr., Parrott, L., O'Connor, L. E., & Wade, N. G. (2001). Dispositional forgivingness: Development and construct validity of the Transgression Narrative Test of Forgivingness (TNTF). *Personality and Social Psychology Bulletin, 27,* 1277–1290.

Brown, R. P. (2003). Measuring individual differences in the tendency to forgive: Construct validity and links with depression. *Personality and Social Psychology Bulletin, 29,* 759–771.

Brown, R. P. (2004). Vengeance is mine: Narcissism, vengeance, and the tendency to forgive. *Journal of Research in Personality, 38,* 576–584.

Brown, R. P., & Phillips, A. (2005). Letting bygones be bygones: Further evidence for the validity of the Tendency to Forgive scale. *Personality and Individual Differences, 38,* 627–638.

Carver, C. S., Scheier, M. F., & Weintraub, J. K. (1989). Assessing coping strategies: A theoretically based approach. *Journal of Personality and Social Psychology, 56,* 267–283.

Casey, K. L. (1998). Surviving abuse: Shame, anger, forgiveness. *Pastoral Psychology, 46,* 223–231.

Clements, C. M., Sabourin, C. M., & Spiby, L. (2004). Dysphoria and hopelessness following battering: The role of perceived control, coping, and self-esteem. *Journal of Family Violence, 19,* 25–36.

DeLongis, A., & Holtzman, S. (2005). Coping in context: The role of stress, social support, and personality in coping. *Journal of Personality, 73,* 1633–1656.

Denton, R. T., & Martin, M. W. (1998). Defining forgiveness: An empirical exploration of process and role. *American Journal of Family Therapy, 26,* 281–292.

Endler, N. S., & Parker, J. D. A. (1994). Assessment of multidimensional coping: Task, emotion, and avoidance strategies. *Psychological Assessment, 6,* 50–60.

Exline, J. J., Baumeister, R. F., Bushman, B. J., Campbell, W. K., & Finkel, E. J. (2004). Too proud to let go: Narcissistic entitlement as a barrier to forgiveness. *Journal of Personality and Social Psychology, 87,* 894–912.

Fincham, F. D., Jackson, H., & Beach, S. R. H. (2005). Transgression severity and forgiveness: Different moderators for objective and subjective severity. *Journal of Social and Clinical Psychology, 24,* 860–875.

Folkman, S., & Lazarus, R. S. (1980). An analysis of coping in a middle-aged community sample. *Journal of Health and Social Behavior, 21,* 219–239.

Follingstad, D. R., Neckerman, A. P., & Vormbrock, J. (1988). Reactions to victimization and coping strategies of battered women: The ties that bind. *Clinical Psychology Review, 8,* 373–390.

Freedman, S. R., & Enright, R. D. (1996). Forgiving as an intervention goal with incest survivors. *Journal of Consulting and Clinical Psychology, 64,* 983–992.

Gordon, K. C., Burton, S., & Porter, L. (2004). Predicting the intentions of women in domestic violence shelters to return to partners: Does forgiveness play a role? *Journal of Family Psychology, 18,* 331–338.

Hynes, G. J., Callan, V. J., Terry, D. J., & Gallois, C. (1992). The psychological well-being of infertile women after a failed IVF attempt: The effects of coping. *British Journal of Medical Psychology, 65,* 269–278.

Konstam, V., Holmes, W., & Levine, B. (2003). Empathy, selfism, and coping as elements of the psychology of forgiveness: A preliminary study. *Counseling and Values, 47,* 172–183.

Lawler, K. A., Younger, J. W., Piferi, R. L., Billington, E., Jobe, R., Edmondson, K., et al. (2003). A change of heart: Cardiovascular correlates of forgiveness in response to interpersonal conflict. *Journal of Behavioral Medicine, 26,* 373–393.

Lazarus, R. S., & Folkman, S. (1984). *Stress, appraisal, and coping.* New York: Springer.

Macaskill, A. (2005). Defining forgiveness: Christian clergy and general population perspectives. *Journal of Personality, 73,* 1237–1265.

Maltby, J., Day, L., & Barber, L. (2004). Forgiveness and mental health variables: Interpreting the relationship using an adaptational-continuum model of personality and coping. *Personality and Individual Differences, 37,* 1629–1641.

Matheson, K., & Anisman, H. (2003). Systems of coping associated with dysphoria, anxiety and depressive illness: A multivariate profile perspective. *Stress, 6,* 223–234.

Mattlin, J. A., Wethington, E., & Kessler, R.C. (1990). Situational determinants of coping and coping effectiveness. *Journal of Health and Social Behavior, 31,* 103–122.

Mauger, P. A., Freeman, T., McBride, A. G., Perry, J. C., Grove, D. C., & McKinney, K. E. (1992). The measurement of forgiveness: Preliminary research. *Journal of Psychology and Christianity, 11,* 170–180.

McCullough, M. E. (2000). Forgiveness as human strength: Theory, measurement, and links to well-being. *Journal of Social and Clinical Psychology, 19,* 43–55.

McCullough, M. E., Bellah, C. G., Kilpatrick, S. D., & Johnson, J. L. (2001). Vengefulness: Relationships with forgiveness, rumination, well-being, and the big five. *Personality and Social Psychology Bulletin, 27,* 601–610.

McCullough, M. E., & Hoyt, W. T. (2002). Transgression-related motivational dispositions: Personality substrates of forgiveness and their links to the Big Five. *Personality and Social Psychology Bulletin, 28,* 1556–1573.

McCullough, M. E., Pargament, K. I., & Thoresen, C. E. (2000). The psychology of forgiveness: History, conceptual issues, and overview. In M. E. McCullough, K. I. Pargament, & C. E. Thoresen (Eds.), *Forgiveness: Theory, research, and practice* (pp. 1–14). New York: Guilford Press.

McCullough, M. E., Rachal, K. C., Sandage, S. J., Worthington, E. L., Jr., Brown, S. W., & Hight, T. L. (1998). Interpersonal forgiving in close relations II: Theoretical elaboration and measurement. *Journal of Personality and Social Psychology, 75,* 1586–1603.

McCullough, M. E., & Worthington, E. L., Jr. (1999). Religion and the forgiving personality. *Journal of Personality, 67,* 1141–1164.

Mullet, E., Barros, J., Frongia, L., Usaie, V., & Shafighi, S. R. (2003). Religious involvement and the forgiving personality. *Journal of Personality, 71,* 1–19.

Nolen-Hoeksema, S., Parker, L. E., & Larson, J. (1994). Ruminative coping with depressed mood following loss. *Journal of Personality and Social Psychology, 67,* 92–104.

Pargament, K. I. (1997). *The psychology of religion and coping: Theory, research, practice.* New York: Guilford Press.

Pargament, K. I., Koenig, H. G., & Perez, L. M. (2000). The many methods of religious coping: Development and initial validation of the RCOPE. *Journal of Clinical Psychology, 56,* 519–543.

Pargament, K. I., Smith, B. W., Koenig, H. G., & Perez, L. M. (1998). Patterns of positive and negative religious coping with major life stressors. *Journal for the Scientific Study of Religion, 37,* 710–724.

Parker, J. D., & Endler, N. S. (1992). Coping with coping assessment: A critical review. *European Journal of Personality, 6,* 321–344.

Ravindran, A. V., Matheson, K., Griffiths, J., Merali, Z., & Anisman, H. (2002). Stress, coping, uplifts, and quality of life in subtypes of depression: A conceptual frame and emerging data. *Journal of Affective Disorders, 71,* 121–130.

Scobie, E. D., & Scobie, G. E. W. (1998). Damaging events: The perceived need for forgiveness. *Journal for the Theory of Social Behaviour, 28,* 373–401.

Seybold, K. S., Hill, P. C., Neumann, J. K., & Chi, D. S. (2001). Physiological and psychological correlates of forgiveness. *Journal of Psychology and Christianity, 20,* 250–259.

Snyder, C. R., & Pulvers, K. M. (2001). Dr. Seuss, the coping machine, and "Oh, the places you'll go." In C. R. Snyder (Ed.), *Coping with stress. Effective people and processes* (pp. 3–29). Oxford: Oxford University Press.

Tennen, H., Affleck, G., Armeli, S., & Carney, M. A. (2000). A daily process approach to coping: Linking theory, research, and practice. *American Psychologist, 55,* 626–636.

Thoresen, C. E., Harris, A. H., & Luskin, F. (2000). Forgiveness and health: An unanswered question. In M. E. McCullough, K. I. Pargament,

& C. E. Thoresen (Eds.), *Forgiveness: Theory, research, and practice* (pp. 254–280). New York: Guilford Press.

Tracy, S. R. (1999). Sexual abuse and forgiveness. *Journal of Psychology and Theology, 27,* 219–229.

Vrba, R. (1964). *Escape from Auschwitz: I cannot forgive.* New York: Grove Press.

Webb, J. R. (2003). Spiritual factors and adjustment in medical rehabilitation: Understanding forgiveness as a means of coping. *Journal of Applied Rehabilitation Counseling, 34,* 16–24.

Witvliet, C. V. O., Ludwig, T. E., & Vander Laan, K. L. (2001). Granting forgiveness or harboring grudges: Implications for emotion, physiology, and health. *Psychological Science, 12,* 117–123.

Worthington, E. L., Jr., Mazzeo, S. E., & Canter, D. E. (2005). Forgiveness-promoting approach: Helping clients REACH forgiveness through using a longer model that teaches reconciliation. In L. Sperry & E. P. Shafranske (Eds.), *Spirituality oriented psychotherapy* (pp. 235–257). Washington, DC: American Psychological Association.

Worthington, E. L., Jr., & Scherer, M. (2004). Forgiveness is an emotion-focused coping strategy that can reduce health risks and promote health resilience: Theory, review, and hypotheses. *Psychology and Health, 19,* 385–405.

Worthington, E. L., Jr., & Wade, N. G. (1999). The psychology of unforgiveness and forgiveness and implications for clinical practice. *Journal of Social and Clinical Psychology, 18,* 385–418.

Ysseldyk, R. L., Matheson, K., & Anisman, H. (2006, June). *Dispositions toward forgiveness and revenge in relation to stress appraisals, coping styles, and psychological well-being.* Paper presented at the annual meeting of the Canadian Psychological Association, Calgary, Alberta, Canada.

Ysseldyk, R. L., Sudom, K., Skomorovsky, A., Matheson, K., & Anisman, H. (2005, January). *The roles of forgiveness and coping in relation to depressive affect among women in abusive dating relationships.* Poster presented at the annual meeting of the Society for Personality and Social Psychology, New Orleans, LA.

Zechmeister, J. S., & Romero, C. (2002). Victim and offender accounts of interpersonal conflict: Autobiographical narratives of forgiveness and unforgiveness. *Journal of Personality and Social Psychology, 82,* 675–686.

9

Potential Dangers of Empathy and Related Conundrums

KATHRYN BELICKI, JESSICA ROURKE, AND MEGAN MCCARTHY

Introduction

This chapter arises from an uneasiness prompted by the often uncritical optimism regarding forgiveness. In the literature, there is a tendency to depict forgiveness as unqualifiedly beneficial: good for physical health, for emotional well-being, for promoting world peace. It is even touted for its benefits to business as a human resource strategy (Kurzynski, 1998). Although individual writers often appreciate the complexities associated with forgiveness, the overarching impression from the literature is glowingly positive.

Concerns *have* been raised, but in response it has been countered that these do not apply to "true" forgiveness; forgiveness properly understood. For example, a typical, well-respected definition of forgiveness is, "a willingness to abandon one's right to resentment, negative judgment, and indifferent behavior toward one who unjustly injured us, while fostering the undeserved qualities of compassion, generosity, and even love toward him or her" (Enright, Freedman, & Rique, 1998, pp. 46–47). As noted in the first chapter of this book, other authors give somewhat different definitions. Nonetheless, despite their differences, many pin forgiveness down to a specific definition that can then be distinguished from other experiences. They use this narrower definition of forgiveness to counter criticisms that the beneficial qualities of forgiveness are offset by liabilities. For example, to the argument that forgiveness undermines justice (e.g., Murphy, 2002), it is sometimes countered that forgiveness is not excusing or condoning or justifying or pardoning (Enright & the

Human Development Study Group, 1991). As such, in the case of a criminal act, a person can forgive, but still allow the legal system to proceed. To the argument that forgiveness is potentially dangerous, placing the injured at risk of being victimized again (e.g., Murphy, 2005), it is countered that it is reconciliation rather than forgiveness that is risky (e.g., Enright & Eastin, 1992).

However, as we shall see, when these counterarguments are examined more closely, they are not as strong as at first they might appear. Moreover, even if they were unquestionably sound, the "true" forgiveness that is espoused lacks some of the power and potential of those riskier forms of forgiveness that are intimately tied to reconciliation or associated with a willingness to entertain excuses. Given this, "true" forgiveness *can* become just another technique for feeling better (although that is *not* the intention of the authors cited earlier), one that can leave the offender completely out of the picture. This is not to demean the value of any technique that contributes to healing, but it seems to us that there is so much more that forgiveness can accomplish if we are willing to grapple with some deeply troubling conundrums.

The Relation of Empathy to Forgiveness

While not every author takes an unambiguously positive view of forgiveness (e.g., Lamb & Murphy, 2002), many of the researchers studying forgiveness *do* assume that it is generally a desirable response to injury. While it is often argued on practical grounds, for example, that people who forgive have better well-being than those who do not (e.g., Freedman & Enright 1996; Karremans, Van Lange, Ouwerkerk, & Kluwer, 2003; McCullough, 2000), it is also argued on moral grounds (e.g., Enright & the Human Development Study Group, 1991). Indeed, within the new "positive psychology" literature, forgiveness is sometimes listed as a character strength (e.g., Peterson, Park & Seligman, 2006). Given these arguments, studies have examined the factors predicting forgiveness.

Empathy is one of the most consistent predictors of forgiveness. Both "state empathy" (empathizing with a specific offender) and "trait empathy" (the dispositional ability to empathize) have been found to be related to increased forgiveness across a wide range of offenses

(Brown, 2003; Coleman & Byrd, 2003; Konstam, Chernoff, & Deveney, 2001; Macaskill, Maltby, & Day, 2002; McCullough et al., 1998; McCullough, Worthington, & Rachal, 1997; Paleari, Regalia, & Fincham, 2005; Wade & Worthington, 2003). In the research conducted by the Brock Forgiveness Research Group, we too have found that empathy correlates with forgiveness of even very horrific injuries. For example, we observed that empathy for the 9/11 terrorists was correlated with forgiveness (Stewart Atkinson, Belicki, & DeCourville, 2003). In addition, in experiments in which we asked participants to imagine themselves as victims in various scenarios, we found empathy to be related to increased forgiveness following having been infected with HIV (Williams, DeMunck, Belicki, & DeCourville, 2005), having had a partner killed by a drunk driver (Williams et al.), domestic violence (DeMunck, Williams, & Belicki, 2004), and sexual infidelity (McCarthy, DeCourville, & Belicki, 2005).

The Benefits of Empathy

Taking a closer look at empathy, there is evidence that it can be argued to be a beneficial quality quite independent of its relation to forgiveness. However, we must differentiate among several concepts, all of which have been called empathy. To begin, we must distinguish between a cognitive process of perspective-taking and several emotional processes (e.g., Davis, 1983). Perspective-taking essentially refers to understanding another person's point of view (Davis). Empathy can also refer to various emotional processes, and here we can distinguish three responses (e.g., Eisenberg et al., 1991). First, a person may experience vicarious emotion, feeling the emotion that the other person feels. Second, a person may also feel concern and compassion for a distressed person, an experience that has been called empathic concern, sympathy, or other-oriented concern. Third, the person may feel a more self-oriented distress such as anxiety in response to the other, an experience that is commonly called personal distress (e.g., Batson, 1998).

Empathic concern and personal distress have different underlying motivations and therefore result in different behaviors. For example, those who experience empathic concern are more likely to act altruistically to relieve another's pain even when they can avoid the situation (Batson, 1998; Eisenberg et al., 1994; Karniol, Gabay, Ochion, & Harari, 1988). In contrast, those experiencing personal distress typically try to escape the situation and may even react aggressively (Eisenberg et al.). If they act altruistically, it is usually because they cannot escape the situation and therefore act helpfully in order to reduce their own distress (Eisenberg, 2002).

How do these four forms of empathy inter-relate? Perspective-taking is understood to have the potential to facilitate vicarious emotion and empathic concern, though neither necessarily (Eisenberg et al., 1994). Vicarious emotion, in turn, is thought to potentially increase either empathic concern or personal distress (Eisenberg et al.). While more research is needed, the evidence would suggest that empathic concern and personal distress operate in opposing directions. For instance, there is evidence that when people are feeling empathic concern their heart rate drops, but when they are feeling personal distress it increases (Eisenberg et al., 1989, 1991). Moreover, there is some developmental evidence that families who encourage the expression of emotion (particularly the softer emotions, like sadness, as opposed to aggressive emotions) and who teach ways to manage emotion, have children who are more likely to respond with empathic concern and less likely to respond with personal distress (Eisenberg et al., 1988; Eisenberg, 2002). In fact, there is some evidence that empathic concern is associated with social competence in children, while personal distress is associated with poorer social skills (Eisenberg et al., 1994; Siu & Shek, 2005).

In terms of forgiveness, very few studies have examined perspective-taking, empathic concern, and personal distress separately. Instead, most studies have focused on emotional forms of empathy and have found a relation to increased forgiveness and reduced vengefulness (see Mullet, Neto, & Rivière, 2005, for a review). Brown (2003) studied both perspective-taking and empathic concern (but not personal distress) and found perspective-taking to be related to forgiveness. In contrast to other studies, he did not find empathic concern to be related; however, he was studying dispositional forgiveness. Konstam et al. (2001) found both perspective-taking and empathic concern to be correlated with state forgiveness (they also examined personal distress and found no relation to forgiveness). Similarly, we found empathic concern and perspective-taking, but not personal distress, to be associated with higher levels of forgiveness in imagined scenarios of grievous harm (DeMunck et al., 2004; Williams et al., 2005). Therefore, as with other studies of empathy, the preliminary evidence is that personal distress and empathic concern pull in different directions. Given that the preferred response of people experiencing personal distress is to escape the situation, forgiveness becomes neither necessary nor desirable if the offender can be avoided. Future research could examine the possibility that those inclined to experience personal distress in a context that encourages empathy with someone who has hurt them would, in the first instance, try to avoid that person (and not be forgiving); however, if avoidance is not possible they may be more likely to express forgiveness to the offender.

In short, not only forgiveness, but also certain forms of empathy—specifically, perspective-taking and empathic concern—are potentially beneficial on both practical and moral grounds. Therefore, it might seem that we should whole heartedly embrace programs that facilitate forgiveness through the nurturance of these forms of empathy. However, a closer consideration of some of the consequences of perspective-taking and empathic concern raises some troubling conundrums.

Perspective-Taking Facilitates Processes That May Undermine Justice

Let us begin with perspective-taking—the ability to understand the other person's point of view. As already noted, there is evidence that this facilitates empathic concern and is positively related to forgiveness. It has also been successfully employed in programs to facilitate forgiveness (e.g., Enright, 2001; Freedman, 2000; McCullough et al., 1997). However, the argument has been made that perspective-taking in the wrong context can be highly inappropriate. Of great relevance to our consideration is that this "wrong context" is exactly one in which talk of forgiveness would be found—that is, following the kinds of grievous wrongdoings that evoke the descriptor "evil."

To illustrate this, consider the outrage that accompanied Ron Rosenbaum's (1999) book, *Explaining Hitler.* At the center of the controversy was the original cover for the book, which sparked a moral outcry. It was described as an obscenity and several countries banned publication until the cover was changed. What could be so profoundly upsetting as to merit, in some minds, complete censorship? A rather touching picture of Hitler as a baby.

Claude Lanzmann, a film-maker who made an epic 9.5-hour documentary on the Holocaust, has been particularly vitriolic about these baby photos, even before one was published on the cover of this book. To quote Rosenbaum (1999):

> A Hitler whose baby faced innocence lures us down the path Lanzmann condemns, seduces us into constructing explanations for the evolution of innocent child into mass murderer—explanations that are, Lanzmann argues, inevitably obscene rationalizations … virtually justifications for Hitler's behavior. … To embark upon the attempt to understand Hitler, understand all the processes that transformed this innocent babe into a mass murderer, is to risk making his crimes "understandable" and thus, Lanzmann implies, to acknowledge the forbidden possibility of having to forgive Hitler. (pp. xvi–xvii)

There is much that could be unpacked from this quote, but let us look more closely at the assumption that understanding leads to justifications that inevitably carry us to forgiveness, even of something that a person might—perhaps ought to—consider unforgivable. Rosenbaum (1999) tells us Lanzmann is not alone; other more moderately voiced scholars are also concerned that understanding leads to justification and thereby forgiveness. When Rosenbaum uses the term "justification," he appears to intend what in the forgiveness literature is typically called excusing. Excusing involves minimizing the injurer's responsibility for an act that was clearly wrong: "The devil—or my childhood, or my unfortunate biochemistry, or current social pressures—made me do it." (In contrast, justification is often taken to mean that in the light of the circumstances surrounding the act, the injurer in fact did no wrong. For example, an injury might be justified if the injurer unambiguously provoked it. See Neu, 2002, for a discussion of this difference.)

What evidence exists for this concern that understanding leads to excusing and from there to forgiveness? Let us begin with the fundamental attribution error. This is a principle now accepted virtually as fact that we tend to view others' actions as being caused by their character, and our own actions as being caused by circumstances. You blew up the other day because you are an angry person; I blew up because I was under tremendous stress. In short, I hold you responsible for your misdeeds, but I make excuses for my own. This phenomenon accounts for the fact that when people first hear about a particularly serious wrongdoing, they invariably assume that the act reflects the character of the injurer (e.g., Miller, Gordon, & Buddie, 1999). However, of more relevance to our discussion is that the wrongdoer is inclined to attribute his or her offense to mitigating circumstances. This raises the real possibility that empathy, particularly perspective-taking, could increase the risk of accepting the excuses of the offender even when that is not fully appropriate.

We know that people are more likely to forgive when an offender apologizes (e.g., Armour & Umbreit, 2005). Furthermore, there is also evidence from McCullough and his colleagues (1997) that empathy mediates the relation between apology and forgiveness. Therefore, an apology makes individuals more likely to empathize with an offender and that, in turn, leads to forgiveness. How is this finding related to our concern that empathy may lead us to accept the excuses of wrongdoers?

One of the variables we have examined in three of our studies is "excuses apologies" in which offenders admit that they are the cause of the offense but, essentially, argue that they are not responsible because the behavior was caused by factors outside their control (DeMunck et al., 2004; McCarthy et al., 2005; Williams et al., 2005). We have contrasted such apologies with "fuller" apologies in which the offenders not only admitted they were the cause but took full responsibility and took steps to make amends or to guarantee that they would change.

What is alarming is that excuses apologies work—in some cases not as well as full apologies, but in some cases just as well. This makes sense: If empathy is the key that makes apologies evoke forgiveness, an excuses apology would facilitate empathy, particularly perspective-taking, because such apologies involve offering a perspective, an explanation. What about when there is no apology? McCarthy et al. (2005) have found that dispositional empathy is related to forgiveness when there is no apology. Here, we have a situation where an offender is not apologizing, so there is every reason to think she or he might re-offend, but people high on empathy are more likely to forgive, anyway.

Perhaps one of the best demonstrations of the potential dangers associated with empathy comes from a study by Seligman and Veenvliet (2003). They presented participants with a scenario in which a man beat his wife into unconsciousness because she had burned the supper. Half were told that he had been abused as a child; half were told nothing. Those who were told about the childhood history were more likely to think that the man had done this before and would do it again—but they were still more likely than the people who were told nothing to feel that the wife should forgive him. So, presumably, empathy led to more forgiveness despite a greater perceived risk of victimization occurring again.

Let us step back and look at the big picture. Many researchers will say that forgiveness is not making excuses. On the other hand, they tend to see forgiveness as beneficial and therefore empathy as helpful because it facilitates forgiveness. However, it seems likely that one of the ways empathy facilitates forgiveness is through making—or accepting—excuses for the offender's behavior. If so, we cannot have it both ways: uncritically praising empathy while criticizing excusing. We should note that Veenstra (1992) has explicitly stated that some forgiveness arises from making excuses for the offender. Veenstra's answer is that we must distinguish between explaining and excusing. Explaining need not result in excusing, Veenstra says (cf. Neu, 2002)—but we would bet that, in practice, it often does.

Before moving on to another potential problem that arises from perspective-taking, let us complicate matters a little further. We have noted that many researchers view excusing as problematic, and we will admit that this tends to represent our own view. However, in the spirit of the first chapter in this book, we note that this is not a universal perspective. For example, Damascene (2002) made an impassioned argument for the necessity of excusing in forgiveness and that such excusing is consistent with Christian morality. He describes the case of a Russian monk, Elder Sampson, who spent 20 years in Communist concentration camps and who forgave those who tortured him. Damascene quotes him as saying, "It is impossible to forgive and not excuse … The heart is made this way … It excuses, it does everything possible to justify and excuse.… That is a Christian quality!" (pp. 287–288). Therefore, we cannot discard excusing as a "false" form of or path to forgiveness without at least stating our grounds for such a dismissal.

Moreover, even outside of any religious system, there may be occasional merits to excusing that deserve further study. While offering an excuse may well be self-serving, it may simultaneously serve the needs of the injured. When we give a full apology for some hurtful act that was intentional, we declare unambiguously that there was at least a moment in which we viewed the person we hurt as unworthy of compassionate, respectful treatment. In contrast, an excuse conveys that we never stopped thinking well of the person we hurt; instead, our behavior was caused by other factors. If the injured is willing to believe us, this is a less hurtful message. Furthermore, when injurers offer excuses for their behavior, they are confirming that their action was wrong and/or hurtful. They are also affirming the value of the moral principle that was violated by their action, and they imply that they continue to embrace that principle as governing their behavior (see Gonzales, Manning, & Haugen, 1992, for a similar argument). Therefore, providing an excuse may be, on occasion, the kindest and most reassuring way for an offender to proceed.

Empathy and, more specifically, perspective-taking may have another troubling effect. Specifically, it is argued that forgiveness does not involve minimizing or denying the injurious impact of an offense (e.g., Enright & the Human Development Study Group, 1991). However, perspective-taking may well encourage a tendency to minimize the hurtful impact, something that is clearly on the minds of Holocaust scholars who have misgivings about the enterprise of explaining Hitler. The first author of this chapter is reminded of a bemused student who once commented, after a discussion of "evil" from a social psychological perspective, "If I take this seriously, it's as if nothing is really bad." This student is not alone in this thinking.

When we turn to psychological literature, we see validation for the concern that understanding may affect the evaluation of the grievousness of a wrongdoing. In his 1997 book on evil, Roy Baumeister describes what he calls the magnitude gap. For victims, the emotional impact of the event is much larger than it is for the perpetrator. While the victim can inherit lasting and deep pain, the perpetrator tends to get only small and fleeting pleasure. Even in robbery, as he points out, the victim loses the full value of the object while the thief, in hocking it, receives only a small portion of its worth. Therefore, the injury is a "smaller," less serious event when viewed through the perpetrator's eyes.

From here, Baumeister (1997) makes a noteworthy assumption that the two perspectives are incompatible. To understand one person's experience, whether victim or offender, necessarily requires jettisoning the other's, as illustrated in the following quote:

> The main goal of this book is psychological understanding, not moral analysis. It will be necessary for me to tune out the overwhelmingly powerful victim's perspective to understand the perpetrator's, and it will be necessary for you, the reader, as well. (p. 20)

At the end of his book, Baumeister notes that endeavors, such as this, to understand perpetrators *do* facilitate forgiving and that there is a risk thereby of losing moral perspective and judgment.

Others have found evidence for Baumeister's concern. For example, Miller et al. (1999) conducted a series of studies examining whether explanations for cruelty resulted in increased "condonation." By condonation, they meant a shift in the direction of greater forgiveness and, in general, a more positive attitude toward an offender. In one study, participants were asked to read scenarios involving serious doing of harm and then half were asked to generate, on their own, a possible explanation for the behavior. Those who gave explanations for the behavior were more condoning of the offender than those who did not. In subsequent studies, Miller et al. examined the effect of reading a social psychological explanation of cruelty. Participants who were exposed to such explanations perceived the social psychologists as being more condoning than participants who read an explanation that stressed the character of the offender. Of particular interest is that in one of the two studies, participants continued to be harsh in their personal evaluation and hence seemed personally unaffected by the social psychological explanation; however, in the other they were more condoning.

Certainly there is evidence that exposure to social psychological explanations can affect judgment. Colman (1991) observed that in the South African courts where, at the time of his writing, death sentences were mandatory for murder except when there were extenuating circumstances, social psychological explanations were accepted as providing evidence of extenuating factors. For example, he cites one case in which the death sentence of five defendants for the murder of a young woman was commuted to 20 months' imprisonment on the basis of arguments drawing on such social psychological principles as conformity, deindividuation, and group polarization.

Therefore, perspective-taking may affect not only how we attribute responsibility for an act, but also our evaluation of the severity of the wrongdoing. It is for good reason that some Holocaust scholars, such as Lanzmann, have such serious misgivings about perspective-taking in the context of particularly horrific acts. However, it is not just perspective-taking, but also empathic concern—the emotional side of empathy—that poses conundrums for forgiveness.

Empathic Concern and Justice

Much of what we have discussed so far concerning perspective-taking would also apply to empathic concern. However, there are unique aspects of empathic concern that might undermine some of the treasured notions of "true forgiveness." As noted previously, empathic concern is associated with decreased heart rate while personal distress is associated with heart rate increase. Most assume that this difference reflects the direction of attention, or orientation, when we are feeling empathic concern versus when we are feeling personal distress (e.g., Eisenberg et al., 1991). Specifically, heart rate goes down when people are focused outside themselves and collecting information about another. As such, decreased heart rate is part of an orienting response.

In contrast, when we are oriented inward—that is, when we are attentive to our own needs and our own safety—heart rate increases. The significance of this for our current discussion is that when we are immersed in one of these processes (orienting out or orienting in), we are, by definition, disconnected from the other process. In other words, there is a certain incompatibility between these two orientations.

Consistent with this, we have already seen how personal distress and empathic concern seem to pull us, psychologically, in differing directions. This distinction in direction of orientation brings to mind Alice Miller's contention that we cannot simultaneously attend to the needs of another and to our own pain. This assumption undergirds her arguments that we should not try to understand those who hurt us.

Alice Miller is a former psychoanalyst who subsequently became an outspoken critic of psychoanalysis. She stands passionately against trying to understand perpetrators of violence, including psychological abuse, and against the pursuit of forgiveness. However, her opposition arises from a concern that is different from those already discussed. Her concern is that understanding and forgiveness distract victims from remembering and appreciating their own pain. She argues that this distraction perpetuates violence and thus has negative consequences—not just for the individual but also for society.

In brief, Alice Miller's theory (1997) is that atrocities arise in the following way: When infants and children are exposed to traumatic experiences, these evoke rage, grief, terror, helplessness, and humiliation. In order to survive emotionally, these powerful emotions are repressed. This is adaptive in the young child, but in the adult results in a person who still has reservoirs of these emotions that if not faced and processed, put the individual at risk to hurt others. This risk arises, in part, because hurting others relieves some of that emotion (e.g., allows the expression of rage, counteracts feelings of helplessness) and because the offender does not remember how it feels to be hurt in this way. She contends that if individuals can undo their repression, they will stop hurting others because, for one thing, no one who remembers how it feels to be hurt would deliberately hurt someone in the same way.

In her thinking, empathy and forgiveness both work against this remembering of pain. She describes both understanding and forgiveness as trying to keep the repression of childhood intact. Consider the following quote in a passage where Miller (1997) begins by citing an imaginary client questioning forgiveness:

> So why should I go on trying to understand and forgive my parents and whatever happened to them in their childhood, with things like

> psychoanalysis and transactional analysis? What's the use? Whom does it help? It doesn't help my parents to see the truth. But it does prevent me from experiencing my feelings, the feelings that would give me access to the truth. But under the bell-jar of forgiveness, feelings cannot and may not blossom freely. Such reflections are, unfortunately, not common in therapeutic circles, in which forgiveness is the ultimate law. The only compromise that is made consists of differentiating between false and correct forms of forgiveness. (p. 135)

"False and correct forms of forgiveness"—does *that* not sound familiar! Whatever one thinks of her theory about the origins of violence, at the heart of her argument is the apprehension that focusing on the concerns of the offender distracts injured people from their own feelings.

One does not have to not agree with Miller's theory; in fact, the opposite argument has been made: that it is the absence of empathic concern for others that leads to violence (e.g., Eisenberg, 2002). However, her basic observation about the incompatibility of what we might call empathic concern and experiencing one's own feelings seems valid. Turning to more moderate, palatable voices, McCullough et al. (1997) have, in fact, suggested that the efficacy of empathy comes from giving a certain perceptual salience to the offender's needs that reduces the salience of the hurtful event, making forgiveness possible. Therefore, we see again the idea that emotionally appreciating the position of the offender somehow reduces our capacity to appreciate our own pain although that was not the point that McCullough et al. intended to make.

Therefore, while, generally speaking, it would appear that empathic concern is a much more desirable response than personal distress—and morally more desirable than complete apathy and disinterest in the face of pain—there may well be contexts where a more self-oriented response is desirable, at least for a time. Wanda Malcolm's chapter on the timeliness of forgiveness talks about such contexts. In addition, those advocating forgiveness as an intervention often make the case that it is important to become aware of the emotional depth of one's injury before contemplating forgiveness (e.g., Enright, 2001; Freedman, this volume).

However, even caveats about addressing emotional injury before forgiving do not eliminate the conundrum. For Alice Miller, there is no appropriate time to forgive, particularly grievous wrongs. Others articulate entirely opposite perspectives: that the time to forgive is as fast as one is capable (e.g., Damascene, 2002) and that one should not wait for feelings of forgiveness before making a deliberate decision to forgive and enacting that as best as one can (e.g., DiBlasio, 1998).

In short, we need much more thought and debate on when one "ought" to look inward versus when one "ought" to look outward in compassion for the other. More fundamentally, we must identify the philosophical and theoretical grounds for such recommendations. The statement of assumptions is all too infrequent in the forgiveness literature. This is not specific to the topic of forgiveness, but a more general problem with the current practice of psychological writing. This general omission has presumably evolved because, in many research areas, there are consensually shared assumptions that, because they have been widely adopted, are no longer stated and therefore have become implicit, if not unconscious. However, there is no such consensus within the study of forgiveness. Writers bring widely varying assumptions and world views; therefore, it becomes particularly important to identify the grounds associated with any position they take on complex issues such as how to balance compassion with inward attention.

Turning to another issue, empathic concern is related to altruism even when one can easily avoid the other person (for review, see Eisenberg, 2002). In other words, when people experience empathic concern, they want to help the person even when they have no personal need to do so. This may have an unintended negative outcome that is, perhaps, best illustrated by an example. It is the observation of the first author in her prior research on childhood abuse that often the most effective and active people fighting abuse are survivors who are still hurting. In contrast, those who are no longer in distress often lack the passion and energy to do the hard work of activism. Furthermore, individuals who are compassionately focused on the concerns of an offender may be less likely to spend their time getting visibly angry about abuse in public forums. In other words, empathic concern may carry a person in quite a different direction than righteous anger would.

In addition, the fact that empathic concern prompts helping behavior brings us to another conundrum: the possibility that empathy and forgiveness increase the risk of being victimized again.

Empathy, Forgiveness, and Reconciliation

We may be tempted to say that it is reconciliation that is risky, not forgiveness, but the thought that forgiveness can be cleanly separated from reconciliation (as many have argued; see first chapter for review) does not represent most people's views. Collectivist cultures are very inclined to see forgiveness as involving, or even being synonymous with, reconciliation (see Sandage & Wiens, 2001, for a fascinating differentiation between collectivist and individualistic cultures in their approaches to forgiveness). For example, in Bishop Tutu's (1999) book about the South African process following the dismantling of apartheid, he uses the words *forgiveness* and *reconciliation* quite interchangeably. Even in this individualistic culture, Kanz (2000) and we (Belicki, DeCourville, Michalica, Stewart Atkinson, & Williams, 2003) have found that the vast majority of people think that if you forgive, you will likely reconcile. In our sample, in response to the question, "Is reconciliation a necessary part of forgiveness?" 86.3% said maybe or yes (and 50% said yes). This tendency to blur forgiveness and reconciliation is not just observed in questionnaire responses. Gordon, Burton, and Porter (2004) have shown that forgiveness was the strongest predictor of an intention to return to an abusive partner in women living in a domestic violence shelter.

Furthermore, the belief that forgiveness and reconciliation go together appears to be rather difficult to change. For example, Hui and Ho (2004) conducted an educational, school-based program with adolescents to increase forgiveness. One of the tenets of their program was that forgiveness should be differentiated from reconciliation. While they had some success in changing students' opinions, after the program a full 73.7% of students still indicated that reconciliation was part of forgiving. Therefore, we have to accept the reality that if empathy facilitates forgiveness, empathy *will* make reconciliation more likely, and that is risky business. However, this very characteristic of forgiveness—that, for many, it is linked to reconciliation—underscores the social benefits of forgiveness. Relying too much on the distinction between forgiveness and reconciliation to manage risk for injustice and re-victimization can downplay the rich benefits that can accrue from a more relational understanding of forgiveness (for a discussion of the benefits of a relational view of forgiveness, see Shults & Sandage, 2003).

However, in addition to any indirect link between empathy and reconciliation through forgiveness, there are characteristics of empathy that independent of forgiveness, may make reconciliation more likely. Specifically, as noted briefly earlier, empathic concern is related to altruism. Therefore, individuals experiencing empathic concern may be more likely to act in kindly ways toward those who have hurt them. In fact, in one of our studies, in which we asked participants to imagine scenarios of becoming infected with HIV or losing a partner in a car accident caused by a drunk driver, we observed that empathic concern was positively related to reaching out to the offender in compassionate ways (Williams et al., 2005).

Therefore, we again come up against a conundrum. Many want to argue that we must distinguish between forgiveness and reconciliation. Some of those same researchers and clinicians have argued for encouraging the development of empathy in order to facilitate forgiveness. However, even as we try to loosen the ties between reconciliation and forgiveness, in actual practice, empathy may tighten those ties.

The Attempt to "Domesticate" Forgiveness Through Restrictive Definitions

It would be easy for a reader to assume, from this chapter, that we join the slim ranks of those who argue against the promotion of forgiveness. In fact, we do not. We hold a decidedly positive view of forgiveness on pragmatic, moral, and, in the case of the first author, theological grounds. We view forgiveness as holding immense potential for personal and societal change; however, we also see it as complicated, difficult, and potentially risky. Others have attempted to reduce the potential liabilities of forgiveness, such as the possibility of undermining justice or increasing the risk of re-victimization, by carefully defining forgiveness in such a way as to surgically excise those meanings that increase the likelihood of a negative outcome.

We have argued that there are several problems with such an approach. First, we have shown that empathy, which many view as desirable (and, for some, because it facilitates forgiveness), increases the likelihood that people will excuse and reconcile as part of the process of forgiving. Second, even if, in the safe confines of research or under the careful supervision of a therapist, we are able to separate empathy and forgiveness from excusing and reconciling, most of humanity will blunder through the forgiveness process without the benefit of such a protective environment. Many of them will make excuses for and reconcile with the offender as part of their process of forgiving. That is the reality we have to face when discussing forgiveness.

Third, we have seen that there may be value to excusing that has not been fully appreciated. In addition, reconciliation in appropriate contexts has merit in its own right. It is tales of heroic reconciliation as a result of forgiveness that catch our attention, thrill our hearts, and make newspaper headlines—not accounts of someone coming to peace through a personal, inner experience of forgiveness that includes never seeing or speaking to the offender again. The latter may well be adaptive, admirable, and even inspirational, particularly when the offense is grievous, but it is not in the same order as parents embracing the murderer of their daughter (e.g., Godfrey, 2007).

Rather than attempt to domesticate forgiveness by tidily trimming out of the definition all the embarrassing and unsafe meanings that can attach to it, we think that we would do better to take seriously and respect these tendencies, for example, to "confuse" forgiveness with excusing and reconciling. More generally, we believe that we should dispense with language of "true" forgiveness and instead document the range of differing experiences that are called forgiveness and study each of these in its own right.

References

Armour, M. P., & Umbreit, M. S. (2005). The paradox of forgiveness in restorative justice. In E. L. Worthington, Jr. (Ed.), *Handbook of forgiveness* (pp. 33–40). New York: Routledge.

Batson, C. D. (1998). Altruism and prosocial behavior. In D. T. Gilbert, S. T. Fiske, & G. Lindzey (Eds.), *The handbook of social psychology* (Vol. 2, pp. 282–316). Boston: McGraw–Hill.

Baumeister, R. F. (1997). *Evil: Inside human violence and cruelty*. New York: Henry Holt and Company.

Belicki, K., DeCourville, N., Michalica, K., Stewart Atkinson, T., & Williams, C. (2003, June). *What does it mean to forgive?* Paper presented at the annual meeting of the Canadian Psychological Association, Hamilton, Ontario, Canada.

Brown, R. P. (2003). Measuring individual differences in the tendency to forgive: Construct validity and links with depression. *Personality and Social Psychology Bulletin, 29,* 759–771.

Coleman, P. K., & Byrd, C. P. (2003). Interpersonal correlates of peer victimization among young adolescents. *Journal of Youth and Adolescence, 32,* 301–314.

Colman, A. M. (1991). Crowd psychology of South African murder trials. *American Psychologist, 46,* 1071–1079.

Damascene, H. (2002). Resentment and forgiveness. *Orthodox Word, 38,* 279–303.

Davis, M. H. (1983). Measuring individual differences in empathy: Evidence for a multidimensional approach. *Journal of Personality and Social Psychology, 44,* 113–126.

DeMunck, K., Williams, C., & Belicki, K. (2004, June). *The influence of empathy on forgiveness across time and apology style.* Paper presented at the annual meeting of the Canadian Psychological Association, St. John's, Newfoundland, Canada.

DiBlasio, F. A. (1998). The use of a decision-based forgiveness intervention within intergenerational family therapy. *Journal of Family Therapy, 20,* 77–94.

Eisenberg, N. (2002). Empathy-related emotional responses, altruism, and their socialization. In R. J. Davidson & A. Harrington (Eds.), *Visions of compassion: Western scientists and Tibetan Buddhists examine human nature* (pp. 131–164). Oxford: Oxford University Press.

Eisenberg, N., Fabes, R. A., Miller, P. A., Fultz, J., Shell, R., Mathy, R. M., et al. (1989). Relation of sympathy and personal distress to prosocial behavior: A multimethod study. *Journal of Personality and Social Psychology, 57,* 55–66.

Eisenberg, N., Fabes, R. A., Murphy, B., Karbon, M., Maszk, P., Smith, M., et al. (1994). The relations of emotionality and regulation to dispositional and situational empathy-related responding. *Journal of Personality and Social Psychology, 66,* 776–797.

Eisenberg, N., Fabes, R. A., Schaller, M., Miller, P., Carlo, G., Poulin, R., et al. (1991). Personality and socialization correlates of vicarious emotional responding. *Journal of Personality and Social Psychology, 61,* 459–470.

Eisenberg, N., Schaller, M., Fabes, R. A., Bustamante, D., Mathy, R. M., Shell, R., et al. (1988). Differentiation of personal distress and sympathy in children and adults. *Developmental Psychology, 24,* 766–775.

Enright, R. D. (2001). *Forgiveness is a choice: A step-by-step process for resolving anger and restoring hope.* Washington, DC: American Psychological Association.

Enright, R. D., & Eastin, D. L. (1992). Interpersonal forgiveness within the helping professions: An attempt to resolve differences of opinion. *Counseling & Values, 36,* 84–103.

Enright, R. D., Freedman, S., & Rique, J. (1998). The psychology of interpersonal forgiveness. In R. D. Enright & J. North (Eds.), *Exploring forgiveness* (pp. 46–62). Madison: University of Wisconsin Press.

Enright, R. D., & the Human Development Study Group. (1991). The moral development of forgiveness. In W. M. Kurtines & J. L. Gewirtz (Eds.), *Handbook of moral behavior and development* (Vol. 1, pp. 123–152). Hillsdale, NJ: Lawrence Erlbaum Associates.

Freedman, S. R. (2000). Creating an expanded view: How therapists can help their clients forgive. *Journal of Family Psychotherapy, 11,* 87–92.

Freedman, S. R., & Enright, R. D. (1996). Forgiveness as an intervention goal with incest survivors. *Journal of Consulting and Clinical Psychology, 64,* 983–992.

Godfrey, R. (2007, January). Murder and mercy. *Chatelaine,* 69–78.

Gonzales, M. H., Manning, D. J., & Haugen, J. A. (1992). Explaining our sins: Factors influencing offender accounts and anticipated victim responses. *Journal of Personality and Social Psychology, 62,* 958–971.

Gordon, K. C., Burton, S., & Porter, L. (2004). Predicting the intentions of women in domestic shelters to return to partners: Does forgiveness play a role? *Journal of Family Psychology, 18,* 331–338.

Hui, E. K. P., & Ho, D. K. Y. (2004). Forgiveness in the context of developmental guidance: Implementation and evaluation. *British Journal of Guidance & Counseling, 32,* 477–492.

Kanz, J. E. (2000). How do people conceptualize and use forgiveness? The Forgiveness Attitudes Questionnaire. *Counseling & Values, 44,* 174–188.

Karniol, R., Gabay, R., Ochion, Y. & Harari, Y. (1988). Is gender or gender-role orientation a better predictor of empathy in adolescence? *Sex Roles, 39,* 45–59.

Karremans, J. C., Van Lange, P. A. M., Ouwerkerk, J. W., & Kluwer, E. S. (2003). When forgiving enhances psychological well-being: The role of interpersonal commitment. *Journal of Personality and Social Psychology, 84,* 1011–1026.

Konstam, V., Chernoff, M., & Deveney, S. (2001). Toward forgiveness: The role of shame, guilt, anger, and empathy. *Counseling & Values, 46,* 26–39.

Kurzynski, M. J. (1998). The virtue of forgiveness as a human resource strategy. *Journal of Business Ethics, 17,* 77–85.

Lamb, S., & Murphy, J. G. (Eds.). (2002). *Before forgiving: Cautionary views of forgiveness in psychotherapy.* New York: Oxford University Press.

Macaskill, A., Maltby, J., & Day, L. (2002). Forgiveness of self and others and emotional empathy. *The Journal of Social Psychology, 142,* 663–665.

McCarthy, M., DeCourville, N., & Belicki, K. (2005, June). *Factors affecting the role of apology in forgiveness*. Paper presented at the annual meeting of the Canadian Psychological Association, Montreal, Quebec, Canada.

McCullough, M. E. (2000). Forgiveness as human strength: Theory, measurement, and links to well-being. *Journal of Social and Clinical Psychology, 19,* 43–55.

McCullough, M. E., Rachal, K. C., Sandage, S. J., Worthington, E. L., Jr., Brown, S. W., & Hight, T. L. (1998). Interpersonal forgiving in close relationships: II. Theoretical elaboration and measurement. *Journal of Personality and Social Psychology, 75,* 1586–1603.

McCullough, M. E., Worthington, E. L., Jr., & Rachal, K. C. (1997). Interpersonal forgiving in close relationships. *Journal of Personality and Social Psychology, 73,* 321–336.

Miller, A. (1997). *Breaking down the wall of silence.* New York: Meridien.

Miller, A. G., Gordon, A. K., & Buddie, A. M. (1999). Accounting for evil and cruelty: Is to explain or to condone? *Personality and Social Psychology Review, 3,* 254–268.

Mullet, E., Neto, F., & Rivière, S. (2005). Personality and its effects on resentment, revenge, forgiveness, and self-forgiveness. In E. L. Worthington, Jr. (Ed.), *Handbook of forgiveness* (pp. 159–181). New York: Routledge.

Murphy, J. G. (2002). Forgiveness in counseling: A philosophical perspective. In S. Lamb & J. G. Murphy (Eds.), *Before forgiving: Cautionary views of forgiveness in psychotherapy* (pp. 41–53). New York: Oxford University Press.

Murphy, J. G. (2005). Forgiveness, self respect, and the value of resentment. In E. L. Worthington, Jr. (Ed.), *Handbook of Forgiveness* (pp. 33–40). New York: Routledge.

Neu, J. (2002). To understand all is to forgive all—or is it? In S. Lamb & J. G. Murphy (Eds.), *Before forgiving: Cautionary views of forgiveness in psychotherapy* (pp. 17–38). New York: Oxford University Press.

Paleari, F. G., Regalia, C., & Fincham, F. (2005). Marital quality, forgiveness, empathy, and rumination: A longitudinal analysis. *Personality and Social Psychology Bulletin, 31,* 368–378.

Peterson, C., Park, N., & Seligman, M. E. P. (2006). Greater strengths of character and recovery from illness. *The Journal of Positive Psychology, 1,* 17–26.

Rosenbaum, R. (1999). *Explaining Hitler: The search for the origins of his evil.* New York: HarperPerennial.

Sandage, S. J., & Wiens, T. W. (2001). Contextualizing models of humility and forgiveness: A reply to Gassin. *Journal of Psychology and Theology, 29,* 201–211.

Seligman, C., & Veenvliet, S. G. (2003). *Perceiving evil.* Paper presented at the meeting of the Society for Personality and Social Psychology, Los Angeles, CA.

Shults, F. L., & Sandage, S. J. (2003). *The faces of forgiveness: Searching for wholeness and salvation.* Grand Rapids, MI: Baker Academic.

Siu, A. M. H., & Shek, D. T. L. (2005). Relations between social problem solving and indicators of interpersonal and family well-being among Chinese adolescents in Hong Kong. *Social Indicators Research, 71,* 517–539.

Stewart Atkinson, T., Belicki, K., & DeCourville, N. (2003, June). *The relation of empathy to forgiveness in the context of September 11th.* Paper presented at the annual meeting of the Canadian Psychological Association, Hamilton, Ontario, Canada.

Tutu, D. M. (1999). *No future without forgiveness.* New York: Doubleday.

Veenstra, G. (1992). Psychological concepts of forgiveness. *Journal of Psychology and Christianity, 11,* 160–169.

Wade, N. G., & Worthington Jr., E. L. (2003). Overcoming interpersonal offenses: Is forgiveness the only way to deal with unforgiveness? *Journal of Counseling & Development, 81,* 343–353.

Williams, C. V., DeMunck, K., Belicki, K., & DeCourville, N. (2005, June). *The role of empathy and apology in the forgiveness of friends vs. strangers.* Paper presented at the annual meeting of the Canadian Psychological Association, Montreal, Quebec, Canada.

10

Reflections of a Study on Forgiveness in Recovery From/Resilience to the Trauma of War

NANCY A. PEDDLE

Introduction

Who Does Us What?

Who does us what?
We're all keyed into one system.
Tied necks only and hung on greed's rod
Our hands suddenly grab the ropes at base, but to no avail;
Suddenly, our once sturdy feet snap loose, dangling helplessly….
No one seems to hear our yelp for help,
Our castrated spirits plead from sunup to sundown.
Yet, all there's to it is catcall-filled laughter,
"Let them burn in Hell. … Forever, forever, forever!"
Us, who yesterday were are, today about not to be.
Our glory becoming gory, our fame flaming into the abyss. …
"away with them, away with them!"
and the last words we hear on our way out;
Who does us what? Who cares our demise?
Who?

©2001 IkpoBari Dumletam Senewo (a refugee of war)

Out of the hell of Mr. Senewo's experiences comes the beauty of his poems. His story of hell was one of over 95 I listened to during my research. His willingness to transform his pain and to reach for beauty awed me as did his hope to forgive one day. The 95 refugees interviewed for this study are part of the 9.2 million refugees and 25 million people displaced by war in their own countries, as of 2006, as documented by the United Nations High Commission for Refugees (UNHCR). Their stories illuminate the UNHCR's findings that extreme acts of violence have reached a new level of cruelty and that no one is safe from atrocity during war. For example, sexual violence—sometimes involving the systematic rape of women and girls—is a weapon of war used by all the fighting forces (Truth & Reconciliation Commission, 2004). In the wars of the 21st century, civilians are targets, victims, forced perpetrators, and expendable persons (Reyes & Jacobs, 2006; Truth & Reconciliation Commission, 2004). As violence to civilians continues to escalate worldwide, especially against children and women, finding new ways of healing is imperative. Previous attempts to promote healing in individuals and countries have not sufficiently stopped enemies from going to war again with each other or their descendents. One way forward may be to address the trauma caused by the conflict and introduce forgiveness to prevent future suffering so that people can build peaceful relationships with former enemies (Borris & Diehl, 1998; Sider, 2001; *UN Chronicle,* 1996).

There is some common ground between trauma recovery and forgiveness, as has been discussed in the literature since the early 1990s. Although still only a handful of studies combine trauma recovery and forgiveness, these have significantly increased in the past 5 years. These range from studies of interpersonal to international conflict, and they link forgiveness with elements of trauma recovery. In so doing, they improve our understanding of how one might alleviate individual and societal suffering. For example, these investigations have studied such outcomes as reduced anger (Coyle & Enright, 1997; Peddle, 2001; Schumm, 1995; van Biema, 1999); reduced likelihood of posttraumatic stress disorder (Noll, 2005; Sider, 2001; Witvliet, Phipps, Feldman, & Beckham, 2004); reduced incidence of violent, vengeful responses to perceived transgressions (Holbrook, White, & Hutt, 1995; McCullough & Worthington, 1995); and escape from an endless cycle of violence (Borris, 2006; Finnegan, 2005; McLaughlin & Davidson, 1994; Minow, 1998; Staub, Pearlman, Gubin, & Hagengimana, 2005).

Moreover, there has been a call for more studies on forgiveness among those who have experienced ethnic conflicts or who are survivors of war (Noll; Worthington, 1998a).

While support for the incorporation of forgiveness into discussions of trauma recovery is growing, there is debate among researchers regarding the role of forgiveness, if any, in trauma recovery (Herman, 1992; Minow, 1998; Richards, 1988), how forgiveness should be defined (Glasse, 2005; Yandell, 1998), and when it should be used (Pargament, McCullough, & Thoresen, 2000). Borris (2006) notes the paradox intrinsic to forgiveness: that it seems to be a form of betrayal to survivors, yet may be necessary for full psychosocial health and may reduce factors that fuel conflicts (Borris; Van Gorp, 2000).

These questions and parallels between forgiveness and trauma recovery suggest the relevance of one to the other as well as a necessary research direction. They also indicate the need for forgiveness and trauma researchers to collaborate—the next step in accelerating the finding of tenable solutions to healing after traumatic experiences (Peddle, 2001; Worthington, 2004).

My desire to see new ways of healing comes from my lived experience of Sierra Leone's May 25th Bloody Coup where children were given AK 47s and told to "get revenge." The research on which this chapter is based was, in part, a way for me to understand my own experience and give witness to the pain, resilience, and recovery of survivors, as well as the forgiveness granted by those who experienced what some would consider "unforgivable" experiences. It was also, in part, my intense reaction to a new political strategy calling for forgiveness after atrocities of ethnic cleansing and violence in the absence of empirical data backing such a strategy. I felt literally called to investigate the quantitative as well as qualitative relationship between trauma recovery and forgiveness. The following is a brief overview of my study's conceptual model, as well as a summary of quantitative and qualitative findings that examine the role of forgiveness in relation to refugees' trauma recovery/resilience. In this study, it is not possible to separate recovery from resilience because retrospective measurement cannot differentiate between them. Therefore, hereafter, the word *recovery* is used to signify both recovery and resilience. This research provided some of the first data on the overlap between forgiveness and war trauma recovery. If you read beyond the numbers, the reward will be the data that reflect the deep and meaningful stories.

Forgiveness and Trauma Recovery

As noted previously, there is common ground between forgiveness and trauma recovery. At the core of both is a perceived traumatic event, injury, or betrayal from which a person recovers or forgives a blameworthy transgressor or injurer. Both trauma recovery and forgiveness have links to lessened anxiety, hopelessness, depression, and low self-esteem. Literatures from both fields describe process models that have conceptual similarities. For example, as described in more detail later, both use the technique of telling one's story. Both describe processes that take time, although forgiveness can transcend such a time-consuming process, as in Wilson's story of immediately forgiving those who caused his daughter's death by bombing, in Northern Ireland (Bolton, 1999) and, more recently, the heroic forgiveness of the Amish community in response to the school shootings there (http://www.npr.org/templates/story/story.php?storyId=6225726).

By their nature, forgiveness and trauma healing require the establishment of security and trust. In the case of refugees, resettlement can provide some safety from the immediate conflict. Once safely resettled, refugees' work toward trauma recovery can begin. Remembering and peeling away the layers of the traumatic experience that may be repressed or forgotten (Herman, 1992; Raundalen, Dyregrov, Steylen, Kleve, & Lunde, 1987)—that is, "telling one's story in truth" (Herman) or "uncovering" the truth (Enright & the Human Development Study Group, 1991)—is described as an important step for both trauma recovery (e.g., Herman) and forgiveness (Enright & the Human Development Study Group). Truth telling is also a core concept guiding the work of truth and reconciliation commissions (Truth & Reconciliation Commission, 2004). This step may help survivors of atrocity gain a sense of forgiveness and tolerance (DeMartino & von Buchwald, 1996) and, some suggest, help foster peacemaking (Borris, 2006; Enright, Gassin, Longinovic, & Loudon, 1994; Flanigan, 1998).

This base led to my development of a conceptual model that combined forgiveness and trauma recovery, and embedded it in an ecological framework (Figure 10.1). It integrates and builds on forgiveness

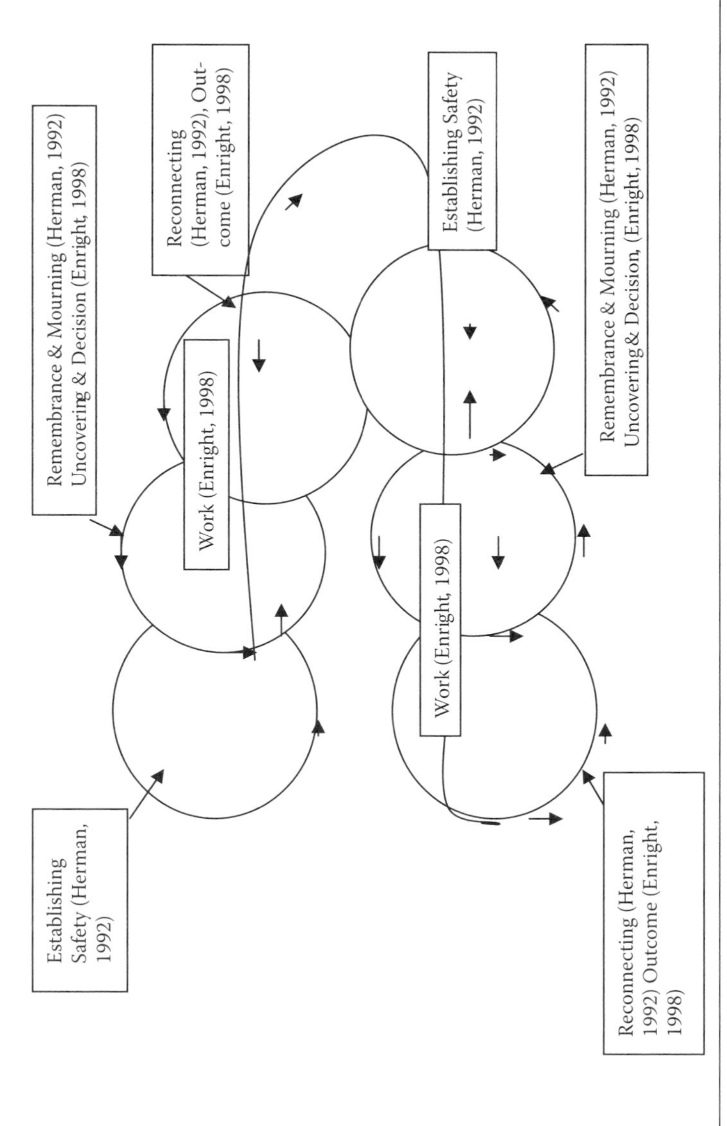

Figure 10.1 Combined trauma and recovery (r/r) and forgiveness conceptual model.

models (Enright & Coyle, 1998; McCullough & Worthington, 1995; Schumm, 1995; Worthington, 1998b) and trauma recovery theory (Dubrow & Garbarino, 1989; Herman, 1992; Pynoos & Nader, 1988; van der Kolk & Greenberg, 1987). Specifically, two conceptual models formed the new model: Enright and the Human Development Study Group's (1991) forgiveness process model and Herman's (1992) trauma and recovery stage model. The Enright forgiveness process model has 20 elements organized into four phases: *uncovering, decision, work,* and *deepening* that incorporate cognition, behavior, and affect. Herman's trauma and recovery stage model has three interrelated elements: *establishment of safety, remembrance and mourning,* and *reconnection.* Telling one's story in truth is common to both Enright's *uncovering* and *work* phases and Herman's *remembrance and mourning* stage.

The integrated model incorporates all the elements of the two models into one that does not require a specific linear sequence and can be unique to each person's healing process. It uses a spiral diagram, in which a person can revisit "earlier" stages at a higher level of integration, double back to certain stages in an effort to move ahead, or simply leap over a stage, as is seen also in Sider's (2001) model of trauma recovery. This combined model enriches and strengthens each of the fields and has the flexibility to integrate other successful healing approaches such as cognitive behavior therapy and energy psychology, have been shown to be helpful in shifting emotional response patterns.

Overview of Study on Forgiveness in Recovery/Resilience From the Trauma of War Among a Selected Group of Adolescent and Adult Refugees

In this study (Peddle, 2001), the process of finding refugees for the research was plagued by barriers from confidentiality laws and trust issues. However, this study had an angel, a social worker from Kosovo who worked at a relief agency. She wanted the atrocities documented, so she went the extra mile to help recruit many of the 95 refugees in and around Chicago, Illinois, for the study. In addition, after completing the study, a number of participants referred other refugees because they found participation to be personally helpful. The final convenience sample included 83 participants (12 of the original 95 did not provide a full set of usable data) whose ages ranged from 13 through 85 years, with 22% under the age of 18. The majority were women (59%). Most (71%) came from the former Yugoslavia; 24% came from Africa and 5% came from Europe. Participants self-identified either as a member of a family (75%), who were interviewed together, or as an individual. Only 25% spoke English. The non-English speakers designated another family member, some less than 13 years of age, to interpret or translate. All identified a religious affiliation (73% Muslim, 27% Christian) and saw faith or religion as playing a role in their war experiences.

Finally, despite having experienced a range of brutal war atrocities, participants were all able to identify a specific transgressor or blameworthy injurer when completing the forgiveness measure. Noll (2005) has noted that the inability to identify a specific, noteworthy injurer can be an obstacle for research with war-affected populations. For instance, one participant who was on the death list at Auschwitz identified a guard named Schultz as his transgressor, a man who inflicted absurd cruelty on those already living a nightmare. In reference to their specific transgressor, the majority (72%) rated themselves on a one-item forgiveness question as not at all forgiving the injurer, while 22% rated themselves as being in the process of forgiving him or her. Only 6% of the participants had completely forgiven the person who injured them.

There were two phases to the study. Inclusion in the first phase required participants to have been refugees, to be 13 years or older, and to have experienced war atrocities. Participation in the second phase required speaking English and having experienced war less than 16 years prior to the study. For the first phase, participants were randomly assigned to two groups: One completed an interview first and one completed a survey first. All were paid $10 and given resource information on trauma from the Red Cross. For the second phase, nine refugees were selected from the 83 participants on the basis of their recovery and forgiveness scores and completed a phone questionnaire from 1 to 3 weeks after the first phase.

The *Multidimensional Trauma Recovery and Resiliency Assessment Manual* (MTRR; Harvey, Westen, Lebowitz, Sunders, & Harney,

1998) was used to assess trauma recovery/resilience. The administration of the MTRR begins with an interview in which the participant tells his or her story. The researcher then rates the participant on 99 items that assess the following areas of psychological functioning that are affected by traumatic exposure: authority over memory, integration of memory and affect, affect tolerance, symptom mastery and positive coping, self-esteem, self-cohesion, and safe attachment. Because members of families chose to be interviewed together, modifications were made to the MTRR (Peddle, 2007).

The Enright forgiveness inventory (Enright & the Human Development Study Group, 1991)—introduced to participants as the "Attitude Scale"—was used to assess forgiveness. It is a self-report measure assessing forgiveness across affective, behavioral, and cognitive subscales and includes a stand-alone forgiveness question, "To what extent have you forgiven the person you rated on the Attitude Scale?" In the second phase, a six item, open-ended questionnaire designed for this study explored a qualitative understanding of forgiveness.

Selected Results

In general, the results revealed that the number of years since the experience of war was associated with better trauma recovery and forgiveness. They also showed that refugees' ages were positively correlated with forgiveness, but there was no relation of age to recovery.

Participants tended to have high MTRR ratings on recovery and low EFI forgiveness scores. Higher forgiveness was associated with better recovery, with significant relations being found between all forgiveness subscales and all domains of the MTRR, but forgiveness was not necessary for recovery. Many refugees had high recovery but low forgiveness scores. However, everyone with high forgiveness scores had high recovery scores. For those 18 years and under, there was a clear difference from the rest of the sample: Forgiveness was lower than average and recovery was higher.

In the second phase, two issues were examined through structured interview by telephone: (1) how war-exposed refugees viewed the person or persons who injured them, and (2) their understanding of forgiveness after the experience of war. The nine participants in the second phase had an average age of 22 years (range 13–41). The majority ($n = 5$) were 18 or under, three were 19 to 39, and one was 41. Most ($n = 8$) had experienced war in the prior 5 years. Participants came from Kosovo ($n = 5$), Bosnia ($n = 2$), Sierra Leone ($n = 1$), and Nigeria ($n = 1$). Most were Muslims ($n = 7$) and women ($n = 6$). Two of these participants had originally self-identified as "individual" and seven identified as "members of a family," with none from the same family.

All participants self-rated their experience as "deep hurt" during the traumatic event of war, as typified by the following partial account from one participant's story:

> March 22. Seeing people crying, running just like animals. Seeing people shot for nothing. We couldn't do anything about it. [We] couldn't help anybody. With what could you help? All the kids were crying. The old people couldn't walk. Three days later it was our time … While we were eating breakfast, someone knocked on the door then broke the door and came in. We were shaking like we were so cold. I remember their faces. My little brother didn't know anything. He said, "I'm not finished, I want to eat." They took him and stopped him eating. One said, "You better get out of here or I'll kill your son." While we were walking, we had to jump over dead bodies, smell the smell of blood. It was really hard to get to our car. Tried to get to Macedonia. We had to drive on landmines. We weren't sure of anything. The human is stronger than anything. I wanted to be dead. I was crying so much but my eyes were still strong, stronger than ever.

Qualitative analysis of the interviews identified five major categories of content: faith, possibility to forgive the unforgivable, struggle to make meaning, view of the injurer, and process of forgiveness. Each of these categories had theme elements for a total of 24 theme elements, all of which had been apparent in the MTRR interviews. However, due to space limitations, the following discussion will focus mainly on the major content categories.

Faith

Faith, along with the related theme elements of religion, spirituality, God, and prayer, was described by many refugees as being key to making it through the experience of war and moving toward forgiveness. Most narratives held stories of God's protection, miracles, and acts of kindness. I was a witness to one such narrative that occurred on a bitter December night during a family MTRR session. It was a particularly emotional recounting of the family forced to leave a father (husband) and uncle (brother) in a concentration camp, where they vanished. AP, 7 years old at the time, continued with her story:

> It was June '92, my mother wanted to get water for us [three children, 11, 7, and 4] because we were thirsty and we didn't drink anything the whole day. We were all in the cattle car on the train. Some people had died. Soldiers made mothers throw their children in the river. It was when we, the Bosnians, were in the hands of the Serbs. They didn't let my mother get any water, and they wanted to kill her. They pointed a gun on her head. The train started moving and she wasn't back yet. [I was] scared she might not come back. Scared to lose both my mother and father.

AP started crying and said, "I miss my dad. Most girls my age have dads." AzraP, her sister, then told her story and said at the end, "Faith helped us. When I wished for something I had it. God gave us what I needed. I didn't miss anything." We were almost finished with everyone's story when a sparrow flew into the room through the kitchen window, startling everyone. The mother, one of the few being treated for PTSD, remained calm as everyone else went flying out of the room. She tenderly picked up the bird and let it back out the window. Everyone returned and burst into laughter. We laughed so hard it was difficult to catch our breaths. When AzraP finally regained her voice she said, "It's like the Spirit [or God] is here. Who could believe we could be so sad and then a bird could come and we could laugh so hard."

Miracles described by the 83 participants in the MTRR interviews included a Serbian border police guard easing a family with no documentation across an impenetrable border; a wave at a stop sign by a Serbian police officer to continue when everyone else was being stopped, searched, beaten, and separated from their cars; a bracelet and ring on a woman's hand sticking as a Serb soldier demanded the jewelry, then mysteriously falling off just as the soldier started to reach for the hand to cut it off; and a prisoner on a camp death list meeting a fellow prisoner and former friend who secretly removed the red death mark beside his name.

Participants who were Christian were more apt to say they were Christian and to quote the Bible or Jesus's teachings of forgiveness. They shared their belief in their religious teachings of forgiveness even if, they said, they could not yet forgive. Two Christian participants quoted the same Bible verse, "vengeance is mine," saying that only God had this power of vengeance. Others expressed the need for God's help to forgive: "The only way I could forgive them is only inside [me] with God's help." For many, praying to God or a higher power helped make recovery possible. "I'm praying to God every night. I pray to forget everything that happened to me, to take it out of my mind and to make my parents happy," said one participant. The spirituality of a number of participants was evidenced as they explained the need to forgive "because good people must do that ... because they're not perfect" and because "we are all human beings with hearts."

Possibility to Forgive the Unforgivable

This theme category included a range of ideas, including forgiving being impossible, the impact of the violation of trust, the impossibility of adequate restitution or compensation, the importance of creating harmony, the role of love, and the need for God's help, which links back to the faith category. The possibility of forgiving the unforgivable is specific to these refugees' experiences of ethnic cleansing, rape, beatings, torture with burning oil, witnessing the killing of relatives and friends, fleeing from burning homes, and other atrocities of war.

Only those under 18 said that it just was not possible to forgive. After additional questions during the interviews, however, a number of young people changed their minds and added that maybe God could help them with forgiveness. Furthermore, most participants felt that there was the possibility to forgive in the future. Nessa, a 16-year-old Muslim, was one who did not change her mind. She felt not only that she could not forgive, but also that she would like to take revenge on those who hurt her and on those she saw hurting others:

> How can I forgive or forget them for the things they did. Kill for no reason. It's just a child. Unfair to kill kids and pregnant women. They had no heart to do that. I would never forget. Wish to see what God would do, what would happen to them in another life. They were laughing when we were crying. I would like to laugh at them. I would do the same to them.

SHB, a 15-year-old Muslim participant, was another who felt she could not forgive. She said:

> I can't forgive them because how they did to my parents. No jobs, no money. And how they killed people and hurt my family and killed many young people and some of my friends and cousin. No, I can never forgive them. Even if they built my house. What about my friends and family? They should think before [acting].

Trust was an issue and it had two sub-elements: (a) Had the injurer changed? (b) Would he or she tell the truth? Participants were more willing to forgive if the injurer met one or both elements. If the injurer had not changed and thus could not be trusted, participants questioned whether they could forgive. The breaking of trust is at the heart of betrayal. AP, a 15-year-old Muslim female from Bosnia, said it succinctly after telling the story of her father's best friend, a guard at one of the Serbian concentration camps. The guard turned his back on her family when they asked for news on her father's whereabouts. "I couldn't live with them anymore," she said. "I wouldn't want to live with them. One day they are your friends. The next, they are your enemies."

Not only did participants feel they could not trust their former friends and neighbors because the same friends and neighbors had been involved in the killings, but they also said they could not regain trust or forgive because of insurmountable obstacles to restitution or compensation. In the aftermath of the killings, it was seen as impossible to make restitution or to compensate those who had lost their lives: "They cannot bring someone back to life."

Even with these obstacles, most participants talked about the possibility of forgiving. Some felt that forgiveness was an expectation of their religion; therefore, they were choosing to work on forgiveness. ES, a Christian, explained why it was important to forgive from a religious standpoint, but also how difficult it was:

> The Bible says we should. So does the Lord's Prayer. If God forgives, we should be forgiving our fellow humans. It's hard because I'm human. Sometimes you forgive and then an event happens [that reminds you of the original event] and it feels like it's happening all over and forgiveness is hard. I know I will, but it will take time.

A few participants expressed harmony or peace as reasons to forgive, even as they struggled with these beliefs with those who had committed the atrocities. AP said, "Peace is most important, I ask God for peace." Yet, she did not think that forgiveness was necessary for peace. Areben, a Muslim from Kosovo, said that "pure hearts, human things. ... We must forgive. Good people, normal people do that." Most called on God to make possible forgiveness. Tony, a 13-year-old, expressed this well: "I can't forgive them forever. [There is] nothing they could do to make me forgive. [Prompt: Is there anything?] If God helped me to do good [forgive]."

Struggle to Make Meaning

Participants struggled to make meaning even as they took part in the interview. Some thought they had come to a resolution, as Areben said, "I'm done with it. I have my own kid, my own life. Back home is in pieces. Now I'm trying to find a way to have a living and happiness with my family." But his struggle did not end here. When asked why the injurer acted in the way he did, Areben answered with a number of themes, including victims becoming victimizers, and the role of the lack of consequences for violence. He struggled to answer the "why" question:

> I thought a lot about [why] but I could never find an answer. They were under pressure ... under someone else. I don't know. Someone living next to you. Then they had freedom. They were like gods and they could do whatever they wanted without responsibility to anyone or without consequences.

AP also struggled with the "why" question and expressed the theme of the oppressed becoming the oppressor: "I thought but never came to a good conclusion. There must be a good reason. Maybe … someone did something to them and they wanted to pay back." Similarly, MBC, a Christian participant, stated, "People might have gone through torture and don't have any more care for humans … vindictive." SHB's response reflected a related, but slightly different, idea that a victim can become a victimizer: "[They] might have done it for their family. If you don't do it, I will hurt your family, or you won't work, or have food, or maybe you'll end up in jail. So they had to."

MB, a 17-year-old Muslim, had multiple themes in her response. These included themes of the importance of cultural history and the lack of consequences:

> I think their parents told them never trust Albanian people. Told them the history of Yugoslavia. "We stole their country, but if they disagree kill them." 'cause he was trying to kill us to get the country, houses, cars, everything. "If I'm going to lose everything let them die." [They had] nothing to lose.

Nessa also suggested that history played a role in what happened to them, specifically because of their nationality. She said, "From the day we were born, we know they are against us because … their parents taught them how to be from the beginning … because we were Albanians."

The struggle with making meaning and answering the "why" question may never be finished, but as many said, they are moving on. They are trying to live the life they now have and be comfortable with their options and their process of recovery.

View of the Injurer

The strongest element in this theme category was morality, and for the younger participants this was characterized as good or bad. The good/bad thinking led to comments of punishment, revenge, and justice; for many respondents, these went hand in hand. During the 83 MTRR interviews, I heard such comments as, "They should be brought to justice and pay a penalty for what they have done," "I believe in love, but they need to be punished first," and more extremely, "I couldn't help it, I felt like killing both the Serbs and the Macedonians for what they were doing to the children." AP's thoughts reflected both the good/bad thinking and that of revenge acted out by God. "I think if God paid … or if they have a good life or if they are having bad times, too. After all, they did if they have a good life or bad. I think maybe a bad life."

Tony's thoughts included, "I think they are bad. They do to old people like that. I think God is going to hurt them or their family." For RE, a 22-year-old, morality is the principle by which one lives: "You know what is good and what is bad." He said, "I don't like any person doing wrong to themselves or others when they know it's bad … what he did was wrong."

Revenge was a theme expressed in forceful terms by a few. Only one person used the word "revenge," but most of the participants mentioned that they hoped the injurer or injurers were not doing well or that God might play a role in payback (as seen in AP's and Tony's earlier responses). Nessa also did not think that the injurers would be happy "because of the God." MB expressed her thoughts on this with a trace of anger in her voice, "Too bad because [now] they're going to apologize because we won. They got kicked out … They don't have houses now. They don't have nothing at all." The responses of those over 18 years did not carry anger. For this age group, justice was more important than revenge, as illustrated in MBC's interview: "They might have regretted what they did. See what they have done to people, like maimed them. People are calling on them for what they have done. They can't be happy."

The last theme, anger, was like the word "revenge" in that, while only a few said the word "angry," many participants' manner of speaking conveyed their anger toward the injurer. AP, when talking about filling out the forms, said, "Oh God I hate them so much. Well, I don't like them. I don't like to hate them." Because of the values she held, AP was working on reducing her anger toward the injurer. MBC was changing her mind as well as she worked on forgiveness and let go of her anger:

> I was bitterly against them. I decided to change my mind. Coming to America has changed my mind. They are open … God is blessing America 'cause it gives to its citizens. If God can bring me to America, I can forgive.

Process of Forgiveness

Themes related to the process of forgiveness came up throughout the interviews as the respondents reflected on what they were saying or on their experience of the actual study. Making an actual decision to forgive or not to forgive was heard many times. For some of those ages 18 and under their decision was not to forgive, now or ever. In contrast, for MBC, the decision to forgive came as a clear fork in the road:

> I was filling out that form [EFI] and at first I was bitter and angry, but when I got to that last question I thought of the Christian principle to forgive and I decided that if I could ask God for forgiveness and he could give it to me, then I could forgive them. That's the way I marked it [the one-item forgiveness question—*complete forgiveness*].

For another, it was something to decide about in the future when he was ready: "Maybe one day I'll decide. When they come for a cup of coffee." MTRR statements supported the idea of forgiveness as a decision—for example: "Maybe one day I'll make up my mind to forgive, but for now, no" and

> I know when Jesus was on the cross he said, "I forgive them for they know not what they do." But these people do. How can I decide to forgive when they may do it again? This is difficult to think about with my faith. I may decide something different later.

An internal/external theme emerged that was related to the process many participants went through in deciding to forgive. For almost all of them, it was an internal process. RE captured this element:

> We don't care about material things. You can't turn back the life of all those innocent people. It's very hard when you're thinking inside yourself. You're always thinking about it inside yourself, but [you] can't trust it won't happen again.

The importance of the passage of time was pervasive. For most participants, their physical health had improved in the year(s) since the traumatic event; they were having fewer or no more nightmares or intrusive thoughts, headaches and other bodily aches and pains had decreased, and they were beginning to trust again and form friendships. Participants were able now to think about the possibility of forgiving, something they said they could not have done right after the event. One person described time as a change agent, "I'm much more committed to a spiritual nature in these 16 years since the war, more commitment to common good now." ES said, "I know I will [forgive], but it will take time." Others said they prayed daily for recovery and forgiveness.

Finally, all participants were asked about the study process and their experience of telling their story. Although the majority expressed the sadness they felt in retelling their story ("I was emotional at times"), they also "felt some release." RE likened telling the story to a Coke: "The fizzes come out and it lets a little pressure out. The healing deal." Most MTRR interviews ended with a thank-you for having someone to tell their story to, one who could understand and document their experiences.

Discussion

Results showed that, for these refugees, forgiveness was related to recovery, although (as discussed in more detail later) it was possible to show strong recovery in the absence of forgiveness. In addition, age, number of years since the beginning of war, and religion were also important predictors of both forgiveness and recovery. These findings are consistent with literature that suggests that both forgiveness and trauma recovery are developmental, wherein those under 18 are shown to be more recovered (Dubrow, Liwski, Palacios, & Gardinier, 1996; McCallin, 1991; Pynoos, 1994), but less forgiving (Enright, Santos, & Al-Mabuk, 1989; Mullet & Girard, 2000).

The overall MTRR ratings were on the high side, consistent with Radan's (1999, as cited in Harvey et al., 2003) ratings of South American women refugees in the Boston area. These refugees with severe traumatic exposure may be more resilient (possible protective factors being faith and family cohesiveness) or more recovered (possible factors being social support and the availability of resources in the United States) or less likely to use the language of psychopathology than trauma survivors in therapy (M. Harvey, personal communication, March 14, 2001). The high MTRR ratings of adolescents may also be linked to their parents' religious or spiritual beliefs, which is consistent with findings that Palestinian refugee children suffered less from the war situation when their mothers were religious (Mahjoub,

1991). While greater resilience may explain why these participants have higher MTRR ratings, research findings caution against taking resilience or recovery for invulnerability, as they are not constant qualities and can vary across time and circumstances (Kinzie, 2006; McCallin, 1991).

Refugees' forgiveness scores were on the low side, which may have been due to the severity of the trauma, the prior relationship between the person and the injurer, and the injurer's subsequent actions—all factors that affect the quality of forgiveness. Those who said they were forgiving were, as expected, high in recovery, and their stories were apt to link their recovery to forgiveness. However, many who rated high in recovery did not rate high in forgiveness, consistent with the findings of Subkoviak, Enright, and Wu (1992). This finding was especially strong in those who had been exposed to the traumatic events of war within 5 years or less of the MTRR interview. They had difficulty in expressing a positive view of the injurer and thus had difficulty forgiving. Expressing positive views is more difficult with many trauma survivors because time has not yet distanced them from the possibility of re-experiencing the event. Data and literature suggest that both forgiveness and trauma recovery/resiliency are developmental, take time, and can be ameliorated by religious belief.

Religion was pivotal to these participants in the way they experienced the trauma, their recovery, and their willingness and ability to forgive. Some examples include "I don't need to say I need to die because I'm a Muslim" and "I prayed not to be touched and I wasn't touched, thank God for help." Many believed that forgiveness is an expectation of their religion: "My religion says to forgive. [I'm] praying for forgiveness to be in my heart, asking God's help with it," which is consistent with other research (Enright & Fitzgibbons, 2000; Pargament, 1997). Most participants used faith, religion, or a belief in God to place their suffering in a larger context: "My faith is what got me through, the Bible is my strength" or afterward: "I prayed to not have nightmares and I didn't," giving evidence found in other research to the critical protective and coping function that religion plays during stressful experiences (McFarlane & van der Kolk, 1996; McFarlane & Yehuda, 1996; Pargament).

Faith was a link with hope for some: "I am in the hands of God, holding on to hope" and "Prayer gave me hope." Most participants conveyed a sense of relief and hope after telling their stories, consistent with literature on exposure to violence (Herman, 1992; Mollica, 1988; Weine, 1996). Theorists posit that organized religion is the most enduring institution for the ritual re-establishment of trust in the form of faith, and trust has been argued to be the source of hope (Erikson, 1963). This re-establishment of trust is the starting point for recovery and forgiveness while hope gives the ability to conceive a future.

The data from this study suggest that forgiveness is a personal choice in the decision to forgive and the ongoing willingness to forgive, supporting Enright and the Human Development Study Group's (1991) process model. While one participant decided to forgive in a moment—a phenomenon that is documented in the literature (Bolton, 1999), the majority of those who chose to forgive said that it was a practice they needed to live intentionally or even have help in doing. Choosing to practice forgiveness may be important to achieve forgiveness and may be part of the forgiveness process, as has been argued by others (Enright & Fitzgibbons, 2000; Friedman & Toussaint, 2006a; Ilibagiza & Erwin, 2006).

The data also suggest that people sometimes need a reason to choose to forgive, such as a belief in God, a religious teaching, or an authority requesting it. Authority figures or leaders such as Rev. Tutu in South Africa and President Kabbah in Sierra Leone have provided the impetus to forgive with positive results (Borris, 2006; Chapman, 2001; Truth & Reconciliation Commission, 2004; Williams, Zinner, & Ellis, 1999), although such leadership also carries grave risks, as seen with the assassination of President Anwar Sadat of Egypt. Furthermore, talk of forgiveness without concomitant healing of the core of the betrayal can leave a person simmering with anger, ready to erupt at the slightest provocation.

Conclusions, Recommendations, and Reflections

It is a thought-provoking and inspiring time as the fields of trauma recovery and forgiveness come together. It is time for a new paradigm, one that is emerging with researchers and practitioners crossing between metaphysical realms and traditional realms. Research is beginning to look at how energy work, miracles, and the role of concepts such as forgiveness and gratitude (Borris, 2006; Feinstein, 2006; Friedman & Toussaint, 2006a, 2006b) transform trauma. Validation of strategies for the restoration of the human spirit and maintenance of recovery are mounting.

However, as the concept of forgiveness as a healing intervention grows, with more research to back its efficacy, so too the expectation to forgive may grow, placing the burden of action on injured people. Indeed, expectations have already been placed on refugees—expectations that border on being policy—to reconcile and reintegrate soon after a conflict is over (Cousens, Jan, & Parker, 1996; Landgren, 1998). We must remember that studies have shown good reasons for which people might choose not to forgive or be reconciled, as former friends and neighbors may have been the injurers (Noll, 2005; Peddle, 2001) or the death of a loved one leaves the perception of an insurmountable obstacle to forgiveness (Peddle; Roth, 2006). Yet, these may be the very situations that need forgiveness in order to avoid condemning the injurer and the injured to an intractable conflict. Helping people see forgiveness as an experience inside one's body that affects one's emotional experience and does not rely on the injurer may be a strategy (Borris, 2006; Worthington, 2004). However, we must give people clear choice concerning the processes and activities around forgiveness and respect their reasons, feelings, or emotional experiences for not forgiving, or we may retraumatize the people we seek to help.

In terms of steps that can be taken, crisis, relief, and development agencies could allocate funds for psychosocial interventions with forgiveness components after a conflict. Peacekeeping forces, relief agencies, and psychosocial interventionists can assist these processes by understanding that their actions are not neutral. It is also important for them to know the issues and tensions among the processes of trauma recovery, forgiveness, reconciliation, and justice (Borris & Diehl, 1998; Keating & Knight, 2004). They must be aware of which interventions work and when, after traumatic events (Feinstein, 2006; Williams et al., 1999). For example, forgiveness interventions are more successful in the context of safety; as one refugee said, "Create a safe place for me and offer me hope of forgiveness." For instance, the Red Cross/Red Crescent is successfully applying forgiveness in the context of development projects to address deep-seated trust issues between communities divided by years of conflict (Patro, 2003). The Taylor Institute worked to increase forgiveness and reconciliation by training people in contact with children and families on how to incorporate forgiveness into their jobs, their community roles, and their daily interactions (Peddle, Monteiro, Guluma, & Macaulay, 1999)—work supported by other successful programs (Peddle, Stamm, Hudnall, & IV, 2006; Staub et al., 2005). At a national level, the replication of models such as South Africa's Truth and Reconciliation Commission could be fully funded within other conflict-ridden countries (Chapman, 2001). The Sierra Leone Truth and Reconciliation Commission was a prologue to this strategy, but it lacked sufficient resources to do its work adequately or to implement the recommendations (Truth & Reconciliation Commission, 2004).

Because the ability to forgive can begin at a young age, as seen in the similarities of family members' forgiveness scores, the use of forgiveness might be effective as a preventive strategy in school and at home. Teaching forgiveness can help with classroom management as it reduces anger (Enright & Fitzgibbons, 2000) and with supporting resilience in children. To this end, we might learn from families that teach forgiveness as a moral value, for the most part, rather than simply a skill. For instance, one man explained, "My father taught us to never forget, but that we should forgive," a moral teaching with which his own 12-year-old son was so familiar that he could mimic his father and complete the rest of the lesson: "It's what I want to pass on to my children." It may be that embedding forgiveness in moral values, when teaching young children, can increase the likelihood that these children will be more able to move toward forgiveness when they reach adolescence, a stage of development linked with a difficulty to forgive. Helping children to develop more complex thinking beyond the good/bad dichotomy that is common to children is supported by studies that have found that those who saw themselves and others as complex people were more likely to have a forgiving attitude (Borris, 2006; Gardner, 1987).

Furthermore, expanded dialogue on the common ground between trauma recovery and forgiveness should continue to be encouraged. Multidisciplinary, scholarly dialogue could bring synergy to the discourse, further advance our knowledge, and expedite recovery from the trauma of war. There is a great deal more to learn from scientific investigation of both these fields. We should not be afraid to include the cutting edge strategies that have been researched, such as the use of gratitude, cognitive behavior therapy, energy psychology, and other strategies that help create the emotional shift needed for recovery (Borris, 2006; Feinstein, 2006; Friedman & Toussaint, 2006a, 2006b).

I can testify to the miracles that occurred as part of the process of this research. Doors opened at exactly the right time despite the strength of the confidentiality laws. I experienced people being transformed through the telling of their stories and embracing forgiveness, and I was moved by the generosity of people sharing what little resources they had and sharing their indomitable spirits. I was witness to the bird flying into the room on an arctic December night and the stories of miracles. Miracles are possible even with stories coming from the depths of the darkness of pain (Borris, 2006; Feinstein, 2006; Friedman & Toussaint, 2006b; Ilibagiza & Erwin, 2006).

References

Bolton, D. (1999). The threat to belonging in Enniskillen: Reflections on the Remembrance Day bombing. In M. B. Williams (Ed.), *When a community weeps: Case studies in group survivorship* (pp. 191–211). Philadelphia, PA: Brunner/Mazel.

Borris, E. R. (2006). The healing power of forgiveness and the resolution of protracted conflicts. In G. Reyes & G. A. Jacobs (Vol. Eds.), *Handbook of international disaster psychology: Vol. 3. Refugee mental health* (pp. 85–100). Westport, CT: Praeger Publishers.

Borris, E. R., & Diehl, P. F. (1998). Forgiveness, reconciliation, and the contribution of international peacekeeping. In H. L. Langholtz (Ed.), *The psychology of peacekeeping* (pp. 207–222). Westport, CT: Praeger Publishing.

Chapman, A. (2001). Truth commissions as instruments of forgiveness and reconciliation. In R. L. Petersen (Ed.), *Forgiveness and reconciliation: Religion, public policy, and conflict transformation* (pp. 247–267). Philadelphia: Templeton Foundation Press.

Cousens, E., Jan, A., & Parker, A. (1996, July). *Healing the wounds: Refugees, reconstruction, and reconciliation.* Paper presented at the Healing the Wounds: Refugees, Reconstruction, and Reconciliation, Princeton University, Princeton, NJ.

Coyle, C. T., & Enright, R. D. (1997). Forgiveness intervention with post-abortion men. *Journal of Consulting and Clinical Psychology, 65,* 1042–1045.

DeMartino, R., & von Buchwald, U. (1996). Forced displacement: Non-governmental efforts in the psychosocial care of traumatized people. In L. Weisaith (Ed.), *International responses to traumatic stress* (pp. 193–218). Amityville, NY: Published for and on behalf of the United Nations by Baywood Publishing Company.

Dubrow, N., & Garbarino, J. (1989). Living in the war zone: Mothers and young children in public housing development. *Journal of Child Welfare, 68,* 3–20.

Dubrow, N., Liwski, N. I., Palacios, C., & Gardinier, M. (1996). Traumatized children: Helping child victims of violence. In L. Weisaith (Ed.), *International responses to traumatic stress* (pp. 327–346). Amityville, NY: Published for and on behalf of the United Nations by Baywood Publishing Company.

Enright, R. D., & Coyle, C. (1998). Researching the process model of forgiveness within psychological interventions. In E. L. Worthington, Jr. (Ed.), *Dimensions of forgiveness: Psychological research and theological perspectives*: *Vol. 1. Laws of the symposia series* (pp. 139–161). Philadelphia: Templeton Foundation Press.

Enright, R. D., & Fitzgibbons, R. P. (2000). *Helping clients forgive: An empirical guide for resolving anger and restoring hope.* Washington, DC: American Psychological Association.

Enright, R. D., Gassin, E. A., Longinovic, T. & Loudon, D. (1994). *Forgiveness as a solution to social crisis.* Paper presented at the Morality and Social Crisis, Institute for Educational Research conference, Beograd, Serbia.

Enright, R. D., & the Human Development Study Group. (1991). The moral development of forgiveness. In J. Gewirtz (Vol. Ed.), *Handbook of moral behavior and development: Vol. 1. Theory* (pp. 123–152). Hillsdale, NJ: Erlbaum.

Enright, R. D., Santos, M., & Al-Mabuk, R. (1989). The adolescent as forgiver. *Journal of Adolescence, 12,* 95–110.

Erikson, E. H. (1963). *Childhood and society* (2nd ed.). New York: W. W. Norton & Company.

Finnegan, A. C. (2005). *A memorable process in a forgotten war: Forgiveness within Northern Uganda.* Unpublished manuscript, Tufts University, Boston.

Flanigan, B. (1998). Forgivers and the unforgivable. In J. North (Ed.), *Exploring forgiveness* (pp. 95–105). Madison: University of Wisconsin Press.

Friedman, P., & Toussaint, L. (2006a). Changes in forgiveness, gratitude, stress, and well-being during psychotherapy: An integrative evidence-based approach. *International Journal of Healing and Caring, 6.* Retrieved March 28, 2007, from http://ijhc.org

Friedman, P., & Toussaint, L. (2006b). The relationship between forgiveness, gratitude, distress, and well-being: An integrative review of the literature. *International Journal of Healing and Caring, 6*. Retrieved March 28, 2007, from http://ijhc.org

Gardner, J. W. (1987). *The moral aspect of leadership*. Washington, DC: Independent Sector.

Glasse, J. (2005, May 14, 2005). *Trauma and forgiveness*. Dart Center for Journalism & Trauma. Retrieved August, 24, 2006, from http:// www.dartcenter.org/articles/headlines/2005/2005_05_14.html

Harvey, M. R., Liang, B., Harney, P. A., Koenen, K., Tummala-Narra, P., & Lebowitz, L. (2003). A multidimensional approach to the assessment of trauma impact, recovery and resiliency: Initial psychometric findings. *Journal of Aggression, Maltreatment, and Trauma, 6*, 87–109.

Harvey, M. R., Westen, D., Lebowitz, L., Sunders, E., & Harney, P. (1998). *Multidimensional trauma recovery and resiliency assessment manual*. Cambridge, MA: The Cambridge Hospital Victims of Violence Program.

Herman, J. (1992). *Trauma and recovery*. New York: BasicBooks.

Holbrook, M. I., White, M. H., & Hutt, M. J. (1995). The vengeance scale: Comparison of groups and an assessment of external validity. *Psychological Reports, 77*, 224–226.

Ilibagiza, I., & Erwin, S. (2006). *Left to tell: Discovering God amidst the Rwandan holocaust*. Carlsbad, CA: Hay House.

Keating, T., & Knight, A. (Eds.). (2004). *Building sustainable peace*. Edmonton, Alberta, Canada: University of Alberta Press.

Kinzie, J. D. (2006). Personal reflections on treating traumatized refugees. In G. A. Jacobs (Vol. Ed.), *Handbook of international disaster psychology: Vol. 3. Refugees' mental health* (pp. 101–114). Westport, CT: Praeger Publishers.

Landgren, K. (1998). *Reconciliation: Forgiveness in the time of repatriation*. U.S. Committee for Refugees. Retrieved March 28, 2007, from http://www.refugees.org/world/articles/repatriation_wrs98.htm

Mahjoub, A. (1991). The theory of stress as an approach to studying psychological responses in a war environment. In M. McCallin (Ed.), *The psychological well-being of refugee children: Research, practice and policy issues* (pp. 24–45). Geneva, Switzerland: International Catholic Child Bureau.

McCallin, M. (1991). The impact of current and traumatic stressors on the psychological well-being of refugee communities. In M. McCallin (Ed.), *The psychological well-being of refugee children: Research, practice and policy issues* (pp. 68–89). Geneva, Switzerland: International Catholic Child Bureau.

McCullough, M. E., & Worthington, E. L., Jr. (1995). Promoting forgiveness: A comparison of two brief psychoeducational group interventions with a wait-list control. *Counseling and Values, 40*, 55–68.

McFarlane, A. C., & van der Kolk, B. A. (1996). Trauma and its challenge to society. In L. Weisaeth (Ed.), *Traumatic stress: The effects of overwhelming experience on mind, body, and society* (pp. 24–46). New York: Guilford Press.

McFarlane, A. C., & Yehuda, R. (1996). Resilience, vulnerability, and the course of posttraumatic reactions. In L. Weisaeth (Ed.), *Traumatic stress: The effects of overwhelming experience on mind, body, and society* (pp. 155–181). New York: Guilford Press.

McLaughlin, C., & Davidson, G. (1994). *Spiritual politics: Changing the world from the inside out.* New York: Ballantine Books.

Minow, M. (1998). *Between vengeance and forgiveness: Facing history after genocide and mass violence.* Boston: Beacon Press.

Mollica, R. F. (1988). The trauma story: The psychiatric care of refugee survivors of violence and torture. In F. M. Ochberg (Ed.), *Post-traumatic therapy and victims of violence* (pp. 295–314). New York: Brunner/Mazel, Publishers.

Mullet, E., & Girard, M. (2000). Developmental and cognitive points of view on forgiveness. In C. E. Thoresen (Ed.), *Forgiveness: Theory, research, and practice* (pp. 111–132). New York: Guilford Press.

Noll, J. G. (2005). Forgiveness in people experiencing trauma. In E. L. Worthington, Jr. (Ed.), *Handbook of forgiveness* (pp. 363–375). New York: Routedge.

Pargament, K. I. (1997). *The psychology of religion and coping: Theory, research, and practice.* New York: Guilford Press.

Pargament, K. I., McCullough, M. E., & Thoresen, C. E. (2000). The frontier of forgiveness: Seven directions for psychological study and practice. In C. E. Thoresen (Ed.), *Forgiveness: Theory, research, and practice* (pp. 299–319). New York: Guilford Press.

Patro, B. (2003). Winning the peace. *The Magazine of the International Red Cross and Red Crescent Movement.* Available from Red Cross, Red Crescent, PO Box 372, CH–1211, Geneva, Switzerland.

Peddle, N. (2001). *Forgiveness in recovery/resiliency from the trauma of war among a selected group of adolescents and adult refugees.* Unpublished doctoral dissertation, Fielding Graduate University, Santa Barbara.

Peddle, N. (2007). Assessing trauma impact, recovery, and resiliency in refugees of war. In U. Tummala-Narra (Ed.), *Sources and expressions of resiliency in trauma survivors: Ecological theory, multicultural practice.* Binghamton, NY: Haworth Press.

Peddle, N., Monteiro, C., Guluma, V., & Macaulay, T. E. A. (1999). Trauma, loss and resilience in Africa: A psychosocial community based approach to culturally sensitive healing. In B. H. Stamm (Ed.), *Honoring differences: Cultural issues in the treatment of trauma and loss* (pp. 121–149). Philadelphia: Brunner/Mazel.

Peddle, N., Stamm, B. H., Hudnall, A. C., & IV, H. E. S. (2006). Effective intercultural collaboration on psychosocial support programs. In G. A. Jacobs (Vol. Ed.), *Handbook of international disaster psychology: Vol. 1. Fundamentals and overview* (pp.113–126). Westport, CT: Praeger Publishers.

Pynoos, R. S. (1994). Traumatic stress and developmental psychopathology in children and adolescents. In R. S. Pynoos (Ed.), *Posttraumatic stress disorder: A clinical review* (pp. 65–98). Lutherville, MD: The Sidran Press.

Pynoos, R. S., & Nader, K. (1988). Psychological first aid and treatment approach for children exposed to community violence: Research implications. *Journal of Traumatic Stress, 1,* 445–473.

Raundalen, M., Dyregrov, A., Steylen, L. H., Kleve, L., & Lunde, L. H. (1987, July). *The impact of war on children.* Paper presented at the Children in Situations of Armed Conflict: Agenda for Action Conference, Nairobi, Kenya.

Reyes, G., & Jacobs, G. A. (Eds.). (2006). *Handbook of international disaster psychology: Vol. 4. Interventions with special needs populations.* Westport, CT: Praeger Publishers.

Richards, N. (1988). Forgiveness. *Ethics, 99,* 77–97.

Roth, J. (2006, August 15). *The ethics of forgiveness* [online edition]. *Science and Theology News.* Retrieved August 25, 2006, from http://stpnews.org/news.htm

Schumm, D. H. (1995). Forgiveness in the healing process. In P. Kilbourn (Ed.), *Healing the children of war: A handbook for ministry to children who have suffered deep traumas* (pp. 267–283). Monrovia, CA: MARC Publications.

Sider, N. G. (2001). At the fork in the road: Trauma healing. *Conciliation Quarterly, 20.* Retrieved on March 28, 2007, from http://www.emu.edu/ctp/pub1.html#sider

Staub, E., Pearlman, L. A., Gubin, A., & Hagengimana, A. (2005). Healing, reconciliation, forgiving and the prevention of violence after genocide or mass killing. *Journal of Social and Clinical Psychology, 24,* 297–334.

Subkoviak, M. J., Enright, R. D., & Wu, C.-R. (1992). *Current developments related to measuring forgiveness.* Unpublished manuscript, University of Wisconsin, Madison.

Truth & Reconciliation Commission. (2004). *Witness to truth: Report of the Sierra Leone Truth and Reconciliation Commission (Vol. 1).*

UN Chronicle. (1996). The Chronicle interview: Archbishop emeritus Desmond Tutu. *UN Chronicle, 23,* 4–6.

van Biema, D. (1999, April 5). Should all be forgiven? *Time Magazine, 153,* 55–58.

van der Kolk, B. A., & Greenberg, M. S. (1987). The psychobiology of the trauma response: Hyperarousal, constriction, and addiction to traumatic reexposure. In B. A. van der Kolk (Ed.), *Psychological trauma* (pp. 63–87). Washington DC: American Psychiatric Press.

Van Gorp, K. (2000). Forgiveness: What it is. What it isn't. What it can be. *FaithWorks Magazine, 3,* 14–17.

Weine, S. M. (1996). *Bosnian refugees: Memories, witnessing, and history after Dayton* [internet document]. U.S. Committee for Refugees. Retrieved March 28, 2007, from http://refugees.org/world/articles/bosnians_wrs96htm

Williams, M. B., Zinner, E. S., & Ellis, R. R. (1999). The connection between grief and trauma: An overview. In M. B. Williams (Ed.), *When a community weeps: Case studies in group survivorship* (pp. 3–17). Philadelphia: Brunner/Mazel.

Witvliet, C. V. O., Phipps, K. A., Feldman, M. E., & Beckham, J. C. (2004). Posttraumatic mental and physical health correlates of forgiveness and religious coping in military veterans. *Journal of Traumatic Stress, 17,* 269–273.

Worthington, E. L., Jr. (1998a). Empirical research in forgiveness: Looking backward, looking forward. In E. L. Worthington, Jr. (Ed.), *Dimensions of forgiveness: Psychological research and theological perspectives: Vol. 1. Laws of the symposia series* (pp. 321–339). Philadelphia: Templeton Foundation Press.

Worthington, E. L., Jr. (1998b). The pyramid model of forgiveness: Some interdisciplinary speculations about unforgiveness and the promotion of forgiveness. In E. L. Worthington, Jr. (Ed.), *Dimensions of forgiveness: Psychological research and theological perspectives: Vol. 1. Laws of the symposia series* (pp. 107–137). Philadelphia: Templeton Foundation Press.

Worthington, E. L., Jr. (2004). Everett Worthington [online edition]. *Science and Theology News.* Retrieved August 25, 2006, from http://www.stpnews.org/Research.htm

Yandell, K. E. (1998). The metaphysics and morality of forgiveness. In J. North (Ed.), *Exploring forgiveness* (pp. 35–45). Madison: University of Wisconsin Press.

11

Restoration of a Moral Universe

Children's Perspectives on Forgiveness and Justice

SANDRA RAFMAN

Introduction

Just as policy makers, caregivers, and other adults have systematically underestimated the suffering experienced by children in situations of illness, death, or war, so also they have neglected children's moral understanding of, and response to, social and political events (Miljevic-Ridjicki & Lugomer-Armano, 1994). In the context of political violence, children experience not only disruption of their physical, relational, and social worlds but also a shattering of their moral universe.

Forgiveness has been considered as a way of restoring relational breaches, but it can also be viewed as a way of restoring moral breaches. I argue, however, for a perspective on forgiveness that does not see it as opposed to justice (as is sometimes the case in the truth and reconciliation commissions) but rather as intricately intertwined with it (Biggar, 2001; Shriver, 1995). In this chapter, I focus on the moral domain and argue that when dealing with these breeches, forgiveness must be situated in the context of moral repair (Walker, 2006).

I hope to demonstrate that not only adults but also children and adolescents see forgiveness as intimately intertwined with creating and sustaining a moral universe, a universe in which both forgiver and forgiven have a stake and to which they wish to belong. I present clinical and developmental findings that support such a framework and show how such a perspective can clarify controversies in the field. For example, it has been argued that efforts aimed at individual recovery following political violence are opposed to measures designed to foster social healing. However, viewing forgiveness as a mode of re-entry into a moral universe serves to counteract this dichotomy. Placing or understanding forgiveness within its historical, philosophical, and ethical setting can enrich models of treatment for children traumatized by social and political violence and betrayal.

Children's Moral Experience in Contexts of War and Political Violence

In contexts of war and political violence, children typically experience or witness moral violations such as torture, mutilation, disappearances, and sexual exploitation. Killing has become intentional and acceptable. The politically organized and socially sanctioned nature of war often makes it difficult to name aggressors or to attribute blame. The perpetrators, whose identities are frequently ambiguous and uncertain, often operate during and after war with impunity, making forgiveness particularly problematic. Often the line between political and criminal violence is not clear (Straker, Mendelsohn, Moosa, & Tudin, 1996): Ideology, ambiguity, meaning, and intention interact to affect the subjective interpretation of a political event or of political violence, and this interpretation often has a more powerful impact than the extent or degree of exposure to violence (Bachar, Canetti, Bonne, Denour, & Shalev, 1997; Kuterovac-Jagodic, 2000; Punamäki, 1996; Slone, Kaminer, & Durrheim, 2002; Wiene et al., 1995).

Additional developmental challenges confront children because they are often the intended or unintended witnesses to violence and injustice. The child is often witness to attacks on a parent and, like Hamlet, feels simultaneously an intense pressure to avenge the parent and a powerlessness to do so. Beside the failure to avenge the loved one, forgiving the perpetrator may feel like another betrayal of the victim, and forgiveness as another injury (Moosa, Straker, & Eagle, 2004).

Children often encounter complex situations that present moral dilemmas (Goenjian et al., 1999) where they may be obliged to engage in acts they view as immoral, such as stealing for food or even killing. In many contemporary armed conflicts, children are conscripted as soldiers and forced to commit atrocities against their own families, placing them in moral dilemmas where relational, moral, and survival imperatives conflict and permit no resolution. After war, they are typically viewed with greater suspicion and distrust than adults who have committed similar acts (Boyden, 2003).

Moral Dilemmas in Children's Play Narratives

In our own research, moral dilemmas were found to underlie the content of play narratives of war-orphaned Central American children of differing clinical status (Rafman, Canfield, Barbas, & Kaczorowski, 1996, 1997). The play narratives of those children, not referred for treatment (from Guatemala, Nicaragua, and El Salvador), who had lost parents through death or disappearance in the context of political violence were compared with war-orphaned children who had been referred to a clinic for various psychological disturbances.

The nonreferred children who had lost parents nonetheless re-created how their parents died or how their parents' bodies were discovered. In play, the children undid or modified the intentionality, the cruelty, and the finality of their parents' deaths, but not the event itself. Murderous attacks became accidents; bodies found bloodied and mutilated were discovered unbloodied. The children's ability to acknowledge their parents' deaths was made difficult by their inability to comprehend how their parents could have died by a willful, violent, human act.

The relational imperative required remembering and mourning the lost parent, but the moral reality of intentional evil left the child too horrified to admit the cause of loss. It was the transgression of a moral edict and the conflict between a relational and moral imperative, rather than the parental loss that froze the child at the moment of the killing. Such conflicts underlie what is termed traumatic grief or complicated mourning, where characteristics of the traumatic event interfere with children's ability to mourn the loss of a loved one adequately and where the need to remember powerfully meets the pressure to deny or forget (Brown & Goodman, 2005; Dunn & Herrera, 1997).

The play of orphaned children referred for psychological consultation was characterized by more disjointed, fragmented, and ambiguous scenes than those of their community-based, nonclinical counterparts. Whereas community-based, nonreferred children re-enacted the killing of their parent, the referred children re-enacted the destruction of their moral universe. The remembered and fantasized scenes were not so much about terrible brutality, but about anguished moral choices that permitted no resolution. The theme of good and evil linked seemingly disparate episodes together. Roles of perpetrator and victim, aggressor, betrayer, and protector shifted rapidly as moral ambiguities permeated their fragmented play scenes. Children often confused the rage of the aggressor with their own rage, further complicating the identification of perpetrator and victim, making forgiveness more complex.*

Children's Moral Development

The research literature supports the view that children form moral judgments and experience moral dilemmas early in development. I will consider literature documenting that children are capable of moral judgment early in development and see how this affects their granting or withholding of forgiveness. Indeed, forgiveness plays such a central role in the child's and adult's life, in part, because moral dilemmas and conflicts are integral to the social and moral reality of individuals, even in societies not mired by armed conflict and political violence (Turiel & Wainryb, 2000). In fact, by the age of 3 years, children are able to invent alternative outcomes to resolve a moral dilemma within a play narrative (Buchsbaum & Emde, 1990). In the right context, conflict may be an important facilitator of children's socio-emotional development. For example, how mothers justify, resolve, and mitigate conflict among themselves, their 2½-year-old children, and their siblings predicts levels of socioemotional development later in childhood (Dunn & Herrera, 1997; Laible & Thompson, 2002).

As forgiveness is often discussed in the context of deep injustice, not mere annoyances, it is critical to recognize that breaches in the moral domain differ from breaches in the social–conventional domain. Smetana, Daddis, et al. (1999) have shown that across social contexts, children judge moral transgressions far more severely than

* Situating oneself with regard to evil has become recognized as a predominant theme in political forgiveness (Digeser, 2004). Bar-on (1990) found that the distinction between themselves and evil was a predominant theme in both the children of Holocaust survivors and the children of the Nazi perpetrators.

they evaluate violations of social–conventional rules. From age 4 and onward, children of varying backgrounds and characteristics (such as violent or nonviolent, perpetrator or victim, maltreated or not; Smetana, Toth, et al., 1999) evaluate moral transgressions resulting in unfairness, physical harm, or psychological harm (Helwig, Zelazo, & Wilson, 2001) as very serious and deserving of punishment. Although violent and nonviolent children differ in their explanations as to why unprovoked violence is worse than provoked violence, both use moral reasoning as explanations (Astor, 1994).

Although social and cultural frameworks may shape the expression of moral judgments, children's sociological frame alone does not determine their moral judgment (Helwig & Jasiobedzka, 2001; Helwig & Turiel, 2002). Turiel and Wainryb (2000) emphasize that across cultures and sex of child, children make complex moral judgments involving rights, justice, tradition, and authority that cannot be explained by appeal to the cultural framework alone.

Despite the moral chaos of war, children are able to exhibit moral judgment and competence distinct from the societal context. For example, in Sri Lanka, a country ravaged by a particularly brutal and vicious civil war, little difference was found between Sinhalese and Tamil youth in their views about the legitimacy of violence. Those in the areas most affected by the violence held similar views to those in areas less affected (Thangarajah, 2002). Although idiosyncratic features exist in such moral judgments, certain universal themes nonetheless emerge, including condemnation of unprovoked violence and the need for remorse on the part of the wrongdoer, as well as the need for social and moral community in the understanding of forgiveness.*

Forgiveness, Justice, and Mental Health

Research on the psychological concomitants of forgiveness has direct implications for policy with war-affected or abused children. Because of the devastating effects of trauma on children (Dyregrov, Gjestad, & Raundalen, 2002; Goldin, Levin, Ake Persson, & Hägglof, 2003;

* Further elaboration of children's moral development in times of political violence and times of peace can be found in Rafman, 2004.

Onyango, 1998), findings that forgiveness has been linked with well-being have led to the active promotion of reconciliation following abuse or political violence. Whether responses to war, however, should be corrected or modified has encountered strong challenges from those who insist that truth-telling and justice must precede forgiveness; otherwise, pressure to forgive may undermine or preclude social and political recovery (e.g., Allan, Allan, Kaminer, & Stein, 2006; Le Touze, Silove, & Zivi, 2005; Lustig, Weine, Saxe, & Beardslee, 2004; Moosa et al., 2004).

Some findings *do* point to an association between unforgiveness and psychological problems in the context of political injustice. For victims of the apartheid era in South Africa, post-traumatic stress disorder and depression were significantly more common in those testifying to the Truth and Reconciliation Commission who were unforgiving than those who were forgiving of the perpetrators (Kaminer, Stein, Mbanga, & Zungu-Dirwayi, 2001). However, findings of the association between forgiveness and mental health are contradictory. Interpersonal forgiveness in children 12 to 14 years of age is a strong predictor of self-reported victimization (Coleman & Byrd, 2003).

One could, however, legitimately ask whether ensuring that perpetrators be brought to justice would not bring about better mental health than teaching forgiveness to the victims. Forgiveness need not be seen as opposed to justice. Indeed, highlighting justice as a value serves to promote forgiveness rather than obstruct it (Karremans & Van Lange, 2005). Karremans, Van Lange, Ouwerkerk, and Kluwer (2003) have shown that the relationship between psychological well-being and forgiveness depends on the nature of the transgression that is being forgiven and the relationship with the forgiver. The relationship between forgiveness and well-being may hold for those to whom we are attached but not necessarily for perpetrators of injustice in other contexts. The relationship is strongest with respect to those toward whom we have mixed or ambivalent feelings. This is particularly relevant for children for whom the relationship with a loved one is critical. As forgiveness involves acknowledging that we are flawed and yet of value (Biggar, 2001), it requires the ability to accept and integrate the good and bad both within ourselves and within the other, an important developmental step (Horwitz, 2005).

Given the intimate link between justice and forgiveness, forgiveness may require moral repair for social healing to occur. Adolescents or youth did not experience a sense of healing following participation in truth and reconciliation commissions in South Africa, East Timor, and Bosnia because they saw that justice was not served, with perpetrators of atrocities enjoying ongoing impunity (Opotow, 2001). Youth in Bosnia referred to war criminals openly walking the streets (Jones, 2002) and in East Timor, they found forgiveness difficult because war criminals had escaped safely to Indonesia, a country intimately linked with the atrocities, but conveniently lacking an extradition treaty with its former colony (LeTouze et al., 2005). By not pursuing justice and by accepting forgiveness as a substitute for social punishment, not only are the innocent retraumatized, but they are also punished once again. Children testify with all the attendant emotional distress, and if the guilty go free, they experience yet another breach in their moral universe.

Forgiveness and Models of Recovery Following Trauma

In addressing the relation between forgiveness and well-being in war-affected children, I will consider two models. One emphasizes narratives of transformation following traumatic events and the other involves concepts of stress, coping, and adaptation. I will illustrate how introducing a moral dimension can enrich the research and the application of either model.

Narrative Models of Transformation

As we have seen, the re-enactment and narratives of the disruptive events in the lives of traumatized children are often ambiguous, partial, and fragmented. The (re)construction of a life narrative following disruptive events is increasingly considered a preferred way of addressing loss and trauma (Omer & Strenger, 1992). The discourse of coping is thus replaced by one of transformation, of which forgiveness can be considered a form. Children's perceptions and narratives of the traumatic events, however, must be seen as embedded within (although not identical with) the perceptions and narratives of the event by the cultures of which the child is a member. Notions of healing, reparation, and justice in the aftermath of war *do* vary between cultures and over time.

But just as political violence devastates the child's assumptive world, it also devastates the assumptive world of his or her culture. Trust in a moral order is shattered for the relevant community or nation as well. Both child and culture may recreate his or her narrative as a means to understanding or overcoming the break in the moral universe and as a way of coming to terms with evil and suffering, trauma and loss. Just as children and adults need to mourn emotional losses, so too they must mourn cultural loss and losses of their assumptive worlds. Although children's understanding occurs within the context of the surrounding society's beliefs and perspectives, this relationship is precisely in flux and at risk in the context of war.

Moreover, narratives are not morally or politically neutral. The ability to create a continuous narrative is viewed as therapeutic, but the question may be posed as to whether all narratives are equal, who controls the content of the narrative, and whose agenda it serves. An examination of the relationship between power and culture may reveal that cultural narratives of trauma and survival can be liberating or repressive (Crossley, 1999). Children and their reference groups often find themselves in the midst of two or more conflicting narratives, as it is for Bosnian, Israeli, Palestinian, Singhalese, and Tamil children, to cite just a few examples. The day of independence in the Israeli narrative is the day of catastrophe in the Palestinian narrative.

In addition, societies and cultures may have "chosen traumata" (Volkan, 2001). They may integrate the mental representation of the trauma into their very identity and relentlessly convey the consequences to the next generation. These social narratives, which can become myths, are created out of a nation's traumatic experiences and may become the national narrative. Some national myths or narratives may prevent mourning and potentially lead the group to see themselves as victims entitled to vengeance (Pick, 2001). Palgi and Durban (1995) demonstrate how cultural symbols intertwine with personal themes to impact the mourning process.

Such narratives may address or suppress the immediate pain of suffering and loss, but they also fuel political violence and constrain forgiveness. As each generation feels pressured to transmit the experience of its own trauma to the next generation, the ability to forgive is thereby affected. Both children's developmental age and family narratives have been found to be critical to their understandings of conflict (Apfel &

Simon, 2000). Biggar (2001) asks how, when a culture is so bereft of agreement on the moral basis of human life, humans locked in any degree of antagonism can presume to make moral judgments of each other. The laborious construction of a narrative on which opposing parties can agree has been chosen as one such path.

If forgiveness, as Paul Ricoeur (2000) writes, gives memory a future, forgiveness can serve as a way of breaking out of the "frozen in time" nature of trauma. Forgiveness then refers not only to a different relation with oneself or the other, but also to a different relation to the past and to the future. For that, the past must be presented; it must be incorporated in the narrative. Bosnian youth, for example, felt that it was important to "put memory before wounds, truth telling before healing. Survivors have a story to tell because they were part of an event, a crime and they want to tell about that experience" (Weine, 1999, p. 360). Consistent with this, participants in the South African Truth and Reconciliation Commission, who were able to forgive the perpetrators, were more likely to have been asked by the Commission panel members to provide details of the violation. In contrast, participants who were unforgiving had typically not been given the opportunity to tell their story (Kaminer, 2006).

Recognition that both the social and moral universes have been disrupted when injustice occurs could counteract the trend to view recovery programs that focus on mental health as being opposed to those that emphasize the need to restore social structures (Summerfield, 2002). Children recognize that the processes of their own recovery are bound up with recovery of their social and political communities (Jones, 2002, p. 1367). Lustig et al. (2004) suggest a testimonial psychotherapy for youth whereby the young person focuses on transcribing personal, traumatic events, situating them in their historical, cultural, and political context. When presented as having the altruistic purpose of education and advocacy, this became an acceptable way for therapists to engage traumatized Sudanese adolescents known as the "Lost Boys."

Models of Stress, Coping, and Adaptation

Stress, coping, and adaptation constitute key notions within a second model of recovery in which a moral dimension is not intrinsically present. Worthington and Scherer (2004) view forgiveness as an emotion-focused coping strategy and unforgiveness as a stress reaction. On the one hand, the concept of post-traumatic stress as a disorder or syndrome does capture many of the psychological "symptoms" following terrifying, uncontrollable, and unpredictable events (Kuterovac-Jagodic, 2003).* Post-traumatic stress refers to both the effort of the child to exclude the traumatic event from awareness and memory and the tendency of the events and emotions to intrude into awareness.

This model fails, however, to acknowledge fully the embeddedness of forgiveness within a social, cultural, and political context. This is particularly striking given that Worthington and Scherer's (2004) review of methods of reducing unforgiveness includes the intrapsychic (denying the hurt, cognitive reframing), interpersonal (successful revenge), legal (redress), ethical (seeing legal justice done, forgiveness), and cultural and political (receiving fair restitution) dimensions.

The inclusion of the moral dimension would be particularly pertinent to understanding an oft-noted feature of post-traumatic stress symptoms—their persistence over time (Dyregrov et al., 2002; Lopes Cardozo, Kaiser, Gotway, & Agani, 2003; Sabian, Lopes Cardozo, Nackerud, Kaiser, & Varese, 2003).† When the terrors, nightmares, re-enactments, and intrusive memories do not abate on their own, and when traumatic grief perseveres, examination of the child's feelings and thoughts around the trauma often reveals unresolved moral dilemmas (Brown & Goodman, 2005; Lopes Cardozo et al., 2003; Rafman et al., 1996). The sense of injustice that often maintains feelings of chronic anger following human-engendered trauma further shows the interdependence of the emotional and the moral.

The psychological and moral impact of events may differ. In some contexts, the immediate psychological benefit of some "coping mechanisms" may have long-term, negative consequences on moral, not to

* Symptoms that are often noted include hyperarousal or vigilance, nightmares, sleep and eating disturbances, intrusive images, repetitive behaviors, loss of interest, restlessness, and increased irritability (Ajdukovic & Ajdukovic 1998; Dyregrov et al., 2002).

† Over a 1-year period it was found that Kosovo Albanians' feelings of hatred toward Serbs and desire for revenge decreased, while social functioning improved among those aged 15 years or older, but post-traumatic stress disorder symptoms increased.

mention political, development. Children in Kabul, interviewed by Berry et al. (2003), were able to distinguish between the short- and long-term effects of different modes of adapting to difficult circumstances. They acknowledged that strategies used by them and their parents, such as not telling the truth, overprotection, the use of physical punishment and violence, and taking revenge, helped and comforted them in their immediate circumstances. Nonetheless, they identified these methods as having negative repercussions for them in the long term. When Jones (2002) interviewed young teenagers who had lived through the war in Bosnia-Herzegovina on opposite sides of the conflict, those adolescents who were not struggling to make sense of the conflict were more likely to be well adjusted by some psychological measures. However, such disengaged adolescents are not likely to engage in attempts to promote reconciliation.

Both the failure to forgive and traumatic responses are strikingly similar with respect to the child's lived relationship to the past. In both unforgiveness and post-traumatic stress disorder, the child is either trapped within the past or is investing all of his or her energy to escape it. Similarly, forgiveness and trauma recovery change the child's relationship to the past and to the future. Both are linked to the alleviation of anxiety, hopelessness, depression, and low self-esteem, as discussed by Peddle (this volume). Her discussions with youth who had experienced political violence revealed that they were often struggling with moral issues related to forgiveness, such as how to view the perpetrators and whether there were unforgivable people or crimes.

Many children are observed to cope well following traumatic events, as measured by the absence of symptoms and by behavioral functioning. For this reason, focus has shifted to studying children's resilience in the face of adversity as researchers and clinicians search for risk and protective factors underlying such resilience. For example, former child soldiers and orphaned adolescents in Sierra Leone experienced complex physical and psychological injuries caused by exposure to terrible violence and loss. They coped well, despite living under highly stressful environmental conditions with severely damaged or nonexistent community resources. Adolescents who could maintain an intact sense of purpose, structured exercise and rituals, effective control of traumatic memories, and successful protection against destructive social isolation through social contact with peers and responsive adults did better psychologically (Kline & Mone, 2003). Maternal mental health, prior traumatic experience, support systems, and the possibility for active participation, among other variables, have also been found to mediate the child's psychological response to the traumatic events of war (e.g., Ajdukovic & Ajdukovic, 1998; McCloskey, Southwick, Fernández-Esquer, & Locke, 1995). The relation of these variables to forgiveness would be important to explore in future research.

As conceptualizations move from perceiving children not only as passive victims, but also as resilient youth and co-constructors of their social world, the associated logic is that they are also constructors of their moral world. By their moral choices and by their offering or withholding acts of reconciliation or forgiveness, children also participate in the construction of their social universe. For example, in an attempt to come to terms with their traumatic experiences, adolescents in Sierra Leone formed a performance troupe and enacted plays that often centered on a specific catastrophic event. In one play, a teenager who had been made to watch as combatants tortured and murdered his family returns to his village. He finds the murderers and has the opportunity to take his revenge. Through the play the actors/adolescents work through their experienced moral dilemmas and conclude with a shouting chorus of "Forgive, yes, but never forget" (Kline & Mone, 2003).

Apologies, Remorse, and Forgiveness: Developmental Considerations

That true regret in the perpetrator is critical to forgiveness supports a perspective on forgiveness as a pathway to moral repair and to re-entry into a social community. Across religion, level of education, sex, and age, the intentionality and consequences of an offense, as well as the victim's relationship with the offender, are important factors. Nonetheless, remorse consistently emerges as the most important determinant of the willingness to forgive a severe offense (Azar & Mullet, 2001; Mullet & Girard, 2000).* Youth and adult participants who forgave

* Azar and Mullet (2001) found that the willingness to forgive a severe offense did not differ among Druze, Shiite, Sunni, Catholics, Maronites, and Orthodox Christian Lebanese as a function of age, sex, or religion.

perpetrators in the South African TRC commissions perceived the perpetrators to be truly sorry (Allan et al., 2006). Gobodo-Madikizela (2002) argues that genuine remorse humanizes perpetrators of gross human rights abuse and transforms their evil from the unforgivable into something that can be forgiven.

That apologies, remorse, and forgiveness can serve to return the transgressor to his or her social group and that punishment is typically applied by children in a rehabilitative fashion are supported by developmental research. Darby and Schlenker (1989) found that children see a remorseful child as less blameworthy, as having better motives, and as having done the damage unintentionally. In their study, the child described as very remorseful was punished least. Relevant to the truth and reconciliation postwar commissions, offending children's reputations determined how their actions were interpreted: Children judged to be "bad" were seen as more worried about punishment when they expressed remorse, and older children thought that "bad" children apologized merely to avoid punishment.

Moreover, apologies and reparative behaviors demonstrate a developmental trajectory (Nakagawa & Yamazaki, 2004). Children's reparative behaviors, after they cause distress, increase with age (Laible & Thompson, 2002). The power of an apology also increases with age. When an offender apologized, fifth graders perceived greater remorse, judged less harshly, and were more prone to forgive than were second graders (Ohbuchi & Sato, 1994). Mullet and Girard (2000) found that the propensity to forgive evolves over the life course, with elderly people more likely to forgive than middle-aged adults, who, in turn, are more likely to forgive than adolescents.

The Role of the Community

Forgiveness is not so much an emotion-focused coping mechanism as it is one part of a mode of re-entry into a moral, communal existence. The other part involves the wrongdoer, who must repent. Only when the wrongdoer repudiates his or her deeds through feelings of regret and makes a commitment not to repeat the offense is moral community with the victim restored (Biggar, 2001). This repentance can take many forms, as is seen in the cleansing rituals devised for re-entry into communal life of child soldiers in Mozambique. Promoting verbalization of traumatic events is considered dangerous both for the person and for the community as it may attract the angry spirits killed during the event (Granjo, 2006). Instead, the community and the former soldier, aided by a healer, engage in a series of ritualized acts that provide for a "fresh start." The veteran assumes his or her past acts and begins a cathartic process, but this is done in a ritualized manner that has more to do with dramatic representation than with revival of the situation and emergence of guilt. In the context of intergroup conflict, forgiveness cannot be only a personal decision, as community leaders must deal with any failure to avenge the dead.

The harm-doer is accountable to the community, which also carries the sense of injury when one of its members is injured or, for that matter, injures others. The child's choice, or scope to forgive, is mediated by his or her political group or community. It is for this reason that there is such value in cleansing rituals or truth and reconciliation commissions. The exposure of the perpetrator's fallibility and flaws in truth commissions is often consoling for children and youth. The perceived omnipotence of the perpetrator is reduced. Particularly for children, care must be taken that offers of forgiveness are not just given to get approval from an authority figure, to restore belief in idealized objects, or as a way to avoid the pain of loss and anger.

Maintaining the relationship with the loved one is of critical importance to the child. Acknowledging this reality underscores the value of considering forgiveness as a mode of re-entry into a moral community. In this way, forswearing resentment, restoring relationship, and fixing a wrong in the past may be involved but none need define forgiveness in every case. One or all may serve to bring about moral and social recovery.

Clinical and Research Implications

Promising areas of research include the examination in children of the precursors and correlates of forgiveness such as empathy and altruism (Scobie & Scobie, 2000), the development of forgiveness (Enright, 1994; Enright, Santos, & Al-Mabuk, 1989), and the study of the contexts and conditions under which forgiveness is developed, facilitated, or constrained (e.g., Horwitz, 2005). A recognition and clarification of the moral, cultural, political, and cultural components or dimensions in these developmental studies could enrich the research. How forgiveness relates to pathological mourning, complicated grief, and trauma could be particularly instructive.

When doing research or providing an intervention focused on forgiveness with children, certain considerations are particularly relevant. First, it is not sufficient simply to define competing or parallel concepts, such as reconciliation, pardon, and condoning, as different. More attention must be paid to the moral impetus, moral community, and moral repair underlying forgiveness that may clarify its link with the emotional sequelae of political trauma and abuse. It is critical to remember that the foundations of forgiveness are not only (if at all) scientific, but are definitely ethical (Biggar, 2001; Kaminer, Stein, Mbanga, & Zungu-Dirwayi, 2000).

Second, developmental considerations, such as the salience of early attachment figures, the impact of early abandonment, the relative power discrepancy between victim and harm-doer, and the devastation of certain betrayals, are realities that should be incorporated into our research. These may play a larger role than acknowledged—in particular, the nature of the relationship prior to or during the offense. Third, bereavement and grief resolution may differ in children, the pain of losing a parent being so great. Overcoming anger and loss may not be identical for adults and children. Fourth, in war and abuse, moral taboos are broken and fundamental moral edicts transgressed. Fractured moral and political relations, rather than just ruptured social relations, become the repositories of a host of socio-moral-psychological dilemmas.

In their narratives and in their play, war-affected children continuously re-enact unresolved emotional and moral issues. The meanings of their narratives and play become clearer when we understand them as attempts to present and to resolve moral dilemmas occasioned by the destruction of moral continuity in their lives, and as struggles to construct a moral order they can once more affirm. Political violence and its associated travesties confront the child with the problem of evil.

Living in the context of a moral universe, where rules govern human relations, proves to be as human a need as living in a world of social and emotional bonds. The loss of such a universe leads to a void as profound as a world bereft of loved ones. A moral order no longer believed in, a covenant betrayed, and a legal system despoiled leave the child as unprotected, as confounded, and as saddened as the loss of a protecting parent does. The restoration of trust and the resolve not to allow the memory of past injury to poison future relations with resentment requires that the impunity of perpetrators be addressed. The proverb that the law and repentance were given on the same day recognizes the individual's potential for evil and, alongside that, the desire for forgiveness; this is something the child understands.

References

Ajdukovic, M., & Ajdukovic, D. (1998). Impact of displacement on the psychological well-being of refugee children. *International Review of Psychiatry, 10,* 186–195.

Allan, A., Allan, M., Kaminer, D., & Stein, D. J. (2006). Exploration of the association between apology and forgiveness amongst victims of human rights violations. *Behavioral Sciences and the Law, 24,* 87–102.

Apfel R. J., & Simon, B. (2000). Mitigating discontents with children in war: An ongoing psychoanalytic inquiry. In A. C. G. M. Robben & M. M. Suarez-Orozco (Eds.), *Cultures under siege: Collective violence and trauma* (pp. 102–130). Cambridge, UK: Cambridge University Press.

Astor, R. A. (1994). Children's moral reasoning about family and peer violence: The role of provocation and retribution. *Child Development, 65,* 1054–1067.

Azar, F., & Mullet, E. (2001). Interpersonal forgiveness among Lebanese: A six-community study. *International Journal of Group Tensions, 30,* 161–181.

Bachar, E., Canetti, L., Bonne, O., Denour, A. K., & Shalev, A. Y. (1997). Psychological well-being and ratings of psychiatric symptoms in bereaved Israeli adolescents: Differential effect of war- versus accident-related bereavement. *Journal of Nervous and Mental Disease, 185,* 402–406.

Bar-On, D. (1990). Children of perpetrators of the Holocaust: working through one's own moral self. *Psychiatry. 53*(3), 229–245.

Berry, J. D., Fazili, A., Farhad, S., Nasiry, F., Hashemi, S., & Hakimi, M. (2003). *The children of Kabul: Discussions with Afghan families.* Westport, CT: Save the Children Federation.

Biggar, N. (2001). Forgiveness in the twentieth century: A review of the literature, 1901–2001. In A. McFadyen & M. Sarot (Eds.), *Forgiveness and truth* (pp. 181–217). Edinburgh, UK: T. & T. Clark.

Boyden, J. (2003). The moral development of child soldiers: What do adults have to fear? *Peace and Conflict: Journal of Peace Psychology, 9,* 343–362.

Brown, E., & Goodman, R. F. J. (2005). Childhood traumatic grief: An exploration of the construct in children bereaved on September 11. *Journal of Clinical Child and Adolescent Psychology, 34,* 248–259.

Buchsbaum, H. K., & Emde, R. N. (1990). Play narratives in 36-month-old children: Early moral development and family relationships. *Psychoanalytic Study of the Child, 45,* 129–155.

Coleman, P. K., & Byrd, C. P. (2003). Interpersonal correlates of peer victimization among young adolescents. *Journal of Youth & Adolescence, 32,* 301–314.

Crossley, M. L. (1999). Stories of illness and trauma survival: Liberation or repression? *Science & Medicine, 48,* 1685–1695.

Darby, B. W., & Schlenker, B. R. (1989). British children's reactions to transgressions: Effects of the actor's apology, reputation and remorse. *Journal of Social Psychology, 28,* 353–364.

Digeser, P.E. (2004). Forgiveness, the unforgivable and international relations. *International Relations. 18*(4), 480–497.

Dunn, J., & Herrera, C. (1997). Conflict resolution with friends, siblings, and mothers: A developmental perspective. *Aggressive Behavior, 23,* 343–357.

Dyregrov, A., Gjestad, R., & Raundalen, M. (2002). Children exposed to warfare: A longitudinal study. *Journal of Traumatic Stress, 15,* 59–68.

Enright, R. D. (1994). Piaget on the moral development of forgiveness: Identity or reciprocity? *Human Development, 37,* 63–80.

Enright, R. D., Santos, M. J., & Al-Mabuk, R. (1989). The adolescent as forgiver. *Journal of Adolescence, 12,* 95–110.

Gobodo-Madikizela, P. (2002). Remorse, forgiveness, and rehumanization: Stories from South Africa. *Journal of Humanistic Psychology, 42,* 7–32.

Goenjian, A. K., Stilwell, B. M., Steinberg, A. M., Fairbanks, L. A., Galvin, M., Karayan, T., et al. (1999). Moral development and psychopathological interference with conscience functioning among adolescents after trauma. *Journal of the American Academy of Child and Adolescent Psychiatry, 38,* 376–384.

Goldin, S., Levin, L., Ake Persson, L., & Hägglof, B. (2003). Child war trauma: A comparison of clinician, parent and child assessments. *Nordic Journal of Psychiatry, 57,* 173–183.

Granjo, P. (2006). *Cleansing rituals and veterans' reintegration in Mozambique.* Instituto de Ceincias Sociais, Universidade de Lisboa. Retrieved from www.ics.ul.pt

Helwig, C. C., & Jasiobedzka, U. (2001). The relation between law and morality: Children's reasoning about socially beneficial and unjust laws. *Child Development, 72,* 1382–1393.

Helwig, C. C., & Turiel, E. (2002). Civil liberties, autonomy, and democracy: Children's perspective. *International Journal of Law & Psychiatry, 25,* 253–270.

Helwig, C. C., Zelazo, P. D., & Wilson, M. (2001). Children's judgments of psychological harm in normal and noncanonical situations. *Child Development, 72,* 66–81.

Horwitz, L. (2005). The capacity to forgive: Intrapsychic and developmental perspectives. *Journal of the American Psychoanalytic Association, 53,* 485–511.

Jones, L. (2002). Adolescent understandings of political violence and psychological well being: A qualitative study from Bosnia Herzegovina. *Social Science and Medicine, 55,* 1351–1371.

Kaminer, D. (2006). Forgiveness attitudes of Truth Commission deponents: Relation to Commission response during testimony. *Peace and Conflict: Journal of Peace Psychology, 12,* 175–187.

Kaminer, D., Stein, D. J., Mbanga, I., & Zungu-Dirwayi, N. (2000). Forgiveness: Toward an integration of theoretical models. *Psychiatry, 63,* 344–57.

Kaminer, D., Stein, D. J., Mbanga, I., & Zungu-Dirwayi, N. (2001). The Truth and Reconciliation Commission in South Africa: Relation to psychiatric status and forgiveness among survivors of human rights abuses. *British Journal of Psychiatry, 178,* 373–377.

Karremans, J. C., & Van Lange, P. A. M. (2005). Does activating justice help or hurt in promoting forgiveness? *Journal of Experimental Social Psychology, 41,* 290–297.

Karremans, J. C., Van Lange, P. A. M., Ouwerkerk, J. W., & Kluwer, E. S. (2003). When forgiving enhances psychological well-being: The role of interpersonal commitment. *Journal of Personality and Social Psychology, 84,* 1011–1026.

Kline, P. M., & Mone, E. (2003). Coping with war: Three strategies employed by adolescent citizens of Sierra Leone. *Child & Adolescent Social Work Journal, 20,* 321–333.

Kuterovac-Jagodic, G. (2000). Is war a good or a bad thing? The attitudes of Croatian, Israeli, and Palestinian children toward war. *International Journal of Psychology, 35,* 241–257.

Kuterovac-Jagodic, G. (2003). Post-traumatic stress symptoms in Croatian children exposed to war: A prospective study. *Journal of Clinical Psychology, 59,* 9–25.

Laible, D. J., & Thompson, R. A. (2002). Mother–child conflict in the toddler years: Lessons in emotion, morality, and relationships. *Child Development, 73,* 1187–1203.

Le Touze, D., Silove, D., & Zwi, A. (2005). Can there be healing without justice? Lessons from the Commission for Reception, Truth and Reconciliation in East Timor. *Intervention, 3,* 192–202.

Lopes Cardozo, B., Kaiser, R. T., Gotway, C. A., & Agani, F. (2003). Mental health, social functioning, and feelings of hatred and revenge of Kosovar Albanians one year after the war in Kosovo. *Journal of Traumatic Stress, 16,* 351–360.

Lustig, S. L., Weine, S. M., Saxe, G. N., & Beardslee, W. R. (2004). Testimonial psychotherapy for adolescent refugees: A case series transcultural. *Psychiatry, 41,* 31–45.

McCloskey, L. A., Southwick, K., Fernández-Esquer, M. E., & Locke, C. (1995). The psychological effects of political and domestic violence on Central American and Mexican immigrant mothers and children. *Journal of Community Psychology, 23,* 95–116.

Miljevic-Ridjicki, R., & Lugomer-Armano, G. (1994). Children's comprehension of war. *Child Abuse Review, 3,* 134–144.

Moosa, F., Straker, G., & Eagle, G. (2004). In the aftermath of political trauma: What price forgiveness? In C. Ransley & T. Spy (Eds.), *Forgiveness and the healing process* (pp. 128–162). New York: Brunner–Routledge.

Mullet, E., & Girard, M. (2000). Developmental and cognitive points of view on forgiveness. In M. E. McCullough, K. I. Pargament, & C. E. Thoresen (Eds.), *Forgiveness: Theory, research, and practice* (pp. 111–132). New York: Guilford Press.

Nakagawa, M., & Yamazaki, A. (2004). Intimacy and apologies in interpersonal conflict situations: Preschool children. *Japanese Journal of Educational Psychology, 52,* 159–169.

Ohbuchi, K., & Sato, K. (1994). Children's reactions to mitigating accounts: Apologies, excuses, and intentionality of harm. *Journal of Social Psychology, 134,* 5–17.

Omer, H., & Strenger, C. (1992). The pluralist revolution: From the one true meaning to an infinity of constructed one. *Psychotherapy: Theory, Research, Practice, Training, 29,* 253–261.

Onyango, P. (1998). The impact of armed conflict on children. *Child Abuse Review, 7,* 219–229.

Opotow, S. (2001). Reconciliation in times of impunity: Challenges for social justice. *Social Justice Research, 14,* 149–170.

Palgi, P., & Durban, J. (1995). The case of a war-orphaned boy. *Ethos, 23,* 223–243.

Pick, T. (2001). The myth of the trauma/the trauma of the myth: Myths as mediators of some long-term effects of war trauma. *Peace and Conflict: Journal of Peace Psychology, 7,* 201–226.

Punamäki, R. L. (1996). Can ideological commitment protect children's psychosocial well-being in situations of political violence? *Child Development, 67,* 55–69.

Rafman, S. (2004). Where the political and the psychological meet: Moral disruption and children's understanding of war. *International Relations, 18*(1), 67–78.

Rafman, S., Canfield, J., Barbas, J., & Kaczorowski, J. (1996). Disrupted moral order and disrupted attachment in war-orphaned children. *International Journal of Behavioral Development, 19,* 817–829.

Rafman, S., Canfield, J., Barbas, J., & Kaczorowski, J. (1997). Children's representation of parental loss due to war. *International Journal of Behavioural Development, 20,* 163–177.

Ricoeur, P. (2000). *La mémoire, l'histoire, l'oubli.* Paris: Editions du Seuil.

Sabian, M., Lopes Cardozo, B., Nackerud, L., Kaiser, R. T., & Varese, R. (2003). Factors associated with poor mental health among Guatemalan refugees living in Mexico 20 years after civil conflict. *Journal of the American Medical Association, 290,* 635–642,

Scobie, G. E. W., & Scobie, E. D. (2000). A comparison of forgiveness and prosocial development. *Early Child Development and Care, 160,* 33–45.

Shriver, D. W. (1995). *An ethic for enemies: Forgiveness in politics.* New York: Oxford University Press.

Slone, M., Kaminer, D., & Durrheim, K. (2002). Appraisal of sociopolitical change among South African youth: The relation to psychological maladjustment. *Journal of Applied Social Psychology, 32,* 318–341.

Smetana, J. G., Daddis, C., Toth, S. L., Cicchetti, D., Bruce, J., & Kane, P. (1999). Effects of provocation on maltreated and nonmaltreated preschoolers' understanding of moral transgressions. *Social Development, 8,* 335–348.

Smetana, J. G., Toth, S. L., Cicchetti, D., Bruce, J., Kane, P., & Daddis, C. (1999). Maltreated and nonmaltreated preschoolers' conceptions of hypothetical and actual moral transgressions. *Developmental Psychology, 35,* 269–281.

Straker, G., Mendelsohn, M., Moosa, F., & Tudin, P. (1996). Violent political contexts and the emotional concerns of township youth. *Child Development, 67,* 46–54.

Summerfield, D. (2002). Effects of war: Moral knowledge, revenge, reconciliation, and medicalised concepts of "recovery." *British Medical Journal, 325,* 1105–1107.

Thangarajah, C. Y. (2002). Youth, conflict and social transformation in Sri Lanka. In S. T. Hettige & M. Mayer (Eds.), *Sri Lankan youth: Challenges and responses* (pp. 177–215). Colombo, Sri Lanka: Friedrich Ebert Stiftung.

Turiel, E., & Wainryb, C. (2000). Social life in cultures: Judgments, conflict, and subversion. *Child Development, 71,* 250–256.

Volkan, V. (2001). Transgenerational transmissions and chosen traumas: An aspect of large-group identity. *Group Analysis, 34,* 79–97.

Walker, U. M. (2006). *Moral repair: Reconstructing moral relations after wrongdoing.* New York: Cambridge University Press.

Wiene, S., Becker, D. F., McGlashan, T. H., Vojvoda, D., Hartman, S., & Robbins, J. P. (1995). Adolescent survivors of "ethnic cleansing": Observations on the first year in America. *Journal of the American Academy of Child and Adolescent Psychiatry, 34,* 1153–1159.

Worthington, E. L., Jr., & Scherer, M. (2004). Forgiveness is an emotion-focused coping strategy that can reduce health risks and promote health resilience: Theory, review, and hypotheses. *Psychology & Health, 19,* 385–405.

12

Does a Humble Attitude Promote Forgiveness?

Challenges, Caveats, and Sex Differences

JULIE JUOLA EXLINE AND
ANNE L. ZELL

Introduction

When reflecting on the offenses of others, it can be tempting to launch into self-righteous thinking. Whether people are reacting to a friend's betrayal or watching a news story about an abusive parent, it can be natural to think, "What kind of person would do something so horrible? I would never do something like that." By distancing themselves from other wrongdoers, people can gain temporary protection for their self-images. Yet, this kind of self-righteous thinking is likely to carry social costs. When people take a morally superior stance, they focus on differences rather than similarities between themselves and others. Empathy becomes difficult, and judgmental attitudes are likely to prevail. But what would happen if people took a different perspective, reflecting on their own shortcomings or misdeeds? We predicted that focusing on one's own capability for wrongdoing could prompt a humble, empathic mindset that would promote forgiving attitudes and merciful judgments.

We have been examining these ideas over the past 8 years, primarily within samples of college students. Our data have often surprised us, in part because we often found unexpected sex differences. The purpose of this chapter is to summarize the main findings from our studies.

Transgression, Forgiveness, and Self-Protection: A Brief Overview of Basic Concepts

When people transgress against others, one result is a state of *inequity*—an unfair status difference in which someone has been treated worse than she or he deserved (Walster, Berscheid, & Walster, 1973). A natural and reasonable response to inequity is to try to restore a sense of fairness. Furthermore, many offenses leave victims feeling humiliated, fearful, or powerless. As such, one of a victim's most pressing aims may be to restore a sense of power (Fagenson & Cooper, 1987). To feel more powerful, offended parties may seek retribution or seek social support for their position: "Can you believe what he did to me?" Another common response is to ruminate, replaying injustices over and over in one's mind. Rumination tends to keep anger inflamed (McCullough et al., 1998), a process that has been documented even at a physiological level (Witvliet, Ludwig, & van der Laan, 2001). A prolonged state of anger is unlikely to be pleasant. Yet, a sense of self-righteous anger may also help people to feel strong and justified—mindsets that many people might choose over feeling helpless and wounded. In short, self-protective and aggressive strategies may help to offset the victim's loss of power and status, at least temporarily.

When people try to forgive others who have harmed them, they turn to a very different strategy. Rather than holding on to anger and defending their position, forgivers attempt to let go of bitter feelings, resentment, and desire for revenge. They may even try to cultivate a positive attitude toward their offenders. Granted, a thoughtful decision to forgive can be an empowering and transcendent choice, but the decision to set aside any type of personal right seems to entail some sense of sacrifice and, perhaps, vulnerability.

Not surprisingly, people who are preoccupied with asserting their rights and protecting their self-images tend to find forgiveness difficult. For example, an inflated, narcissistic sense of entitlement has been linked with readiness to take offense (McCullough, Emmons, Kilpatrick, & Mooney, 2003), unforgiveness (Brown, 2004; Exline, Baumeister, Bushman, Campbell, & Finkel, 2004), and aggressive retaliation (Bushman & Baumeister, 1998). Shame-prone persons, who are chronically fearful of "losing face," also tend to be vengeful when provoked (Tangney et al., 1996). A self-righteous attitude is another likely predictor of grudges, as evidenced by studies showing that people are less forgiving if they cannot see themselves as capable of committing a similar misdeed (Exline et al., 2006).

To summarize, a growing body of evidence demonstrates that a self-protective or self-righteous stance could easily impede forgiveness. We wanted to see whether it would be possible to intercept this process using experimental methods: Is it possible to counteract an offended party's self-protective stance and to facilitate a more humble, empathic outlook? If people can be prompted to think in more humble ways, might they then become less harsh and more forgiving in their judgments of others? We predicted that they would. However, we were unprepared for the complexities that would arise when we tried to get our participants to adopt a humble frame of mind.

The Prisoner's Dilemma: Assessing Short-Term Responses to Provocation

People often think of forgiveness as a long-term process, and this is usually the case for serious hurts. However, a complementary way to think about forgiveness centers on short-term responses to provocation: Can a person tolerate an offense without retaliating? We chose to focus on retaliation in our initial studies. Granted, actions are an imperfect gauge of attitudes. A person might choose not to retaliate but still harbor a private grudge. Nonetheless, we reasoned that a willingness to forego or delay retaliation could be a useful behavioral indicator of a forgiving stance. Our first set of studies focused on retaliation in the context of a laboratory-based game. Because these studies have not been published elsewhere, we review them here in some depth.

Overview of the Prisoner's Dilemma. A classic game called the Prisoner's Dilemma (Axelrod, 1980) allows researchers to examine the dynamics of cooperation and retaliation. Our version of the game involves two players. For each turn of the game, each player has to make a decision: whether to cooperate with the other player or to defect (i.e., not to cooperate). If both players cooperate on any given turn, both win a modest four points. If both defect, they both lose two points.

However, the dynamics change dramatically if one player cooperates when the other defects: Under these conditions, the defector receives a sizable eight points while the cooperator loses five points. Participants were paid 20 cents for each point they earned. In short, the Prisoner's Dilemma presents a situation in which people may be tempted to betray each other by defecting—but only if they can assume that the other player will cooperate.

Our studies required players to complete 10 turns of the game, deciding on each turn whether to cooperate or defect. The game was computerized. Although participants were actually playing against a computer program, they were led to believe that the other player was a student of the same sex as themselves. After each turn, the display was updated to show the choices of both players, the shift in points as a result of the turn, and the ongoing point totals.

Pilot Study

Before introducing hypotheses about humility, we conducted a pilot study to collect baseline data. We found that 80% of our college student participants cooperated on the first turn of the game, with women being more likely to cooperate than men. We also confirmed that having the computerized opponent defect on the very first turn was an effective way of setting an adversarial tone for the game, resulting in many defections by participants and low point totals at the game's end.

Overview of Methods

Because we wanted to create a situation in which forgiveness and retribution would be immediately relevant, both of our subsequent studies used a design in which the participant's computerized opponent always defected on the first turn (as well as the 7th and 10th turns). For the remaining turns, the program used a *tit-for-tat* strategy (Axelrod, 1980), mirroring the participant's action from the prior turn. So if a participant cooperated on turn 1, the other (programmed) player would cooperate on turn 2; if a participant defected on turn 8, the program would defect on turn 9, and so on.

Participants in both of our Prisoner's Dilemma studies were Introductory Psychology students at a private research university in the midwestern United States. All received partial course credit for participating. Our main aim was to see whether participants' tendencies to retaliate would be influenced by their frame of mind before playing the game—in particular, by whether they were induced to feel humble versus proud. As described later, we used autobiographical essays in an attempt to elicit humble and prideful states of mind.

Because the effects of experimental primes often wear off quickly, it was important to have participants write the essays immediately before playing the game. However, we did not want to arouse suspicion. We settled on the following strategy: After explaining the rules of the game, experimenters told participants that they had inadvertently left the essay-writing sheet out of the background materials gathered at the start of the study. They asked participants to complete the essay before starting the game.

Study 1: Feeling Humble Versus Important

The first study included 65 undergraduate participants (46 men and 19 women). After completing a background questionnaire and learning about the game, participants were randomly assigned to one of three conditions. The first was a control condition with no essay. In the second condition, participants were asked to write about a specific incident from their own lives—one in which they felt humble or had a sense of humility. In the third condition, participants recalled a time when they felt important or had a sense of importance. The resulting cell sizes were uneven for two reasons. First, because sex differences were not considered central when we designed the study, we did not attempt to equalize the number of men and women. Also, because we wanted to examine some supplemental hypotheses regarding humility, we assigned more participants to the humility condition (n = 35) than to the importance (n = 14) or control (n = 16) conditions.

Initially, we simply predicted that participants in the humility condition would be more cooperative than those in the importance condition. Recall that there were 10 turns in the game, and the programmed (bogus) participant always defected on the first turn. We predicted that those in the humility condition would wait longer before defecting than those in the importance condition, with the control group scoring in the middle. However, the turn number of the first defection did not differ based on experimental condition.

After seeing the null finding, we began to have some doubts about our hypothesis: Perhaps inducing a sense of humility does not make people more forgiving. We also found a wide range of material in the humility essays. Some focused on positive themes such as gazing at the stars or enjoying a major achievement, while others focused on transgressions or shame-inducing events (in one case, throwing up on a friend!). Obviously, we needed to make our humility primes more specific to reduce the range of events that participants were recalling.

In later analyses of the data set, we noticed some unexpected sex differences. Results revealed a significant interaction between sex and experimental condition, $F(2, 59) = 3.28$, $p < .05$. Men behaved in a manner consistent with our hypotheses, waiting longer to defect if they wrote the humble essay ($M = 4.3$, $SD = 3.7$) as opposed to the important essay ($M = 2.2$, $SD = 1.1$), $t(43) = 2.03$, $p < .05$. Women did just the opposite, waiting longer to defect if they wrote the important essay ($M = 4.3$, $SD = 2.3$) than if they wrote the humble essay ($M = 1.8$, $SD = 0.8$), $t(16) = 3.78$, $p < .01$. We did not want to draw any firm conclusions from these data, both because of the small number of women and because we had not predicted any sex differences. However, the results piqued our curiosity about whether men and women might respond differently to being humbled.

Study 2: Pride Versus Two Ways of Being Humbled

While finishing Study 1, we discovered some new theorizing (Tangney, 2000) suggesting that humility could involve an existential focus: People may feel humble if they see themselves as a small part in the larger scheme of things. Some of our Study 1 participants chose to write humility essays along existential lines, and initial analyses suggested that they may have cooperated more as a result. Seeking to follow these promising leads, we designed Study 2 to pit an existential humility condition against two others: one focusing on pride and another focusing on negative self-views.

The design was similar to Study 1, using three essay conditions before having participants play the Prisoner's Dilemma game. Participants were randomly assigned to recall and describe one of three types of experiences: one in which they felt that they were just a small part in the larger scheme of things (existential humility), one in which they felt bad about themselves, and one in which they felt proud about how they were doing compared to other people. Our intention for the pride condition was to prime a smug or cocky sense of superiority, and we expected to see shame-related stories in the negative self condition. As such, we predicted that those primed to reflect on the "small self"—the existential aspect of humility—would be more cooperative than those in the other groups, taking longer to defect. But once again the data surprised us.

There was a marginally significant difference between the groups in terms of how long they waited to defect, $F(2, 30) = 3.16, p = .06$. But the results did not support our predictions. Instead, those primed to feel proud waited longer to defect ($M = 3.7$, $SD = 2.8$) than those in the "bad self" condition ($M = 2.0$, $SD = 0.6$), $t(30) = 2.38, p < .05$. Those in the existential condition had intermediate scores that did not differ from those of the other groups ($M = 2.4$, $SD = 0.7$). Manipulation checks confirmed that the essays were effective in eliciting the mind-sets that we were seeking; they simply did not seem to affect behavior during the game. These results again made us question whether a humble frame of mind would actually promote forgiving behaviors.

As in Study 1, supplemental analyses revealed some sex differences. Unlike in Study 1, participants' sex did not moderate their choices about when to defect. However, we did find sex differences in participants' attitudes toward the other (bogus) participant at the end of the game. We averaged five items to assess negative attitudes: mistrustful, betrayed, resentful, hurt, and offended ($\alpha = .90$). With negative attitudes as the dependent variable, we found a pattern reminiscent of Study 1, with a significant interaction of sex and condition, $F(2, 27) = 4.81, p < .05$. Women harbored more negative attitudes toward the other player if they had written the "bad self" essay ($M = 4.7$, $SD = 1.8$) rather than the proud essay ($M = 2.0$, $SD = 0.9$), $t(11) = 2.77, p < .05$, or the existential essay ($M = 2.2$, $SD = 1.8$), $t(11) = 2.46, p < .05$. In contrast, men reported marginally greater negative attitudes if they wrote the proud essay ($M = 5.2$,

$SD = 2.1$) as opposed to the "bad self" essay ($M = 3.2$, $SD = 2.6$), $t(16) = 1.80$, $p < .10$. Men's scores on the existential essay were intermediate ($M = 3.9$, $SD = 1.4$) and did not differ from those of the other groups.

Reflections on Prisoner's Dilemma Findings

Due to the small sample sizes and unexpected, post-hoc findings, neither Study 1 nor Study 2 permitted firm conclusions. We still were not clear about whether humbling prompts would make people more forgiving in response to provocation. Study 2, in particular, suggested that positive self-attitudes might lead to more forbearance than negative self-attitudes. Yet, both studies suggested the need to look at sex differences more closely in future research. We observed that, in several cases, prompts focusing on pride seemed to make men less forgiving and women more forgiving. For women, prompts that led to bad feelings about the self seemed to increase hostility toward the other player as well.

Although the possibility of sex differences had begun to intrigue us, we were still unsure about whether these were meaningful or spurious findings. As such, we were reluctant to speculate about them until more systematic studies had been conducted. We also wanted to switch to a different methodology. Although the Prisoner's Dilemma game yielded some provocative findings, the method raises problems of interpretation. For example, does defection necessarily imply aggressive intent? Or could it simply indicate mistrust or a competitive desire to win the game? We were also frustrated by the somewhat artificial gaming focus of the studies, seeking instead to study forgiveness in contexts that had more direct relevance for the everyday lives of our college student participants.

Considering One's Own Potential to Harm Others

Our Prisoner's Dilemma studies focused on humility in a broad sense. A later manuscript (Exline, Campbell et al., 2004) gave us a chance to refine our conceptualization of humility, which we began to view as a nondefensive willingness to consider one's strengths and limitations. Another empirical study (Exline & Geyer, 2004) also revealed that people have many different ideas about what humility means, ranging from low self-esteem and humiliation to existential awe and modesty about their achievements.

We eventually decided that if our research goal was to examine people's responses to transgressions, it might be wise to ensure a closer match between participants' essays and the offenses to which they were responding. So we decided to have people focus on their own potential for transgression (Exline et al., 2006). Our main question was: Would people be more forgiving toward others if they could see themselves as capable of committing a morally similar offense? We predicted that they would.

In various pilot studies, we tried different techniques to encourage people to reflect on their own propensity for wrongdoing. For example, after having people read about a hypothetical offense, we asked them to list reasons for which they might do something similar. We also asked them to describe hypothetical situations in which they might do something similar. Neither of these techniques seemed to have any effect on people's willingness to forgive. However, there was one technique that did show promise: having people focus on a similar offense that they had actually committed at some point. This was the angle that we took in our next set of studies, which are summarized next.

Please note that full descriptions of the moral humility studies appear in another empirical manuscript (Exline et al., 2006). As such, we include less detail here than we did for the Prisoner's Dilemma studies. We suggest that interested readers turn to the empirical paper for full methodological details and statistics.

Scenarios

We began with several studies using scenario methods. Undergraduates first read brief, standardized descriptions of hypothetical offenses, and we assessed their subsequent ratings of how forgivable the offenses were. The most frequently used scenario centered on two college roommates of the same sex as the participant. In the scenario, one student confides in the other about some painful and embarrassing childhood memories. It is clear that the disclosing roommate wants the information kept secret. Later, while gossiping with friends, the confidante reveals the roommate's secret. Everyone laughs, and word of the betrayal eventually makes it back to the roommate. Pilot studies showed that most people can recall betraying someone in this way, but the offense is still seen as fairly serious.

Although the conditions varied slightly across the studies, each study included at least two key conditions. In one condition, participants were asked to recall a time when they committed a similar offense. They then rated the forgivability of the offense from the scenario. In the control condition, participants evaluated the scenario offense without recalling a similar offense of their own.

Several studies using this design yielded a consistent pattern of results: Men behaved in a way consistent with our predictions, rating the scenario offense less harshly if they had been assigned to recall a similar offense of their own. Yet, women did not become more forgiving in response to recalling a similar offense. Supplemental items from one study suggested that, for women, reflecting on their own offense actually made the scenario offense seem larger. We also discovered that, regardless of sex, it was crucial for participants to recall an offense of their own that was similar in severity to the scenario offense. If they saw their own offense as being relatively mild, they were more severe in their judgments of the other offense. It is easy to picture a person thinking, "What I did was nowhere near as bad as what she or he did," with this self-righteous stance prompting a harsher judgment of the other's offense.

Studies of Real-Life Offenses

Next, we wanted to move beyond scenario methods to focus on real-life experiences. In our first study, we asked undergraduate participants to recall and describe a time when another person seriously hurt or offended them. Once again, we randomly assigned participants to one of two conditions: a control condition or one in which they were asked to recall a similar offense of their own.

Results revealed sex differences that paralleled those of the scenario studies. In this case women reported more forgiving attitudes than men, on average. However, men who were assigned to recall a similar offense reported more forgiving (i.e., less vengeful) attitudes toward the offender immediately afterward. In fact, the men appeared just as forgiving as the women under these circumstances. Consistent with our conceptualization, men's attitudes toward their offenders became gentler, in part because of a heightened self-awareness and increased empathy. That is, they became more aware of their potential for committing a similar misdeed, and they were better able to understand the other person's offense. Among women, however, we found no effect of the experimental manipulation on subsequent forgiveness and, in replication of one of the scenario studies described previously, women once again reported that focusing on their own offenses made the other person's offense seem larger.

We conducted one final study to tie up some conceptual loose ends from the prior work. Each of the studies described earlier included only two conditions: one in which people recalled a similar offense and another in which they did not. But what if our humility prompts facilitated forgiveness in men simply by encouraging self-focus? With this idea in mind and also remembering that prideful recollections led to some positive results in the Prisoner's Dilemma studies, we included a self-affirmation condition: People in this group recalled a situation in which they had positive feelings about themselves.

Another goal was to examine empathy more closely. Empathy has been shown to be a robust predictor of forgiveness (see Malcolm, Warwar, & Greenberg, 2005, for a review). Our aim in these studies was to help people empathize with others by focusing on their own potential for wrongdoing, but we realized that there might be more straightforward ways to encourage empathy. As such, we reasoned that it would be wise to include a clear-cut empathy condition in which participants were asked to take the perspective of the person who had offended them. In terms of facilitating forgiveness, we predicted that this condition would be about as effective as the condition in which people recalled a similar offense—at least for men. We were also curious about whether empathy or self-affirmation might have the power to make women more forgiving.

Results suggested that, as predicted, men were less vengeful in the similar-offense and empathy conditions than in the control condition. The self-affirmation condition did not seem to have any effects on men's forgiveness. Once again, none of the conditions seemed to influence forgiveness for women. We did supplemental analyses to ensure that women reported the expected emotional responses to the essays, and they did, but their emotional responses to the essays did not influence their forgiveness ratings.

Why the Differences Between Men and Women?

Taken together, the studies described here suggest that recalling a similar offense of their own may indeed make people more forgiving, especially if they recall an offense of similar severity. Focusing on one's own misdeeds has the potential to facilitate empathy. Yet, in virtually all studies described here, being humbled seemed to facilitate forgiveness only for male participants. Men's attitudes toward other offenders became less harsh when they recalled a similar offense of their own, and this strategy was about as effective as asking them to take the offender's perspective.

Based on these findings, we suggest that perspective-taking and an emphasis on one's own transgressions are both worth considering as tools to help facilitate empathy and forgiveness among men. The notion that the empathy/forgiveness link may be especially strong for men is supported by several recent studies (e.g., Fincham, Paleari, & Regalia, 2002; Toussaint & Webb, 2005). The evidence is mixed, however, with some research suggesting that the link between empathy and forgiveness holds regardless of sex (e.g., Macaskill, Maltby, & Day, 2002).

We do not want to overstate the sex differences that our research revealed or to overgeneralize. Most of our studies were not designed with sex differences in mind, and the research relied on samples of young adults from American universities. It is also possible that there were ceiling effects for women, who generally reported more forgiving attitudes than men at baseline. Nonetheless, because the sex differences were quite consistent across the studies, we would like to speculate about some possible reasons for the differences. (Note that none of these proposed explanations has yet been empirically confirmed.)

One possibility is that women may empathize with others more naturally than men do. If this is the case, then being asked to focus on their own transgressions might serve as a mere distraction for women, breaking the flow of the normal empathy process. Worse, focusing on one's moral failings might raise negative emotions that then have to be managed. Another study from our laboratory offers some data relevant to this idea. Note that this study did not focus on forgiveness; instead, it emphasized the mood and self-esteem effects of focusing on one's faults.

The study was conducted with a sample of 73 undergraduates (42 women and 31 men). First, participants completed a measure of state self-esteem. Next, they were asked to list as many of their personal weaknesses as they could within a 5-minute period, with the incentive that they would be paid 10 cents for each weakness listed. Women listed more weaknesses than men. (For women, $M = 14.6$, $SD = 6.1$; for men, $M = 10.9$, $SD = 5.4$, $F(1, 70) = 7.19$, $p < .01$.) Furthermore, women showed a larger drop in state self-esteem after this exercise ($M = -2.1$, $SD = 6.4$) than men did ($M = 0.9$, $SD = 5.4$), $F(1, 70) = 4.32$, $p < .05$.

Although tentative, these findings suggest that when compared with men, women may be slightly more aware of their faults or more willing to admit them. However, women may also be harder on themselves than men are when attention is drawn to their shortcomings. These possibilities seem consistent with research suggesting that women engage in more depressive rumination than men (Nolen-Hoeksema, Larson, & Grayson, 1999). If women experience reduced self-esteem or dampened mood after focusing on their faults, they may then become distracted with mood regulation or self-enhancement goals. Either of these goals could divert them from attempts to empathize with another person.

Challenges of Trying to Induce a Sense of Humility

Before concluding, we would like briefly to describe some challenges that we have encountered when trying to get people to adopt a humble mindset. Most importantly, we have found the need to strike a delicate balance when encouraging people to focus on their limitations or moral failings. For example, several altruism studies have suggested that anything that makes people feel bad about themselves tends to inhibit generosity (e.g., Exline & Fisher, 2005). At the end of one of our similar-offense studies (Exline et al., 2006, Study 5), we asked participants to reflect on how much negative emotion (e.g., embarrassment, guilt, shame) they experienced when reflecting on their offenses. Women reported slightly more negative emotion than men in this situation, and the worse people felt in response to the essay-writing task, the harsher were their judgments of the other person's offense. Among women in particular, self-focused rumination may begin when attention is focused on their shortcomings. This self-focused rumination may, in turn, make it difficult for a person to forgive others.

Another challenging aspect of encouraging people to reflect on their own offenses is that it can be tempting for people to recall offenses that are relatively trivial. We found this pattern in several data sets. If people focus on a comparatively small offense of their own, the offenses of others may loom even larger in comparison. Under these circumstances, the technique of recalling an offense of their own might actually backfire and make people more severe in their judgments of others. We found this pattern to be especially clear for women.

Setting sex differences aside for the moment, we would like to note another obvious limitation of asking people to focus on similar offenses: If the offense to which they are reacting is particularly unusual or heinous, people may not be able to envision themselves doing something similar. Can most people see themselves capable of becoming torturers or sadistic killers, for example? Some people who have spent time focusing on the dark sides of their own personalities—or human nature in general—may be able to envision a situation in which they would do grievous harm to another person, but many people may see themselves as being utterly incapable of such actions. This problem suggests an upper limit to the practical use of the technique.

Rather than trying to picture themselves committing heinous offenses, some individuals may benefit from a technique used in research by Wohl and Branscombe (2005). Several of their studies focused on attitudes of Jewish participants regarding perpetrators of the Holocaust. Participants reported more forgiving attitudes if the Holocaust was framed in terms of human nature (i.e., how humans behave aggressively toward other humans) rather than the offense of one specific group against another (i.e., how Germans had behaved aggressively toward Jews). This subtle change in wording made a major difference in how people responded to the offenses. In everyday life, then, people may be less severe in their judgments of others if they focus on the flawed or fallen aspects of human nature that we all share. By focusing on our common humanity and connections with each other, individuals may be able to cultivate a sense of self-compassion (see Neff, 2003a, 2003b) that could foster compassion toward others as well.

Although reflecting on human universals is one way to facilitate forgiveness, the data reported here suggest that a willingness to reflect on one's own personal offenses may also be a useful technique—at least for men. But how can we help people to tolerate looking at their flaws without lapsing into despair or defensiveness? Perhaps explaining some of the benefits of considering one's limitations would be helpful, so that people can see the humbling exercise as purposeful and constructive rather than condemning. Also, as described in more detail elsewhere (Exline, 2006; Exline, Campbell et al., 2004), we propose that people will be more likely to tolerate looking at their flaws if the exercise is preceded by positive input that will help them to feel secure, valuable, and accepted. In clinical settings in particular, the role of a strong, accepting therapeutic relationship seems especially important before encouraging people to consider their misdeeds and faults. A highly accepting relationship context might be particularly important for women, given their tendency to ruminate about their shortcomings.

Conclusion

We were surprised by the many challenges that arose when we began to study the link between humble attitudes and forgiveness. Initially, the major hypothesis behind this research seemed straightforward to us: If people can see their own limitations or capability for wrongdoing, they should find it easier to forgive others. Our data did offer some support for this prediction—but mainly among men. We still need a better understanding of techniques that will help women to forgive. These studies have also reminded us that it is a delicate undertaking to challenge people's self-protective defenses. Nonetheless, we remain optimistic that humbling techniques, when implemented with skill, respect, and care, may help many people to become more forgiving and compassionate toward one another.

References

Axelrod, R. (1980). Effective choice in the Prisoner's Dilemma. *Journal of Conflict Resolution, 24,* 3–25.

Brown, R. P. (2004). Vengeance is mine: Narcissism, vengeance, and the tendency to forgive. *Journal of Research in Personality, 38,* 576–584.

Bushman, B. J., & Baumeister, R. F. (1998). Threatened egotism, narcissism, self-esteem, and direct and displaced aggression: Does self-love or self-hate lead to violence? *Journal of Personality and Social Psychology, 75,* 219–229.

Exline, J. J. (2006). Humility: A means of taming the wild ego? In J. Bauer & H. Wayment (Eds.), *Quieting the ego: Psychological benefits of transcending egotism.* Washington, DC: American Psychological Association.

Exline, J. J., Baumeister, R. F., Bushman, B. J., Campbell, W. K., & Finkel, E. J. (2004). Too proud to let go: Narcissistic entitlement as a barrier to forgiveness. *Journal of Personality and Social Psychology, 87,* 894–912.

Exline, J. J., Campbell, W. K., Baumeister, R. F., Joiner, T., Krueger, J., & Kachorek, L. V. (2004). Humility and modesty. In C. Peterson & M. Seligman (Eds.), *Character strengths and virtues: A handbook and classification* (pp. 461–475). New York: Oxford.

Exline, J. J., & Fisher, M. L. (2005, January). *Sentimental journeys and balanced accounts: Emotion, social exchange, and decisions to "pass on" acts of kindness.* Poster presented at the annual meeting of the Society for Personality and Social Psychology, New Orleans, LA.

Exline, J. J., & Geyer, A. L. (2004). Perceptions of humility: A preliminary study. *Self and Identity, 3,* 95–114.

Exline, J. J., Baumeister, R. F., Zell, A. L., Kraft, A., Witvliet, C. V. O. (2007). *Not so innocent: Does seeing one's own capability for wrongdoing predict forgiveness?* Manuscript submitted for publication.

Fagenson, E. A., & Cooper, J. (1987). When push comes to power: A test of power restoration theory's explanation for aggressive conflict escalation. *Basic and Applied Social Psychology, 8,* 273–293.

Fincham, F. D., Paleari, F. G., & Regalia, C. (2002). Forgiveness in marriage: The role of relationship quality, attributions, and empathy. *Personal Relationships, 9,* 27–37.

Macaskill, A., Maltby, J., & Day, L. (2002). Forgiveness of self and others and emotional empathy. *Journal of Social Psychology, 142,* 663–665.

Malcolm, W. M., Warwar, S., & Greenberg, L. (2005). Facilitating forgiveness in individual therapy as an approach to resolving interpersonal injuries. In E. L. Worthington, Jr. (Ed.), *Handbook of forgiveness* (pp. 379–391). New York: Routledge.

McCullough, M. E., Emmons, R. A., Kilpatrick, S. D., & Mooney, C. N. (2003). Narcissists as "victims": The role of narcissism in the perception of transgressions. *Personality and Social Psychology Bulletin, 29,* 885–893.
McCullough, M. E., Rachal, K. C., Sandage, S. J., Worthington, E. L., Jr., Brown, S. W., & Hight, T. L. (1998). Interpersonal forgiving in close relationships II: Theoretical elaboration and measurement. *Journal of Personality and Social Psychology, 75,* 1586–1603.
Neff, K. D. (2003a). Self-compassion: An alternative conceptualization of a healthy attitude toward oneself. *Self & Identity, 2,* 85–101.
Neff, K. D. (2003b). The development and validation of a scale to measure self-compassion. *Self & Identity, 2,* 223–250.
Nolen-Hoeksema, S., Larson, J., & Grayson, C. (1999). Explaining the gender difference in depressive symptoms. *Journal of Personality and Social Psychology, 77,* 1061–1072.
Tangney, J. P. (2000). Humility: Theoretical perspectives, empirical findings and directions for future research. *Journal of Social and Clinical Psychology, 19,* 70–82.
Tangney, J. P., Barlow, D. H., Wagner, P. E., Marschall, D., Borenstein, J. K., Santfer, J., et al. (1996). Assessing individual differences in constructive vs. destructive responses to anger across the lifespan. *Journal of Personality and Social Psychology, 70,* 780–796.
Toussaint, L., & Webb, J. R. (2005). Gender differences in the relationship between empathy and forgiveness. *Journal of Social Psychology, 145,* 673–685.
Walster, E., Berscheid, E., & Walster, G. W. (1973). New directions in equity research. *Journal of Personality and Social Psychology, 25,* 151–176.
Witvliet, C. V. O., Ludwig, T. E., & van der Laan, K. L. (2001). Granting forgiveness or harboring grudges: Implications for emotion, physiology, and health. *Psychological Science, 121,* 117–123.
Wohl, M. J. A., & Branscombe, N. R. (2005). Forgiveness and collective guilt assignment to historical perpetrator groups depend on level of social category inclusiveness. *Journal of Personality and Social Psychology, 88,* 288–303.

13

Repentance in Intimate Relationships

VIRGINIA TODD HOLEMAN

Introduction

Forgiveness research has moved beyond its infancy into perhaps its early childhood, as demonstrated by a growing body of scholarly literature (see Scherer, Cooke, & Worthington, 2005, for a comprehensive bibliography). While there is much yet to discover about forgiveness (Worthington, 2005), researchers are beginning to turn their attention to concepts that are distinct from, yet intimately related to, forgiveness, such as reconciliation and apology. Regarding marital reconciliation, an explicit reconciliation intervention received early attention from Worthington and Drinkard (2000), and Worthington (2001, 2003, 2006) has subsequently refined this reconciliation model. Holeman (2000, 2004) conducted a qualitative study that resulted in the elucidation of factors that contribute to marital reconciliation. Not surprisingly, forgiving and repenting featured prominently in the 12 case studies.

Regarding apology, psychological research has focused primarily on apology from the perspective of victims or from the viewpoint of observers. For example, researchers reported that apologies facilitated forgiveness (i.e., Estrada-Hollenbeck, 1997; Girard, Mullet, & Callahan, 2002; McCullough, Worthington, & Rachal, 1997; Tavuchis, 1991). In addition, studies suggested that observers thought better of wrongdoers who sincerely apologized than those who did not apologize or who offered excuses (Bennett & Dewberry, 1994; Darby & Schlenker, 1989; Ohbuchi & Sato, 1994).

Some researchers have looked at apology and forgiveness from the transgressor's perspective. Sandage, Worthington, Hight, and Berry

(2000) explored personality and developmental factors that might promote seeking forgiveness. They reported that neither religiosity nor age predicted seeking forgiveness and that narcissism and self-monitoring inhibited forgiveness seeking. Witvliet, Ludwig, and Bauer (2002) examined emotional responses as participants imagined seeking forgiveness from someone they had hurt. They found that wrongdoers reported lower levels of sadness, anger, and guilt and higher levels of hope and gratitude when these transgressors also imagined that injured parties forgave them or were reconciled with them. Most recently, Exline, DeShea, and Holeman (2007) explored factors that impacted offenders' choices to offer an apology or to refrain from apologizing, and factors that influenced whether offenders experienced regret about their choice regarding apology. Participants reported more regret about nonapology than apology. Regrets about apology were associated with mutual grudges, protests of innocence, unsafe relationships, and apologies seen as somehow inadequate. Regrets about nonapology were associated with persistent remorse, self-punishing attitudes, and seeing the offended party as innocent of wrongdoing.

This chapter continues to explore relationship repair from the transgressor's perspective. First, apology and repentance are defined and differentiated from other practices. Second, a model of repentance is presented. The chapter closes with recommendations for clinical application and future research.

Differential Accounting Practices

When someone has acted badly in an intimate relationship, the alleged violator and the perceived victim exchange interpretations of the wounding event. For the most part, people act in ways that make sense *to them,* although these same actions may baffle others. "What were you thinking? Why did you do that? I thought I knew you?" are concerns voiced by presumed injured parties to which suspected wrongdoers must respond. In the process of responding, transgressors reveal for which actions they believe they should or could be held accountable, what it means for them to take responsibility for their actions, the degree to which they credit the injured party's experience and interpretation of their relationship, and the extent to which they engage in blaming and defensive strategies or the extent to which they expose "a broken and contrite heart" through expressions of sorrow, regret, and guilt and through demonstrations of changed behavior over time.

These interpretive negotiations can continue for months, even years, when participants desire reconciliation (Holeman, 2004). "Successful restorying" promotes the restoration of love and trustworthiness as partners reach a common understanding of what happened and why, who is responsible for what, and what reparative or compensatory steps are required (Hargrave, 1994, 2001). However, in many relationships, couples have accumulated histories of mutual offending (rather than a single, discrete offense) that result in long-standing patterns of tit-for-tat. Previous research (Baumeister, Stillwell, & Wotman, 1990) has established that victims and perpetrators remember different aspects of their own and the other's behavior so that the process of untangling the webs of guilt and innocence is indeed challenging. In these situations "story consensus" means that partners assume responsibility for their own words and deeds over the course of time and acknowledge the *differential* impact that each had on the relationship (Holeman). Because the "pure victim" and the "pure villain" are myths (Baumeister, 1997) in such cases, each partner learns not only forgiveness, but also apology and repentance. Conversely, many wounded relationships are "restored" in ways that lead to termination rather than repair. This section briefly differentiates among several account-giving strategies that offenders employ. Readers may refer to Schönbach (1980) for a detailed taxonomy of these practices.

When transgressors refute any knowledge of, or participation in, an alleged offense, they engage in denial. Typical statements of denial include: "I don't know what you are talking about." "You're mistaken." "How can you even think that?" Holeman (2004) described how several unfaithful partners used denial to dismiss their mate's suspicions. These particular transgressors chose denial because they wanted to avoid the consequences that would follow if partners' worries were verified. Wrongdoers who use denial may experience guilt or shame. Denial may be a way to reduce these emotions. Denials become a corrosive form of secret keeping. They establish alliances between offenders and those who also know and protect the secret while injured parties struggle to find alternative explanations for their perceptions (Friedman, 1985; Imber-Black, 1998).

A justification is the transgressor's reason for having committed the offense. "I did it because ..." is a typical justification format. Justifications make sense to offenders, and justifying offenders hope that their reasons also make sense to injured parties. If wounded partners accept the justification as valid, presumed offenders can acknowledge the distressing impact that their action had on their partner without abandoning their own belief that they acted in an appropriate manner. Injured parties reinterpret events in light of this new information. Justifications are most likely to work when a perceived offense is small or *truly understandable* given the offender's context.

Sadly, perpetrator justifications are also successful in situations when the offender's relational power outstrips that of the victim, as in cases of domestic violence. Clearly, in any type of abuse, no justification is acceptable. According to contextual therapy (Boszormenyi-Nagy & Krasner, 1986), these justifications arise from a sense of destructive entitlement where offenders believe that they are "entitled" to their actions because of what they are "owed" due to their own experiences of being abused or neglected.

Generally, when transgressors offer excuses, they are in some way saying that they are not accountable for what occurred. Excuses externalize the responsibility for harm done. "I did it but ..." is a classic excuse form. Excuses may help wrongdoers save face (Goffman, 1959, 1967) even as they diminish the image of the wrongdoer in the eyes of an injured party (Fukuno & Ohbuchi, 1998; Ohbuchi & Sato, 1994).When wrongdoers offer excuses, they hope that injured parties find them not culpable. Injured parties accept excuses when they conclude that mitigating external circumstances exist (Ohbuchi & Sato).

What is the difference, then, between a justification and an excuse? According to Langer (2002):

> If I give an explanation that makes sense to us both, the explanation is taken as a reason [justification] for my action. When it is not accepted, a reason becomes an excuse. When it is not accepted, the actor's perspective

> is denied. The attribution of excuse-making allows the person to whom the excuse is made to feel superior, at least for the moment. The cost is loss of genuine interaction and understanding. (pp. 224–225)

The nature of apology has been discussed from psychological (Lazare, 2004) and sociological (Tavuchis, 1991) perspectives. In addition, the psychology of the person who apologizes has been explored in an earlier publication (Goffman, 1971). An apology is a special way of saying, "I'm sorry." Lazare defines apology as "an encounter between two parties in which one party, the offender, acknowledges responsibility for an offense or grievance and expresses regret or remorse to a second party, the aggrieved" (p. 23).

Lazare (2004) proposes that several components comprise successful apologies. They include (a) an adequate and accurate acknowledgment of the offense; (b) an appropriate expression of regret, remorse, or sorrow; (c) a suitable offer of repayment or restitution; and (d) a pledge for behavior reform to ensure that the offense is not repeated. He also observes that apologies can fail if any one of these components is missing or is inadequately presented. For example, wrongdoers may minimize the offense (inadequate acknowledgment) or they may not recognize the offense that the injured party identifies (inaccurate acknowledgment). In one case study involving inadequate and inaccurate acknowledgment, a husband saw his terminated "emotional" affair as the major offense that was upsetting his wife, whereas his partner was actually *more* angry when he confessed to her the degree to which he had deceived her about the full extent of sexual contact that he had had with his ex-lover (Holeman, 2004). Given that research has documented the differential recollection of transgressor and victim accounts (Baumeister, 1997; Baumeister et al., 1990), many apologies are doomed to fail before they get started. Fortunately, additional research suggests that victims may find inadequate apologies better than none (Ohbuchi & Sato, 1994).

Repentance: A Step Beyond Apology

Sincere apologies can repair broken relationships. With the cessation of offensive behaviors, couples may return to the status quo. However, when severe violations of relationship covenants or contracts (Ripley, Worthington, Bromley, & Kemper, 2005) occur between intimate partners, it may take more than apologies to restore love and trustworthiness. I propose that the "more than" process is repentance. The conceptualization of interpersonal repentance that follows emerged from within a larger qualitative project on marital reconciliation (Holeman, 2004). An abridged methodological description will set the stage for the subsequent discussion. Readers may refer to existing publications for a full report of the research design, description of research participants (Holeman, 2000), and a comprehensive presentation of the findings (Holeman, 2004).

The qualitative project used multiple-case, in-depth, phenomenological interviewing (Seidman, 1998). The 12 participating couples met the following criteria: They (a) were over age 18, (b) had experienced a relationship event that seriously threatened their marriage from *their* perspective, and (c) had successfully restored their marriage for at least one full year. I conducted three 90-minute interviews with each couple. The first two interviews were individual so that I could hear the marital story from the perspective of the transgressor and the injured party. A third conjoint interview focused on the couple's process of relationship restoration. A grounded theory of reconciliation developed from the themes and trends that emerged through analyses of the interviews.

What Is Interpersonal Repentance?

In describing forgiveness, Emmons (2006) writes, "Forgiveness is not an emotion per se, but can be thought of as a spiritual process that has emotion-regulating properties" (p. 75). A similar thing can be said about repentance. Repentance practices are found in Buddhism, Christianity, Hinduism, Islam, and Judaism (Holeman, in press). Repentance is most often associated with an experience of personal conviction about sin that subsequently leads sinners to confess their wrongdoing, commit to changed behavior, and make amends. These acts of contrition are offered to God or they are practiced to bring about good karma and diminish bad karma that was generated by the wrongdoing. A Christian understanding of repentance forms the basis for my conceptualization of interpersonal repentance (Holeman, Matsuyuki, & Tzou, 2005).

From a Christian perspective, repentance is most often pictured as a 180-degree change in one's life direction. In an individual's relationship with God, this involves a drastic turning away from anything that blocks that relationship and a complete turning toward full commitment to God. The changes do not stop there. According to Green, McKnight, and Marshall (1992):

> Repentance involves acknowledgement of one's sinfulness. … as well as a new and holy pattern of daily behavior in relation to others. … Thus it is clear that repentance … does not simply consist of a "change of mind," but a transformation of the entire person. (p. 670)

It is this "transformation of the entire person" that is key to differentiating repentance from apology.

Regarding interpersonal repentance, one can picture it as

> a decisive turning away from thoughts, words, and deeds that have betrayed love and trust, and a wholehearted turning toward attitudes and activities that can restore love and trust to the relationship. [It] includes confession and a commitment to consistent changed behavior over time. (Holeman, 2004, p. 238)

The goal of interpersonal repentance is the restoration of love and trust that happens through a transformation of the transgressor and subsequently, the intimate relationship. As already noted, apology may set a wounded relationship on steadier ground, but it does not necessarily imply the personal and relational transformation of repentance. While apology is difficult, repentance is even more challenging because it is all-encompassing. It is a humbling experience that requires transgressors to see themselves and their actions through the eyes of the injured party, and then to credit that perspective with the power to effect drastic change.

Wounded spouses from the qualitative study (Holeman, 2004) wanted *much more* than apology. Apologies were merely a good start. They were looking for consistent and dramatic changes of heart within their transgressors. Transgressors also affirmed the necessity for this transformation. Neither victim nor victimizer was content to return to the way things had been. These 12 couples affirmed that if their relationships were going to survive, some quantum change had to happen. That change often started with offenders' embodiment of interpersonal repentance. Several factors motivated repentance. Some transgressors discovered that their call to repentance came hand in hand with spiritual conviction and renewal. For others forgiveness elicited repentance. The majority of participating transgressors repented out of an intense, and sometimes desperate, desire to save their marriage, particularly in the face of outraged mates' confrontations.

Paradoxically, repentance happens at discrete moments and over the course of time. Several offenders in the previously mentioned study (Holeman, 2004) remembered specific, pivotal instances in which they expressed intense guilt, grief, remorse, and sadness about the offense and the pain they had caused. On the other hand, all transgressors from the study observed that rebuilding trustworthiness, an important element in repentance, took time. This process unfolded over the course of months, even years. Consistent commitment to changed behavior over time was essential.

What relationships might exist among guilt, shame, and repentance? Observations from the narrative data (Holeman, 2000, 2004) suggested that participating transgressors expressed moral emotions of both guilt and shame. Psychologists differentiate between guilt and shame. Tangney (1995) proposed that shame denotes an intense sense of pain about "who I am" while guilt reveals distress about "what I did," with guilt being less debilitating than shame. Tangney's research suggested that shame inhibited repair attempts whereas guilt spurred them on. However, the transgressors from Holeman's (2000, 2004) study dedicated themselves to relationship repair *and* expressed shame about their moral failures. Nevertheless, from the interviews it was clear that for some offenders, Tangney's "shame-proneness" ruled for some time. These offenders felt horrible about their offense and wanted to stop, but they also wanted to avoid humiliation if others found out. When they had "come clean" with their partner (through victim confrontation or offender disclosure), a change seemed to take place. Rather than avoiding conversation about the offense, they welcomed it. Rather than defensively blaming their partner, they took ownership. Rather than avoiding and withdrawing, they engaged in connection and self-disclosure. This would imply that these transgressors eventually experienced another form of shame that supported repair rather than inhibiting it. What explanation might account for this?

Woodruff's (2001) work on reverence may shed light on this conundrum. Woodruff writes:

> Reverence begins in a deep understanding of human limitations; from this grows the capacity to be in awe of whatever we believe lies outside our control—God, truth, justice, nature, even death. The capacity for awe, as it grows, brings with it the capacity for respecting fellow human beings, flaws and all. *This in turn fosters the ability to be ashamed when we show moral flaws exceeding the normal human allotment.* (p. 3, emphasis added)

Woodruff agrees that shame can become a destructive force, arguing, however, that the virtue of reverence prevents this because "virtues are capacities for having feelings in the right way" (p. 73) and at the right time. For Woodruff, shame is a powerful emotion that can move an individual to make appropriate sacrifices for the sake of others.

All study participants (Holeman, 2000) practiced conservative forms of Christianity, which emphasized the reality of human limitations and underscored the awesomeness of God. Transgressors revered God, but rather than revering their mates, they had begun to take their mates for granted and showed disrespect toward them, opening the door for moral offense and failure. As these offenders reclaimed the virtue of reverence for their partners, they experienced the type of shame consistent with Woodruff's position, which allowed for feeling ashamed and making amends. Reverence neutralized shame's corrosiveness.

A Model of Interpersonal Repentance

Because reconciliation is the desired outcome of interpersonal repentance, readers who are familiar with Hargrave's (1994, 2001) model of family forgiveness will find resonance between his approach to forgiveness and this presentation of repentance. Like forgiveness, repentance makes reconciliation possible, but *not inevitable.* Nevertheless, one can imagine that they reflect the two sides of a reconciliation coin, forgiveness being one side and repentance the other (Holeman 2004; Worthington, 2001, 2003, 2006).

Repentance unfolds in two major movements: awareness and accountability. Each movement comprises additional components. Empathy and humility combine to increase transgressors' *awareness* of how their hurtful actions have wounded another. Confession and rebuilding trustworthiness unite to bring about *accountability*. Awareness happens *within* a transgressor. This is parallel to how many psychologists currently define forgiveness (Worthington, 2005). Accountability, on the other hand, happens *between* injured parties and wrongdoers. It is an interactive process and is more akin to what forgiveness researchers would term reconciliation. This model of repentance is not linear. Accountability can precede and support awareness just as awareness can elicit accountability.

Awareness

When transgressors develop awareness, they see themselves, those they wounded, and the offensive action in a new light. Behaviors that offenders had at one time preserved or defended through denial, justifications, or excuses are now viewed as harmful and inexcusable. Baumeister (1997) refers to a "magnitude gap" that exists between the perspectives of victims and perpetrators in terms of the nature of the offense and its impact. Empathy and humility help to close this gap. These moral emotions enable offenders to take the focus off self (humility) so that they can experience the hurtful event through the eyes of the other who has been injured (empathy).

In terms of repentance, humility enables transgressors to admit to their capacity for doing harm without restricting their self-image to only that of a harm-doer. Persons who experience humility have a modest and appropriate estimate of their strengths and weaknesses. Tangney (2002) asserts that humility results in a "forgetting of the self" (p. 411). According to Hargrave (2000), humility helps partners recognize that they "have limitations, problems, inadequacies that can, and should be improved" (p. 55). Humble people are open to learning because they do not see themselves as being better than others (Templeton, 1997).

Humility is not equivalent to low self-esteem or shame-proneness (Emmons, 2003; Tangney, 2002). It is incompatible with arrogance (Templeton, 1997). One can posit that humility's opposites are narcissism and pride. Narcissism has been shown to impede apology (Sandage et al., 2000). Obviously, a sense of moral superiority may also squeeze out humility, and sabotage expressions of repentance. For example, in a study on forgiveness, Exline, Baumeister, Bushman, Campbell, and Finkel (2004) noted that research participants who were primed to feel morally superior judged another person's transgression more harshly and as less forgivable. One can extrapolate from this to repentance. In relationships where mates practice tit-for-tat offending, any attitude of moral superiority contributes to each mate seeing his or her actions as "more right" and "less bad" than their partner's offenses. Therefore, they do not need to apologize—let alone repent.

How did study participants (Holeman, 2004) manifest humility? Consistent with humility, offenders admitted their mistakes, accepted consequences and conditions assigned by their partner, and sought counseling to help them make and maintain salient changes. In addition, they ceased defensive blaming and stopped justifying their actions. In effect, they found themselves "without excuse." Humility enabled these offenders to accept full responsibility for their actions without reference to how a partner's actions may have contributed to or influenced their bad choices. For example, two case studies revolved around alcoholism. The two alcoholic spouses accepted full responsibility for their drinking *without* reference to the caustic, biting, and belittling language of their partners, which they previously claimed had driven them to drink.

Empathy has received considerable attention in forgiveness studies. Batson, Ahmad, Lishner, and Tsang (2002) defined empathy as "an other-oriented emotional response elicited by and congruent with the perceived welfare of someone else." Research findings support a positive association between empathy and forgiving (Malcolm, Warwar, & Greenberg, 2006; Worthington, 1998, 2006). Empathy allows injured parties to imagine the world through the eyes of their offenders. This same visionary process is essential to interpersonal repenting. While humility opens transgressors' eyes to see *themselves* differently, empathy enables them to see their *wounded partners* in other ways. Empathy helps offenders to reframe their actions from the perspectives of injured parties, and to credit these experiences and interpretations. Humility's "forgetting of the self" (Tangney, 2002) supports empathy. Empathy is not simply a trite expression of "I feel your pain." Transgressors' ability to resonate authentically with victims' experiences lets victims know that offenders truly understand the nature of the offense at an emotional level, not merely at a cognitive level ("I know I hurt you"; Holeman, 1997). Empathy helps transgressors respond to the question: "What if something strange happened and you were suddenly transformed into your partner? Knowing how you treated [him or her], how would you feel? What would it be like being in an intimate partnership with you?" (Jory, Anderson, & Greer, 1997, p. 408).

Regarding repentance, empathy's emphasis is on perpetrators' prioritizing of their partners' welfare above their own ease and comfort. This is of critical importance during accountability when reparative demands of injured parties become personally uncomfortable and emotionally distressing for transgressors. This discomfort can last longer than perpetrators may at first imagine. In my clinical experience, it is typical for transgressors to become discouraged when their repair efforts have no positive emotional impact on their partners. When offenders empathize with injured parties' fear of being victimized again, transgressors are better able to sustain reparation from an internal locus of control rather than an external one.

Accountability

The previous paragraphs described awareness, one of the two movements in repentance. The following paragraphs explore the other movement, accountability. Accountability is where the "rubber meets the road." Transgressors can develop awareness through humility and empathy, but if they do not show changed behavior over time, then offenders' words of sorrow and contrition become "all talk and no action." Worthington (2003) identifies an "injustice gap" that exists between how victims and perpetrators view the way things are and how they ought to be. Accountability bridges the injustice gap. Mutual accountability is a facet of healthy, intimate relationships. Partners balance the distribution of giving and receiving (Hargrave, 2000) so that they experience equitable numbers of relationship benefits and burdens. All offenses disrupt this balance and severe offenses threaten to break the scales (Hargrave, 2001). Accountability helps to rebalance scales of giving and receiving through confession and rebuilding trustworthiness.

As previously mentioned, this aspect of repentance closely resembles what most forgiveness researchers call reconciliation (Enright & Fitzgibbons, 2000; Worthington, 2005, 2006). They correctly note that reconciliation happens *between* injured party and wrongdoer. I concur with this position, and in addition, I propose that these "between" processes overlap with repentance. The theological understanding upon which this model is constructed requires more than a change of mind (I agree that I hurt you and that it was wrong). It requires a change of heart, demonstrated through a changed life ("and here is how I am going to be different"). Therefore, an intrapersonal process alone is insufficient.

Confession involves an admission of guilt and sorrow over what has happened and how it has impacted the present. It includes the transgressor's vow to stop the offending behavior. Unfortunately, not all confessions are "good confessions." Two factors influence this: (a) the degree of expressed and experienced guilt and remorse, and (b) the degree of intended and actual behavioral change. When combined, these factors yield four types of confessions.

If offenders have no intent to change and feel no guilt or remorse about their offenses, then they offer an *acknowledgment*. "I did it, so what?" is a standard form of acknowledgment. Acknowledgment may be offered from a defensive and hostile stance. Tangney's (1995) research suggests that shame-proneness may partially fuel such a confession. On the other hand, if offenders experience guilt and remorse, perhaps because they have been confronted with irrefutable evidence, but have no intent to change, then their confession takes the form of *account-giving* (Augsburger, 1996). Like an excuse, account-givers minimize their degree of responsibility through externalization. "I did it, but …" is a standard account-giving format.

Offenders who commit to change, but feel no guilt and remorse offer an *acquiescence*. This is an attempt to appease perceived injured parties. This form of confession represents a "peace at any price" position. Unfortunately, changed behaviors are not likely to persist over time. Finally, an *authentic confession* or authentic apology would express sincere guilt and remorse about the wounding event with the promise to change, and change would happen. For example, in a dramatic move to "come clean," one offending spouse (Holeman, 2004) mailed letters to a number of people who had been hurt by her repeated affairs. In these letters she stated specifically what she had done and how she had hurt people, and she asked for their forgiveness. In addition, she willingly complied with her partner's stipulations and created a few of her own. She wanted to show that she had made a sincere confession.

The shape of a "good confession" may change over time. In Holeman's (2004) study, successful confessions initially included admission of guilt and regret, with pleas for another chance. Justifications were excluded (Holeman, 1997). At this point wrongdoers were desperate to save their marriages and they were willing to comply with the demands of injured parties. As transgressors grew in awareness, their confessions expanded. Now, they also included statements that reflected their new understanding of the offense.

Rebuilding trustworthiness is the other component of accountability. When offenders rebuild trustworthiness, they establish new patterns of behavior so that "their word" will once again mean something to injured parties. In many damaged relationships, victims stipulate what changes must happen (Holeman, 2004). Rebuilding trustworthiness includes faithfully fulfilling those requirements. The burden of untrustworthiness is a price that offenders pay. As previously mentioned, the difficult part of rebuilding trustworthiness is the dedication that is required to maintain salient, changed behaviors in the face of few or no external rewards or "pats on the back." What seems to be central to this process is the transgressor's ownership of it. When offenders internalize the impetus for change, injured parties can more easily risk trusting again.

Krastner and Joyce (1995) observed a tight relationship between truthfulness and trustworthiness. When truthfulness was in question, so was trustworthiness. Deception often gave life to relationship betrayal, particularly in case studies involving affairs (Holeman, 2004). Injured parties believed transgressors' lies. Then the "truth came out." Transgressors not only had to rebuild their trustworthiness, they also had to establish new evidence of truthfulness. Krastner and Joyce propose that residual trust—that is, trust that was earned as a result of the offender's past investments in the relationship—is the basis upon which injured parties accept initial repair attempts. Victim and victimizer engage in direct address, where each one speaks his or her truth and respectfully receives the truth of the other. Study participants repeatedly emphasized the pivotal role that persistent, total honesty and consistent communication played in reconciliation. Eventually, direct address supported merited trust, where injured parties recognized and credited repair attempts. By this point, injured parties were willing to take their partners at their word.

Repentance has internal (awareness) and interpersonal (accountability) aspects. Wrongdoers may engage the four components (humility, empathy, confession, rebuilding trustworthiness) in any order, and they may cycle back at any time to one of the four as necessary. Restoration is the goal of repentance. However, many relationships will not realize this goal. Repentance makes reconciliation possible, but not inevitable.

Repentance and Related Processes

Two assumptions upon which this model is based require further discussion. First, this model also assumes that transgressors will experience relief from guilt and shame. What additional processes are required when their emotional pain does not end and they have repented? Second, this model of repentance assumes that injured parties are involved through their reception of a good confession and by their openness to repair attempts. What options are open to offenders when victims are deceased or have terminated the relationship?

This model depicts repentance as an interpersonal practice. Therefore, enactments of changed behaviors remain a pivotal part of the model even when the original injured party is unavailable (e.g. death, distance, terminated relationship). In these situations, others, who stand in for injured parties, can receive a confession and witness behavioral changes. Clergy and clinicians often play this role when a person is repentant of an offense from the distant past. Pastors and mental health professionals who facilitate delayed repentance and those who may subsequently benefit from wrongdoers' change of heart may be considered "repentance surrogates." Although they have not been hurt by the offender, they now stand in the place of the original injured party. In this way the interactive component is maintained.

When repentance or forgiveness fails to assuage the conscience of a repentant transgressor, self-forgiveness is the next step. Hall and Fincham (2005) defined self-forgiveness as

> a set of motivational changes whereby one becomes decreasingly motivated to avoid stimuli associated with the offense, decreasingly motivated to retaliate against the self (e.g., punish the self, engage in self-destructive behaviors, etc.), and increasingly motivated to act benevolently toward the self. (p. 622)

Hall and Fincham suggested that self-forgiveness can facilitate healing for offenders who experience debilitating guilt and shame. Self-forgiveness takes time as offenders find ways to live with themselves again. Readers may refer to these authors for a full discussion of their theoretical model of self-forgiveness.

Conclusion

> What do I do to make you want me? What have I got to be heard? What do I say when it's all over? Sorry seems to be the hardest word.... It's sad, so sad. Why can't we talk it over? And sorry seems to be the hardest word. (Taupin, 1976)

These words, made famous by Elton John, reflect the sentiments of many transgressors whose words made no impact on injured parties. This chapter suggested that perhaps these offenders offered denials, justifications, or excuses as they tried to "talk it over." While no guarantee exists that repentance will restore lost love, it is possible that had this wrongdoer repented, a different chorus might have been penned.

If "sorry" is the hardest word, repentance may be among the hardest practices. More than words are required. Through awareness, offenders gain insight into and understanding about the offense, themselves, and injured parties. Through accountability, they confess (i.e., authentic apology) and demonstrate their trustworthiness through consistent, changed behavior over time. As these facets are internalized by transgressors, personal and relational transformation unfolds. Repentance addresses the past and can offer hope for the future.

How might mental health professionals use this model of repentance? Lazare (2004) observes that many people do not know how to make a good apology. Fewer still may know how to repent. Clinicians may find this model helpful as a heuristic tool for therapy. For example, is it necessary for the offender to develop awareness? If so, to what degree does the offender understand the nature of the offense from the injured party's perspective? Is the transgressor operating out of a sense of destructive entitlement that will thwart repentance or is humility beginning to surface? On the other hand, is it necessary for the offender to establish accountability? Has the offender made a good confession? Does he or she know how to do that? In what ways might offenders show changed behavior over time? If the offenders are only following through when injured parties challenge or threaten them, how might counselors support a greater degree of ownership of this process? Future outcome research is required to establish the efficacy of this model in clinical settings.

How might researchers interact with this model? Clearly, the theoretical model itself requires investigation. Apology has been operationalized in previous studies as cited throughout this chapter. Repentance has not. Quantitative explorations are needed to test the assumptions upon which this model is built. Do humility and empathy motivate repentance? What other moral emotions might be associated with this construct? The relationship between self-forgiveness and repentance requires additional exploration. Do people who repent find self-forgiveness easier? Under what circumstances might an inverse relationship exist between repentance and self-forgiveness? It will take additional empirical research to answer these questions.

Qualitative studies may address other "big picture" questions. For example, the 12 couples who participated in Holeman's (2004) qualitative study on marital reconciliation all embraced a sincere commitment to the Christian faith tradition. The couples all affirmed that faith acted as a constraint against divorcing their partner and a motivator to pursue reconciliation. Given that many committed Christian couples divorce, one wonders what differences may emerge from the retrospective accounts of sincere Christians who chose divorce rather than reconciliation. Do these individuals find support for marital dissolution within their Christianity? If not, how do they square their decision to terminate their marriage with their Christian faith?

What impact does religiosity have on repentance in terms of conceptualization and implementation? This present model is founded on a Christian theological understanding of repentance. Just as Holeman et al. (2005) explored the ways that Buddhism and Christianity might shape therapeutic approaches to forgiveness, scholars from other religious traditions can compare other theological beliefs with those presented here. For example, Judaism has a long standing emphasis on *teshuva,* the process of return (Dorff, 1998; Schimmel, 2002). Is this model merely a restatement of that ancient practice? How does a religious belief in karma affect interpersonal repentance?

Regarding culture, does a given culture view repentance as a discrete event or a process of reparation that unfolds over time? An exchange that I had with a doctoral student highlights this. An individual of Native American descent, who has been involved in racial reconciliation events, was among a group of students with whom I was speaking about interpersonal reconciliation. He expressed his concern about racial reconciliation conferences. He views these as apology events, and from his perspective, this event begins the apology rather than delivering it as a finished product. He asked, "How do you get the White man to stay at the table?" His culture conceptualizes apology as a process of relationship restoration that incorporates statements of apology (Woodley, 2004). When the White man "left the table" prematurely, the restoration process was arrested.

This chapter has discussed repentance on a small, person-to-person scale. Repairing individual relationships is important as they comprise the scope of the world in which people live. Yet, perhaps these reflections have larger applications. For example, the 1990s witnessed a number of public apologies for past offenses by public governmental officials (Lazare, 2004). Were they effective? Might this model of repentance have application for such occurrences? Given that horrendous evils continue to be committed against entire people groups on a worldwide level, humanity must find ways to live peaceably together. In addition to forgiveness, repentance may help pave the way for that day. Perhaps then, "sorry" will no longer be the hardest word.

References

Augsburger, D. W. (1996). *Helping people forgive.* Louisville, KY: Westminster John Knox Press.

Batson, C. D., Ahmad, N., Lishner, D. A., & Tsang, J. (2002). Empathy and altruism. In C. R. Snyder & S. J. Lopez (Eds.), *Handbook of positive psychology* (pp. 159–171). New York: Oxford University Press.

Baumeister, R. E. (1997). *Evil: Inside human violence and cruelty.* New York: W. H. Freeman and Company.

Baumeister, R. E., Stillwell, A., & Wotman, S. R. (1990). Victim and perpetrator accounts of interpersonal conflict: Autobiographical narratives about anger. *Journal of Personality and Social Psychology, 59,* 994–1005.

Bennett, M., & Dewberry, C. (1994). "I've said I'm sorry, haven't I?" A study of the identity implications and constraints that apologies create for their recipients. *Current Psychology: Developmental, Learning, Personality, Social, 13,* 10–20.

Boszormenyi-Nagy, I., & Krasner, B. (1986). *Between give and take: A clinical guide to contextual therapy.* New York: Bruner/Mazel.

Darby, B. W., & Schlenker, B. R. (1989). Children's reactions to transgressions: Effects of the actor's apology, reputation and remorse. *British Journal of Social Psychology, 28,* 353–364.

Dorff, E. (1998). The elements of forgiveness: A Jewish approach. In E. L. Worthington, Jr. (Ed.), *Dimensions of forgiveness: Psychological research and theological perspectives* (pp. 29–55). Radnor, PA: Templeton Foundation Press.

Emmons, R. A. (2003). *The psychology of ultimate concerns: Motivation and spirituality in personality.* New York: Guilford Press

Emmons, R. A. (2006). Spirituality: Recent progress. In M. Csikszentmihalyi & I. S. Csikszentmihalyi (Eds.), *A life worth living: Contributions to positive psychology* (pp. 62–81). New York: Oxford University Press.

Enright, R. D., & Fitzgibbons, R. P. (2000). *Helping clients forgive: An empirical guide for resolving anger and restoring hope.* Washington, DC: American Psychological Association.

Estrada-Hollenbeck, M. B. (1997). Forgiving in a world of rights and wrongs: Victims' and perpetrators' role in resolving interpersonal conflicts through forgiveness. *Dissertation Abstracts International, 58,* 2749.

Exline, J. J., Baumeister, R. F., Bushman, B. J., Campbell, W. K., & Finkel, E. J. (2004). Too proud to let go: Narcissistic entitlement as a barrier to forgiveness. *Journal of Personality and Social Psychology, 87,* 894–912.

Exline, J. J., DeShea, L., & Holeman, V. T. (2007). Is apology worth the risk? Predictors, outcome, and ways to avoid regret. *Journal of Social and Clinical Psychology,* 26(4), 479–504.
Friedman, E. (1985). *Generation to generation: Family process in church and synagogue.* New York: Guilford Press.
Fukuno, M., & Ohbuchi, K. (1998). How effective are different accounts of harm-doing in softening victims' reactions? A scenario investigation of the effects of severity, relationship, and culture. *Asian Journal of Social Psychology, 1,* 167–178.
Girard, M., Mullet, E., & Callahan, S. (2002). The mathematics of forgiveness. *American Journal of Psychology, 115,* 351–375.
Goffman, E. (1959). *The presentation of the self in everyday life.* New York: Anchor Books.
Goffman, E. (1967). *Interaction ritual: Essays on face-to-face behavior.* New York: Aldine.
Goffman, E. (1971). *Relations in public.* New York: Basic Books.
Green, J. B., McKnight, S., & Marshall, I. H. (Eds.). (1992). *Dictionary of Jesus and the gospels.* Downers Grove, IL: InterVarsity Press.
Hall, J. H., & Fincham, F. D. (2005). Self-forgiveness: The stepchild of forgiveness research. *Journal of Social and Clinical Psychology, 24,* 621–637.
Hargrave, T. D. (1994). *Families and forgiveness: Healing wounds in the intergenerational family.* New York: Brunner/Mazel.
Hargrave, T. D. (2000). *The essential humility of marriage: Honoring the third identity in couples therapy.* Phoenix, AZ: Zeig, Tucker, and Theisen.
Hargrave, T. D. (2001). *Forgiving the devil: Coming to terms with damaged relationships.* Phoenix, AZ: Zeig, Tucker, and Theisen.
Holeman, V. T. (1997). Couples forgiveness exercise. *The Family Journal: Counseling and Therapy for Couples and Families, 5,* 263–266.
Holeman, V. T. (2000). Thinking about reconciliation. *Marriage and Family: A Christian Journal, 3,* 373–386.
Holeman, V. T. (2004). *Reconcilable differences: Healing and hope for troubled marriages.* Downers Grove, IL: InterVarsity Press.
Holeman, V. T. (2007). The role of forgiveness in religious life and within marriage and family relationships. In J. D. Onedera (Ed.), *The role of religion in marriage and family counseling.* New York: Taylor & Francis.
Holeman, V. T., Matsuyuki, M., & Tsou, J. (2005). *A counselor's guide to Buddhist and Christian perspectives on forgiveness.* Unpublished manuscript.
Imber-Black, E. (1998). *The secret life of families: Truth-telling, privacy, and reconciliation in a tell-all society.* New York: Bantam.
Jory, B., Anderson, D., & Greer, C. (1997). Intimate justice: Confronting issues of accountability, respect, and freedom in treatment for abuse and violence. *Journal of Marital and Family Therapy, 23,* 399–419.
Krastner, B. R., & Joyce, A. J. (1995). *Truth, trust, and relationships: Healing interventions in contextual therapy.* New York: Brunner/Mazel.

Langer, E. (2002). Well-being: Mindfulness versus positive evaluation. In C. R. Snyder & S. J. Lopez (Eds.), *Handbook of positive psychology* (pp. 214–230). New York: Oxford University Press.

Lazare, A. (2004). *On apology*. New York: Oxford University Press.

Malcolm, W., Warwar, S., & Greenberg, L. (2006). Facilitating forgiveness in individual therapy as an approach to resolving interpersonal injuries. In E. L. Worthington, Jr. (Ed.), *Handbook of forgiveness* (pp. 379–391). New York: Routledge.

McCullough, M. E., Worthington, E. L., & Rachal, K. C. (1997). Interpersonal forgiving in close relationships. *Journal of Personality and Social Psychology, 73,* 321–336.

Ohbuchi, K., & Sato, K. (1994). Children's reactions to mitigating accounts: Apologies, excuses, and intentionality of harm. *Journal of Social Psychology, 134,* 5–17.

Ripley, J., Worthington, E. L., Jr., Bromley, D., & Kemper, S. (2005). Covenantal and contractual values in marriage: Marital values orientation toward wedlock or self-actualization (Marital VOWS) Scale. *Personal Relationships, 12,* 317–336.

Sandage, S. J., Worthington, E. L., Jr., Hight, T. L., & Berry, J. W. (2000). Seeking forgiveness: Theoretical context and an initial empirical study. *Journal of Psychology and Theology, 28,* 21–35.

Scherer, M., Cooke, K. L., & Worthington, E. L., Jr. (2005). Forgiveness bibliography. In E. L. Worthington, Jr. (Ed.), *Handbook of forgiveness* (pp. 507–556). New York: Routledge.

Schimmel, S. (2002). *Wounds not healed by time: The power of repentance and forgiveness.* New York: Oxford University Press.

Schönbach, P. (1980). A category system for account phrases. *European Journal of Social Psychology, 10,* 195–200.

Seidman, I. (1998). *Interviewing as qualitative research: A guide for researchers in education and the social sciences.* New York: Teachers College Press.

Tangney, J. P. (1995). Shame and guilt in interpersonal relationships. In J. P. Tangney & K. W. Fischer (Eds.), *Self-conscious emotions: The psychology of shame, guilt, embarrassment, and pride* (pp. 114–139). New York: Guilford Press.

Tangney, J. P. (2002). Humility. In C. R. Snyder & S. J. Lopez (Eds.), *Handbook of positive psychology* (pp. 411–419). New York: Oxford University Press.

Taupin, B. (1976). Sorry seems to be the hardest word [recorded by Elton John]. On *Blue moves* [record album]. London: Big Pig Music Limited.

Tavuchis, N. (1991). *Mea culpa: A sociology of apology and reconciliation.* Stanford, CA: Stanford University Press.

Templeton, J. M. (1997). *Worldwide laws of life.* Philadelphia: Templeton Foundation Press.

Witvliet, C. V. O., Ludwig, T. E., & Bauer, D. J. (2002). Please forgive me: Transgressors' emotions and physiology during imagery of seeking forgiveness and victim responses. *Journal of Psychology and Christianity, 21,* 219–233.

Woodley, R. (2004). *Living in color.* Downers Grove, IL: InterVarsity Press.
Woodruff, P. (2001). *Reverence: Renewing a forgotten virtue.* New York: Oxford University Press.
Worthington, E. L., Jr. (1998). An empathy–humility–commitment model of forgiveness applied within family dyads. *Journal of Family Therapy, 20,* 59–76.
Worthington, E. L., Jr. (2001). *Five steps to forgiveness: The art and science of forgiving.* New York: Crown Publishers.
Worthington, E. L., Jr. (2003). *Forgiving and reconciling.* Downers Grove, IL: InterVarsity Press.
Worthington, E. L., Jr. (2005). More questions about forgiveness: Research agenda for 2005–2015. In E. L. Worthington, Jr. (Ed.), *Handbook of forgiveness* (pp. 557–573). New York: Routledge.
Worthington, E. L., Jr. (2006) *Forgiveness and reconciliation: Theory and applications.* New York: Routledge.
Worthington, E. L., Jr., & Drinkard, D. T. (2000). Promoting reconciliation through psychoeducational and therapeutic interventions. *Journal of Marital and Family Therapy, 26,* 93–101.

14

The Timeliness of Forgiveness Interventions

WANDA MALCOLM

Introduction

> There is a time for everything, and a season for every activity under heaven:
> A time to be born and a time to die,
> A time to plant and a time to uproot,
> A time to kill and a time to heal,
> A time to tear down and a time to build,
> A time to weep and a time to laugh,
> A time to mourn and a time to dance,
> A time to scatter stones and a time to gather them,
> A time to embrace and a time to refrain,
> A time to search and a time to give up,
> A time to keep and a time to throw away,
> A time to tear and a time to mend,
> A time to be silent and a time to speak,
> A time to love and a time to hate,
> A time for war and a time for peace.
>
> **Ecclesiastes 3:1–8, New International Version**

I have been involved in the study of forgiveness-oriented, emotion-focused therapy for several years now: first with individual clients (Malcolm & Greenberg, 2000; Malcolm, Greenberg, & Warwar, 2002; Malcolm, Warwar, & Greenberg, 2005; Warwar, Greenberg, & Malcolm, 2006), and then with couples (Greenberg, Warwar, & Malcolm, 2007; Malcolm, Greenberg, & Warwar, 2003; Malcolm & Waldorsky,

2005). Along with these research projects, I have worked with clients in my private practice who struggle to come to terms with the hurtfulness they have experienced (and caused) in relationships that matter to them. I have also read the literature and paid attention to the theoretical and empirical knowledge brought to bear on the topic of forgiveness by my colleagues in the field. This chapter affords me the opportunity to pause and reflect on an important aspect of the forgiveness process that we may be at risk of overlooking when we get caught up in investigating and advocating the potential benefits of forgiveness and forgiveness interventions in psychotherapy.

I am going to begin with what might sound like an odd opinion from a self-proclaimed advocate of forgiveness: It is not a good idea to make forgiveness an a priori goal of therapy. In our enthusiasm to investigate and gather evidence in support of the potential physical, mental, and interpersonal health benefits of forgiveness, we may overlook the fact that, by virtue of having volunteered to participate and then completed an intervention, most participants in forgiveness studies like those reported in the current forgiveness literature (e.g., Coyle & Enright, 1997; Freedman & Enright, 1996; Warwar, Greenberg, & Malcolm, 2002) have already demonstrated some degree of openness to forgiveness as a means of positive change. When it comes to clients in private practice, however, we do not know whether their stance toward forgiveness will be open, closed, or deeply ambivalent. Thus, caution is warranted when presenting forgiveness as a beneficial route to recovery after interpersonal hurtfulness.

On a related note, Worthington et al. (2000) point out that forgiveness may not unfold in predictable ways in its naturally occurring state, and they observe:

> When one studies *interventions* to promote forgiveness, one is learning not about forgiveness per se, but about one way to guide people toward forgiveness. Outcome research investigates how effective intervention is at directing people's attention along the paths that are advocated. (p. 4)

Furthermore, when clients engage in a forgiveness-oriented intervention, the process and outcome are both likely to be impacted, possibly in unpredictable ways, by things such as their personality (Exline,

Baumeister, Bushman, Campbell, & Finkel, 2004; Mullet, Neto, & Rivière, 2005), overall relationship history, the severity of the injury, and the importance of their relationship with the hurtful other (e.g., Cann & Baucom, 2004; Finkel, Rusbult, Kumashiro, & Hannon, 2002). All of these factors are even more complexly interactive in couples' therapy when both partners are attempting to come to terms with a hurtful interaction or series of mutually hurtful interactions. That these factors interact in complex ways increases the potential for frustration if a clinician holds a predetermined conviction that forgiveness is the best response to interpersonal hurtfulness. The frustration of trying to persuade a reluctant individual or couple of the benefits of forgiveness may lead the therapist to see such clients in pathological terms instead of being motivated to help them explore and understand their reluctance to forgive.

Clients who come to therapy because of a relationship injury typically do so because they are dissatisfied with the way they or the hurtful person has responded so far, and therapy becomes the means of finding a better, more satisfying response. When it comes to private practice, the therapist who decides in advance and advocates a particular form of resolution runs the risk of disempowering clients whose sense of self-worth and self-efficacy has already been eroded and diminished by the hurtfulness they have experienced and/or caused. Aside from the usual tasks involved in establishing a good working alliance, which has been shown to predict outcome (Horvath & Greenberg, 1989), there are several therapist tasks germane to recognizing when, and when not, to facilitate a forgiveness-oriented intervention. Given space constraints, this chapter will focus on two closely related therapist tasks: (1) helping clients differentiate and explore what it is about the hurtfulness that they continue to hold against the hurtful other and (2) respecting the "timeliness" of forgiveness. They are closely related because the first task necessitates the second one: It requires time for the injured person to figure out exactly what it is about the hurtfulness that he or she resents and holds against the other person.

It also takes time to figure out what (if anything) the injured person wants and needs from the hurtful other before she or he can let go of her or his resentment or is willing to cultivate compassionate understanding toward the hurtful other. In couples' therapy, it also takes time to establish a therapeutic space that is safe enough for the hurtful partner to experience the difference between *being shamed* by others and *feeling ashamed* of the way in which she or he has hurt a loved one. The former involves being "wiped out" as a person of basic worth by others' harsh negative judgments; the latter involves being enabled, by virtue of a supportive therapeutic working alliance, to tolerate the painful awareness of, and appropriate regret for, having hurt a loved one. This, in turn, motivates adaptive change.

The Human Development Study Group (1991) was among the first of those to highlight the notion that forgiveness takes time, and Worthington et al. (2000) observed that "anything done to promote forgiveness has little impact unless substantial time is spent at helping participants think through and emotionally experience their forgiveness" (2000, p. 18). This observation is consistent with the number of sessions involved in the work that Suzanne Freedman has done with incest survivors (Freedman & Enright, 1996) and is also consistent with our finding that despite statistically significant improvements in symptomatic distress and progress in forgiveness from pre- to post-therapy, 10 sessions of individual emotion-focused therapy did not always provide enough time for clients to reach complete forgiveness (Warwar et al., 2006).*

What this means is that the right moment to forgive in the face of betrayal and hurt will often not come until after some measure of understanding has taken place. By hurrying to forgive, people may hope to avoid suffering on several fronts. They may not want to learn that a loved one cannot always be trusted implicitly and that even the most important relationships may bring hurt. They may not want to accept that one's beliefs in and attempts to do what is right in relationships are not always strong enough to prevent unfairness and injustice. For those who rely on their faith tradition as a source strength and insight, the attempt may be to avoid the suffering involved in discovering that one's faith does not ensure that God will not let anything horrible happen.

For therapists who come alongside a client in the wake of a relationship injury, premature efforts to facilitate forgiveness may be a sign

---

* Complete forgiveness as judged by the client himself or herself in response to a measure of forgiveness where 1 = *not at all* and 5 = *very much*.

of our reluctance to witness our client's pain and suffering and may unwittingly reinforce the client's belief that the pain and suffering is too much to bear and must be suppressed or avoided. The way to avoid conveying this message is to develop the skills that will allow us to be present with and helpful to clients while they work through the process of differentiating and exploring what it is about the hurtfulness that they continue to hold against the hurtful other. What follows is a description of how this worked with one woman who sought therapy.*

Efforts to Facilitate Forgiveness May Be Premature Immediately After an Interpersonal Injury

Margaret called my office to make an appointment for couples' therapy because she and her partner were at a crossroad in their relationship, despite a history of considerable affection and respect for one another. In her initial phone conversation, she described her partner as someone for whom acting with integrity was of utmost importance. The past year had been a difficult one; they had talked about whether it was time to formalize their relationship, but both had expressed reservations and stepped back from the relationship for a time, weighing and measuring what they had together, knowing they were the kind of people who, once they had made a commitment, would not abandon it lightly. Margaret knew that even while she was moving toward commitment, her partner was moving away from it. The situation had come to a head when her partner suddenly seemed sure that the time had come to end their relationship—that they just did not have that deeper passionate love he knew was out there with the "right" person. He agreed, with considerable reluctance, to undertake some couples' therapy first, and it was at that point that Margaret contacted me to make an appointment. It was her hope that they would be able to figure out what had caused the creeping malaise in their relationship and find ways to nurture and share a deeper, more passionate love for one another.

Unfortunately, when Margaret came for the appointment, she came alone. Her hope for the future had been eroded to bedrock, and pain

* Personal information about the clients whose stories are presented in this chapter has been changed to ensure privacy and preserve confidentiality.

radiated from her in palpable waves. Though she had not, at the time, been able to put her finger on why she had become suspicious, she had found herself wondering about the speed with which her partner was terminating their relationship and the depth of his reluctance to join her in couples' therapy. When pressed for an explanation, he had denied any pivotal event that would explain his desire to end the relationship and Margaret had been partially reassured. Still, she wondered, and then she did something wholly uncharacteristic of the way they had conducted their relationship: She went to her partner's house when he was not there and systematically checked for signs that he had been stepping out on her. Sure enough, an unfamiliar telephone number showed up as a regular incoming and outgoing call in recent weeks, and when she dialed the number she connected with the other woman. When confronted, Margaret's partner insisted there was no reason for Margaret to feel betrayed. From his perspective no wrong had been done because he had told her, before he got intimately involved with the other woman, that the time had come to end their relationship.

In acute grief, she sat with me and wondered how this person could be the man she knew and loved—a man who was known for his integrity and who surely ought to have anticipated that what he was doing would devastate her. Instead he bewildered and shocked her by barely pausing to see if she was still alive before he moved out of her life and on to life with another woman. This stranger, who seemed so cold and uncaring, could not be reconciled with the man she knew and loved. She was baffled by the confidence with which he assumed he had given ample warning of his intent to leave the relationship and by his sureness that they had been on the same page about the inevitable demise of their relationship. It was incomprehensible to her that he could claim that he had not cheated on her because he had expressed reservations about the future of their relationship.

In the weeks after the emotional, runaway train had roared through her life and left it in shambles, Margaret sat with me and wept over the fact that she could hold a view of her partner as a good man who had done a bad thing and forgive him for cheating on her, but that she could not forgive him for his breathtaking assumption that she would not be hurt by what he had done. She could not reconcile the man she knew with this person who was surprised that his actions left her stunned and in excruciating pain and who seemed impatient for her to pick up the pieces and get on with her life. We agreed that her first task was to do for herself what he had not done: to stop and assess the damage and see what had to be done to help her get back on her feet.

Once she had identified what she really could not forgive him for, talk about forgiveness disappeared from the therapeutic work. Our focus was on the self-affirming and self-validating work of learning what she needed to know about herself and her capacity to recover, rather than on her ex-partner and whether she could or should forgive him for what he had done. There was no reason to promote forgiveness; it was more important to support her through the process of grieving the irrevocable loss of the man she knew and loved, and to stand beside her while she sorted through the detritus of an irreparably broken relationship. To grieve and to say goodbye are as healthy as forgiving when the hurtful other moves out of one's life, insistent on refusing to take responsibility for the damage done.

If Margaret does forgive him some day, it will come as the culmination of an unfolding process of discovery, after she has recovered a sense of herself as strong enough to bear the pain of his betrayal. It is also possible that before she is willing to forgive him, she will need him to acknowledge that he had not, in fact, been clear about his intent to end their relationship and that as far as she was concerned, he had been unfaithful because he had not properly ended his relationship with her before he started a new one with someone else. If he were to do this, he might be restored as the man she had known and loved and, in so doing, become someone she could forgive—a good person who had done a bad thing.

Efforts to Facilitate Forgiveness May Be Contraindicated When Work on Self Needs Priority

Wade and Worthington (2003) have noted:

> Whereas most people do not like to experience unforgiveness and want to reduce it, clearly not everyone values forgiveness as a primary way to eliminate unforgiveness. There are situations in which clients may not want to or cannot pursue forgiveness. (p. 351)

Another client who was seen for individual therapy, Jennifer, grew up in a highly dysfunctional family where she felt she had always been the brunt of other family members' criticism and rejection despite heroic efforts on her part to draw her family of origin together in mutual support and unity. In early sessions, she dispassionately recounted poignant memories of severe childhood rejection and cruelty that had taught her that she was of no value except as someone who would serve those more deserving of affection and acceptance. For Jennifer, the goal of therapy was to put down the burden of endlessly trying, but failing, to earn approval and acceptance. She had somehow surrounded herself with family and friends whose need seemed endless and insatiable, and she was weary of giving.

The death of one of her parents and the subsequent scattering of the rest of the family had forced Jennifer to face the reality that she was never going to have the family she so desperately wanted. First, she slid into a depression and then she gathered herself up in moral outrage against those who had not come to her aid when she was grieving the irrevocable loss of her dream of a loving, unified family. Week after week, she protested against the unfairness of her life and bitterly rehearsed the instances of thoughtless neglect of those she had thought she could count on.

I did not raise the topic of forgiveness for some time but, eventually, I wondered out loud whether forgiveness might be a means of putting down the burden of her anger and bitterness. When she roundly dismissed that as a possibility, I expressed curiosity about why she felt so strongly opposed to forgiveness. Her reply went something like this:

> I used to be completely forgiving and look what it got me! People abused me and took advantage of me, and I just kept on trying to get them to love me the way I loved them. I dare not forgive any more because if I do, I will forget how dangerous it is to want and need their approval. I'll open myself to the hope that I will be loved and accepted, and I will get hurt again ... I can't bear to be hurt like that again.

Her need, as she saw it, was to keep her anger alive and use it to beat off the "takers" in life. So far, just about everyone she had met wanted something from her and she was forcing herself to remember so she could quiet the hope of ever finding anyone who would simply see that she longed to be loved and cared for unconditionally. Given that it was so melded for her with weakness and danger, I stopped talking about forgiveness. Accepting her anger and not trying to convince her to give it up permitted me to focus on what had happened that day or week to re-evoke the need to protect herself. Then, we could turn together to the task of uncovering and working with the hurt and loss that underlay her self-protective anger.

Would it be good for her to forgive? I am sure that it would serve her well to put down her self-protective weapons of outrage and heightened sensitivity to potential hurt. Accepting the reality of what had happened instead of fighting against the unfairness of it would allow her to take all that emotional energy and put it to the task of figuring out how to get the love she needs and longs for. I am equally sure that both the decision and the timing are not mine to determine. For Margaret, the one-time betrayal of a lover-turned-stranger inflicted a wound that was still too fresh; grieving and letting go of the relationship were more important than forgiving her ex-partner. For Jennifer, the work of establishing a sense of herself separate from the people who had hurt her so badly was more important than forgiving them. It takes a strong sense of self as an autonomous agent to empower an individual to choose and to take responsibility for how he or she chooses to come to terms with interpersonal injury and loss.

Efforts to Facilitate Forgiveness May Need to Be Delayed Until Issues of Relational Safety Are Addressed

Only after the damage has been faced and assessed may we begin to wonder with our clients what they need to do (or need to have done for them) in order to get back on their feet emotionally and find their place in the world again—and sometimes that is going to be a new place that requires change in an ongoing relationship. Part of the recovery process may involve accepting that the hurtful other is not able and/or willing to change a problematic behavior and thus cannot guarantee that she or he will not be hurtful again. The work then is for the injured person to decide whether he or she can live with what has been revealed by the hurtfulness. When this is the case, the issue may have more to do with whether it is wise and safe to re-enter the relationship, with its attendant risk of re-injury, than with the decision of whether to forgive or withhold forgiveness.

In couples' therapy, another part of the process may involve exploring, with the therapist's guidance and support, how each partner may be undermining the other's willingness and ability to make the kinds of changes that are needed to ensure that the same hurtfulness does not recur. This was the case with a couple who volunteered to participate in the study of forgiveness-oriented, emotion-focused couples' therapy* in hopes of restoring trust and safety after the husband had had an extramarital affair.

Bev came to their marital relationship with a strong need for others to agree and fall in line with her view of reality. A strong, articulate woman with passionate convictions, she could reduce Chris to feeling like an inadequate child if she suspected that he was not being entirely honest about something. Chris, in turn, came to the relationship with a strong need to be accepted and affirmed. He resented Bev's ability to run circles around him verbally and would resist her inquisitions by withdrawing and resentfully focusing on how she did not care about him or try to understand him. What Chris did not understand fully was that Bev was usually feeling small and powerless, and acting in self-protective ways when she made a crusade out of pursuing the truth of a situation. Bev had been the victim of incest, with a mother who had steadfastly refused to believe the truth of what Bev was telling her when she came for help to get her father to stop—a situation that persisted until Bev was old enough to square off with him and demand that he leave her alone. The cost to her was to be "orphaned": Both parents refused to deal with what had happened in Bev's bedroom, and she had to live with the fact that insisting on the truth was excruciatingly lonely. The lesson she learned was that if she were going to have to stand up for herself, she had better do so right from the beginning and never back down when she felt someone was behaving badly.

Before Chris could be forgiven for having an affair, they had to change the very ground of their relationship. Each had to become aware

* The York Forgiveness Project (2001–2004) was funded by The Campaign for Forgiveness Research and led by primary investigator Les Greenberg, with Serine Warwar as project coordinator, and Wanda Malcolm as co-investigator.

of the sensitivities they brought to their marriage and appreciate how these sensitivities made them vulnerable to being hurt by one another. The strength of their commitment was seen in Chris's not excusing himself for having the affair and in Bev's not claiming to be an innocent victim. Both agreed that what Chris had done was inexcusable *and* that it might not have happened if Bev had realized how she was driving him away when she put the truth of things ahead of understanding and affirming Chris.

With the therapist's guidance and support, Bev began to work on regulating the anxiety that compelled her to go to any lengths to establish the truth of a situation, so that she would be able to see, and to back down, when Chris was feeling attacked. She also worked at becoming better at reassuring Chris that even when she felt compelled to go after the truth, she still admired and loved him. For his part, Chris began to work on regulating his resentment and speaking up instead of retreating in the face of verbal attack. As he became better able to do this, he was able to see when Bev was being driven by anxiety and was more willing to reassure her that he was not hiding the truth from her. What follows is an excerpt from a session that fell at the midpoint of therapy. Bev had just previously been describing how her determination to state and defend the truth was driven by the fear that if she did not have the courage to speak up, she would be violated again.

Therapist [to Bev]: Tell us what it's like to feel that anxiety and the stirrings of the fear that things aren't what they ought to be.

Bev: I can feel a pressure rising inside my body, and I can feel my heart starting to beat faster, and I can feel like, it's like bells start going off in my head.

Therapist: Danger! Danger!

Bev: Absolutely!

Therapist: Okay ... the whole alarm system is getting ready to take action, and that's where you're pointed and that's where you're going to go. Okay ... What about you, Chris? I could hear the frustration in your voice, and the wanting to stake your territory, "don't intrude" ... is that it?

Chris: Yeah.

Therapist: Okay, describe it a little bit.

Chris: I guess I feel small, if that's a feeling; I feel small when it comes to those things you know but at the same time I'm also anxious because I want to say things that would make sense, but I just don't know how, so I can't … I'm apprehensive of getting into that whole thing …

Therapist: It's like Bev is asking for something you are afraid you can't deliver.

Chris: Yeah.

Therapist: It's like "I'm not up to this task. I can't." And then you feel like "I've got to make her see that I can't."

Chris: Yeah, and usually it doesn't work.

Therapist: There's some kind of feeling of … inadequacy? [Chris sighs] Like, "I'm frightened because I see what you want from me and I don't think I can do it"?

Chris: Yeah, at that moment, that's how I feel.

Therapist: Okay, that's important because you feel vulnerable and at risk, so you feel small.

Chris: Yeah, that's a big thing. I mean I feel like I'm failing is some way at that point. I'm not coming to terms with things … that I need to sort of sell it, and I can't. So I feel small, that's my word for it, I can't think of any other word for that you know.

Therapist: And that's got to feel uncomfortable; not a nice place to be … [Therapist turns to Bev] And as you hear him say that, Bev, what happens?

Bev (crying): It hurts me.

Therapist (speaking softly and gently): Are there some words to the tears? … Don't forget to breathe. Don't hold your breath … It's okay … Let the tears come … and put some words to the feeling … Stay with your feelings.

Bev: It's such a—disconnect from how I see him. I don't see him as small. I see him as having so much power over me because his actions can make me feel so good or make me feel so scared or, like he has such control over me that it's so crazy to me, that he in fact is feeling the exact opposite [of how I see him] … You know I don't want to be doing anything that makes Chris feel less of anything.

Therapist: "This is not what I want."

Bev: It's the opposite!

Therapist: "This is not what I intended."

Bev: No!

Therapist: Can you say that to Chris: "I don't want to make you feel small. … I don't want to be hurtful"?

Bev (sighs): I hate that.

Chris: I know you do … It's honestly like I get that feeling from somewhere else, you know I know that it's not you! It's my feeling. Obviously I've felt that before and it's from the past and I know you don't want to hurt me … [And] obviously, I don't want to hurt you either.

Therapist: So, "I bring the small me into the relationship. I bring it with me and I recognize that it's there also." [Turning to Bev] Okay, it's important for you to hear that he recognizes that you don't want to make him feel small. [Turning to Chris] But she evokes that feeling of being small in you, which you carry somewhere inside of you … And what do you need from Bev when you feel small?

Chris: Compassion. You know when we're in that place I just … sometimes I just need a smile, a lightening of it all. It just becomes so heavy, you know, that I guess that's when the small me comes around, because it's just so heavy and I just need a smile or something you know that shows me that we're, yeah …

Therapist: [It's like you're asking her] "Can you reassure me that it's going to be okay?"

Chris [after Bev cries quietly for 22 seconds]: I don't need you to—come out so hard. I just—you know, I'm there to listen but I need you to reassure me that we're okay; just a reassurance that we're working on this together … because it looks like we're so apart, like we're just two different people, we're not a couple [anymore].

These were neither self-evident nor easy tasks and would not have been possible if our focus had been on getting Bev to let go of her anger and pain so that she could forgive Chris for having an affair. The goal to work toward a restoration of trust and making the relationship safe enough to relax into affection again involves giving voice to the feelings of pain evoked by what had happened, as well as the letting go of anger and guardedness toward the hurtful person. The latter is accomplished by the cultivation of realistic feelings of compassion and understanding toward the hurtful other that would replace feelings of anger and guardedness. Forgiveness also requires that the injured person see the hurtful other as a "good," lovable person who did something "bad." Part of the horror in being hurt by someone we love is that she or he becomes a stranger to us—we cannot reconcile this person with the person we love and trust. Part of the gift of forgiveness lies in the heroic effort of the injured person who works to retrieve a view of the hurtful other as someone who is loved for good reason. In doing this work, the hurt person redeems what is good in the other person and holds it in higher esteem than the equally real hurtful behavior.

The injured person is apt to hold and rehearse his or her pain and anger as a self-protective strategy against forgetting how vulnerable he or she is in the relationship when the hurtful person refuses to stay in the room and hear the story of what she or he has done. In contrast, as Virginia Holeman has already noted (this volume), a good repentance that includes a heartfelt apology and the shouldering of responsibility for harm done goes a long way to presenting oneself as that remembered, good person. Demonstrating repentance is most effectively accomplished when the hurtful other stays beside the one she or he has hurt, and really hears and appreciates what she or he has done. The listening and empathic understanding validate the experience of the one who has been harmed and permits him or her to relinquish the hurt.

Some of this comes through in the letters that Chris and Bev were asked to write to each other after session seven. Having agreed that the crucial offense in the relationship was his affair, Chris had the task of writing a "three Rs" letter: what he *regretted*, what he took *responsibility* for, and what he *resolved* to do in order to ensure that the offense did not happen again. Segments of that letter are reproduced here:

> My first regret was letting our relationship get to the point where I could go out willingly and take a mistress and involve her [in] our perfect healthy life. It was the most naïve, immature and reckless thing I have ever done.
>
> What hurts me the most about my behavior is the pain it has cost you and … the irreparable damage it has done to our lives. I remember the night when I told you [what I had done] … [W]hen I told you

about the affair your reaction was calm and dignified and strong, but it was what you didn't show that scared me. No matter what our relationship brought to us or where it took us, there had always been a sense of security and trust in each other and belief that our relationship could take anything. By breaking that trust I put our relationship on a tightrope, with me being the first to fall. A couple of months later, I would feel the damage I had caused. You were always strong and loyal and true, but I had put a dent in your armor. Watching you cry and have your heart ache with pain was one of the hardest things to watch …

[I take responsibility for my] role in this mess and the cause of your injury … I was the one who [stepped out of our marriage]. I was irresponsible when it came to the well being of my family … I take complete responsibility when it comes to never being able to have those precious days back. The days I could have been involved in the future of my family, and love I could have given to my wife and child are lost forever …

[I resolve] to help you heal the injury I have given you. I am trying to be compassionate, to communicate with you and to show love and understanding. I will be there no matter what you need, no matter how ludicrous … I can't imagine how you feel about the affair, but I can imagine how you will feel if I show you how important you are … [I will give you] compassion because it's what you show to someone you have hurt. [I will work on] communication because it's the beginning or the end of any relationship. With it, things are explained and understood and out in front. Without it, things are in the dark and become a slowly sinking ship. [I will work on] understanding because to understand what has happened and the will to better oneself is part of making the road to healing a success. And lastly, love, because without love I wouldn't be writing this letter and with it I have the renewed energy to build on it and cherish you as long as I live. I love you!!

Bev had a corresponding letter to write and wrote it at the same time as Chris was writing his; as such, it is not a response to his letter. Her task was to identify and describe where she was in the process of healing. What she wrote is reproduced here:

When we began this journey together I was unsure where it would take us. I felt very betrayed and it was almost as if our relationship was irreparably broken. I couldn't stand living with you, without trusting you. I didn't want to feel the panic if I saw you talking to someone I didn't know or if a weird phone call came in. I can't live with a stranger … someone scary and undependable that could hurt me so easily.

The time we spent with [our therapist] has somehow created or allowed us to create the delicate strands that bind us again. These strands have made it possible for us to rediscover each other … feel empathy and kindness and love.

Before, I couldn't ever imagine truly forgiving you; holding on to the pain and hurt made me feel somehow protected. My guard was up and I was prepared for anything you could do to me. What an awful way to live. Like that movie "Living with the Enemy." Yuck.

But … along the way, you have shown me that you are open to learning about yourself and us as a couple. You have shown me that you care to learn more about *me*. You have magically made me feel loved again. Your desire to be supportive of me has been like a gift. Thank you.

Last week I noticed something quite amazing … I felt freed from the past hurts. I felt understanding of you and your mistakes. I FORGAVE you! I didn't want to talk about it right away until I was sure that the feelings were solid and real. They are.

In order for me to feel safe and happy with you, I need you to stay open and honest with me. I love you and support who you are … faults and all. By *you* trusting *me*, I am free to trust you. Thank you for making the effort. Thank you for being open and compassionate. I LOVE you.

Conclusion

While I am quite sure that forgiveness is a good way to resolve relationship hurts, I cannot, in good conscience, go into working with an individual or couple with the a priori intent to move them toward forgiveness. Not all clients share my conviction about the value of forgiving, and even when they do, many of them have already attempted to deal with the hurtfulness by turning to family and friends, needing to give voice to their pain and outrage, only to be told that if they would just forgive the other person then what the other person did to them would not "get to them" any more and they would feel better. For me to urge forgiveness as a solution to hurt and anger would be to join the chorus of voices saying, "Don't hurt. Don't be angry. Don't let it get to you."

The fact is that the hurtfulness that comes to us from someone we love and thought we could trust *does* get to us; it is excruciatingly painful and it evokes fury in the face of being treated so badly. Before we therapists talk about solutions to this reality, we may have to do for our clients what the hurtful other has not done: spend as much time as necessary to really hear how the hurtfulness has undone the client's sense of self and self in the world, validate their experience of having their world jerked out from under them, and affirm the unfairness of what happened. Only when our clients have had the time to figure out what it is that they resent and hold against the other, and what they need in order to get to their feet again, will they be able to move to the next step of relinquishing the hurt and deciding whether they can or should forgive the hurtful other.

References

Cann, A., & Baucom, T. R. (2004). Former partners and new rivals as threats to a relationship: Infidelity type, gender, and commitment as factors related to distress and forgiveness. *Personal Relationships, 11,* 305–318.

Coyle, C. T., & Enright, R. D. (1997). Forgiveness intervention with postabortion men. *Journal of Consulting and Clinical Psychology, 65,* 1042–1046.

Exline, J. J., Baumeister, R. F., Bushman, B. J., Campbell, W. K., & Finkel, E. J. (2004). Too proud to let go: Narcissistic entitlement as a barrier to forgiveness. *Journal of Personality and Social Psychology, 87,* 894–912.

Finkel, E. J., Rusbult, C. E., Kumashiro, M., & Hannon, P. A. (2002). Dealing with betrayal in close relationships: Does commitment promote forgiveness? *Journal of Personality and Social Psychology, 82,* 956–974.

Freedman, S. R., & Enright, R. D. (1996). Forgiveness as an intervention goal with incest survivors. *Journal of Consulting and Clinical Psychology, 64,* 983–992.

Greenberg, L. S., Warwar, S., & Malcolm, W. M. (2007). *Emotionally focused couples' therapy and the facilitation of forgiveness.* Manuscript in preparation.

Horvath, A., & Greenberg, L. S. (1989). Development and validation of the Working Alliance Inventory, *Journal of Counseling Psychology, 36,* 223–233.

Human Development Study Group. (1991). Five points on the construct of forgiveness within psychotherapy. *Psychotherapy, 28,* 493–496.

Malcolm, W. M., & Greenberg, L. S. (2000). Forgiveness as a process of change in individual psychotherapy. In M. E. McCullough, K. I. Pargament, & C. E. Thoresen (Eds.), *Forgiveness: Theory, research, and practice* (pp. 179–202). New York: Guilford Press.

Malcolm, W. M., Greenberg, L., & Warwar, S. (2002, June). *Emotional injuries: The role of empathy, forgiveness, letting go, and holding the other accountable.* Paper presented at the International Society for Psychotherapy Research, Santa Barbara, CA.

Malcolm, W. M., Greenberg, L., & Warwar, S. (2003, November). *A grounded analysis of couples' narratives about forgiveness and psychotherapeutic change.* Paper presented at the annual meeting of the North American Society for Psychotherapy Research, Newport, RI.

Malcolm, W. M., & Waldorsky, C. (2005, May). *Restoring power and connection through forgiveness and reconciliation.* Paper presented at the Women's Perspectives on Forgiveness Conference, Mississauga, Ontario, Canada.

Malcolm, W. M., Warwar, S., & Greenberg, L. (2005). Facilitating forgiveness in individual therapy as an approach to resolving interpersonal injuries. In E. L. Worthington, Jr. (Ed.), *Handbook of forgiveness.* New York: Routledge.

Mullet, E., Neto, F., & Rivière, S. (2005). Personality and its effects on resentment, revenge, forgiveness, and self-forgiveness. In E. L. Worthington, Jr. (Ed.), *Handbook of forgiveness* (pp. 159–181). New York: Routledge.

Wade, N. G., & Worthington, E. L., Jr. (2003). Overcoming interpersonal offenses: Is forgiveness the only way to deal with unforgiveness? *Journal of Counseling & Development, 81,* 343–353.

Warwar, S., Greenberg, L., & Malcolm, W. M. (2002, June). *Differential effects of emotion focused therapy and psychoeducation for resolving emotional injuries.* Paper presented at the International Society for Psychotherapy Research, Santa Barbara, CA.

Warwar, S., Greenberg, L., & Malcolm, W. M. (2006). *Differential effects of emotion focused therapy and psycho-education in facilitating forgiveness and letting go of emotional injuries.* Manuscript under review.

Worthington, E. L., Jr., Kurusu, T. A., Collins, W., Berry, J. W., Ripley, J. S., & Baier, S. N. (2000). Forgiving usually takes time: A lesson learned by studying interventions to promote forgiveness. *Journal of Psychology and Theology, 28,* 3–20.

Index

T